AF322591

Education Reform in Afghanistan

Ending the Cycle of Poverty, Instability, Inequity, and Dependency

By

Belal A. Kaifi

and

Mohammad Haris Azimi

Education Reform in Afghanistan

Ending the Cycle of Poverty, Instability, Inequity, and Dependency

© Belal A. Kaifi and Mohammad Haris Azimi

ISBN: 979-8-218-42972-0

Printed in the United States of America.

Institute of Management, Education, and Arts Development
Mountain House, California

*Dedicated to the late
Mohammad Haroon
Azimi*

Acknowledgements

Many people have contributed directly or indirectly to the preparation of this book. Students in various classes that we have taught have provided us with the inspiration and feedback that helped shape the organization and the content of the book. Discussions with colleagues and graduate students have helped sharpen our thinking. To all of those people, we say thank you. We thank our editors and reviewers (Wajma Aslami, Katie Weinstein, and Karen Hesse) who gave us wonderful suggestions. Finally, we thank our families for all of their love and support.

Table of Contents

Preface

After years of research, numerous conversations, and gathering primary and secondary data, the authors decided to write a book to help Afghanistan end the vicious cycle of poverty, instability, inequality, and dependency by focusing on improving the country's outdated and sub-optimal education system.

As such, this book is a comparative and critical analysis of the Afghan education system with plausible solutions based upon decades of teaching and educational administrative experience both inside and outside of Afghanistan. Some of the added features in this book include: (1) important interviews conducted with subject matter experts, (2) a focus group of 20 Afghan students sharing their experiences and perspectives on the education system in Afghanistan which helped form the topics, chapters, and structure of this book, (3) occasional text translation into the Farsi and Pashto languages, (4) best practices from countries throughout the world mentioned for learning and benchmarking purposes, (5) information written and presented in a simple manner for native English speakers and also English language learners, and (6) potential for this book to be used by many nations around the world to help improve their education systems.

This book is not criticizing the Afghan citizens. The reality is that most Afghans had neither a fair nor equitable opportunity to acquire a quality education. They are the victims and should be praised and commended for their ongoing resilience and patience.

Consequently, it is time for education to become a major priority in Afghanistan.

In the case of Afghanistan, neglect by the leaders coupled with a laissez-faire mentality of depending on foreigners "for funding" or to "figure it out for us" has resulted in a country that is severely crippled and unable to function according to modern day standards.

Therefore, it is important for the authors of this book to acknowledge and emphasize that many Afghan leaders are responsible and to blame for their negligence and shortcomings of providing a quality education to the people of Afghanistan. Unfortunately, the outcome of decades of educational neglect is what Afghanistan is currently dealing with – endless pain and suffering (e.g., poverty, instability, inequity, and dependency). Due to this neglect, Afghanistan has always struggled to compete with or even catch up to many nations around the world.

Over the years, there were some qualified Afghans who noticed this educational neglect and genuinely wanted to help improve the education system in Afghanistan. For example, it is worth mentioning a commendable and patriotic individual by the name of Dr. Abdul Kayeum (former Minister of Education from 1968 - 1971) who completed his doctoral degree in Education from the University of Denver and then returned to Afghanistan in 1948, where he described his work over the next 25 years as helping Afghanistan *"catch up with the caravan of civilization."*

As a practical example of playing "catch up" during the 1960s, the leaders of the U.S. focused on sending a person to the moon, which they accomplished in 1969; during that same time period, Afghan leaders had just realized and officially acknowledged that members of their Royal Family should not hold high positions in the Afghan government. In 1964, the ruling Afghan dynasty opted for the introduction of a Western-style constitutional monarchy. As a result, Article 24 of the new Afghan Constitution of 1964 mentioned that, "Members of the Royal Family were not permitted to hold the offices of Prime Minister or Minister, Member of Parliament or Justice of the Supreme Court" (Grote, 2004, p. 898).

<table>
<tr><td>Article 24</td><td>The Royal House is composed of the sons, the daughters, the brothers and the sisters of the King and their husbands, wives, sons and daughters; and the paternal uncles and the sons of the paternal uncles of the King.

In the official protocol of the State, the Royal House comes after the King and the Queen.

The expenditure of the Royal House shall be fixed in the budget of the Royal Expenses.

Titles of nobility are exclusively confined to the Royal House and shall be assigned in accordance with the provisions of the law.

Members of the Royal House shall not participate in political parties, and shall not hold the following offices:

1. Prime Minister or Minister

2. Member of the Shura (Parliament)

3. Justice of the Supreme Court

Members of the Royal House shall maintain their status as members of the Royal House as long as they live.</td></tr>
</table>

While the US was busy exploring the moon and space in the 1960s, Afghanistan was just understanding and publicly acknowledging the social, political, legal, and economic consequences of nepotism and cronyism in government affairs.

It should be mentioned that the 1960s and the first half of the 1970s is considered the *"Golden Age"* in

Afghanistan by many Afghans. This is because there was no serious conflict, and the country was gradually progressing and trying to implement changes in order to "catch up" to other nations, as the example above illustrates.

Since then, the situation in Afghanistan has regressed due to 40+ years of war, becoming dependent on foreign aid and resources, and internal conflict. As a case in point, Afghanistan went from having Cabinet members (e.g., Minister of Education, Prime Minister, and other Ministers) with doctoral degrees from prestigious American and European universities coupled with decades of experience in their respective fields, to Cabinet members with questionable degrees and limited experience.

The authors understand that their book will most likely not be used by current or future regimes in Afghanistan. However, they are hopeful that administrators, faculty members, researchers, NGOs, and students alike will consider implementing some of the recommendations and suggestions to help build a fully literate, prosperous, and independent Afghanistan that can contribute to the rest of the world in a meaningful manner.

Rabindranath Tagore once said, "The one who plants trees, knowing that he will never sit in their shade, has at least started to understand the meaning of life."

Respectfully,
Belal and Haris

1

INTRODUCTION

"An investment in education gives the best returns."
— Benjamin Franklin

*E*ducation is a journey—a journey that starts a person on the right path to the rest of his or her life. Education is a Latin word that means "to evolve from within". Consequently, many believe that education is the key to success for creating a civil society in order to continuously prosper and evolve. Countries that have embraced and invested in education have reaped the benefits. The transformation of Finland's education system began some 40 years ago as the key driver of the country's economic recovery plan. For instance, Finland pays their teachers as much as medical doctors and as a result, Finland has a 100% literacy rate. To further illustrate this point, in 1949, the Costa Rican government abolished their military, stating that their army would be an "army of teachers" and began using their defense funds towards free public education. Costa Rica now boasts a 98% literacy rate. As a final example to illustrate this point, Allan E. Goodman, President of the Institute of International Education mentioned that in the year 2007, "America had 4,000 colleges and universities and the rest of the world combined had 7,768 institutions of higher education. In the state of California alone, there were about 130 colleges and universities. There are only 14 countries in the world that have more than that number." Although this shocking statistic is from 2007, it clearly shows how much the US has invested in education. The ancient proverb: "If you give a man a fish, you feed him for a day. If you teach a man to fish, you feed him for a lifetime" has many implications for developing countries such as Afghanistan. Unfortunately, for many of the country's children, completing primary school remains a distant dream – especially for girls and those in rural areas. In the poorest and most remote areas of the country, enrollment levels vary extensively and girls still lack equal access. Moreover, an estimated 3.7 million children are out-of-school in Afghanistan – 60% of them are girls (UNICEF, 2023). As such, this book is merely an attempt to provide research and recommendations to Afghan leaders and government officials for implementing a progressive, sustainable, and equitable educational system in Afghanistan that produces life-long learners who are critical thinkers. According to Patrinos (2023), "One extra year of schooling amounts to an annual rate of return of 9 per cent for the individual, according to a recent World Bank study. For measure, that is greater than the annualized price return of the S&P 500 over the past half century. Education additionally drives untold gains for society and the economy too."

Afghanistan

The history of Afghanistan can be traced back to many cultures that have traveled throughout the country. Afghanistan's strategic location has always connected the rest of the world to Afghanistan, dating back to the Silk Road. According to Ewans (2002), "Afghanistan has also over its long history been a highway of conquest between west, central and southern Asia" (p. 10). Different empires have traveled throughout Afghanistan, from China in the East to Rome in the West. Thus, Afghans have truly been exposed to the world of cultures and traditions. Throughout Afghanistan, there are different traditions, languages, and even physical characteristics because of the different empires that have traveled throughout the country (Kaifi, 2009, p. 6).

Afghanistan is a landlocked country that is bordered by Turkmenistan, Uzbekistan, and Tajikistan in the north, by China in the northeast, by Pakistan in the southeast, and by Iran in the west. According to Tapper (2001), "The mountain ranges of the region run from east to west. The principal rivers carve deep gorges through them as they flow northwards into Turkistan" (p. 165). The country is divided east to west by the famous Hindu Kush mountain range and "several of its mountains are among the highest in the world" (Ewans, 2002, p. 1). The majority of the country is covered by mountains and valleys that have assisted Afghanistan during wars. Some two-thirds of it lies above 5,000 feet, and several mountains are among the highest in the world (Ewans, 2002).

Afghanistan currently has a very young population with a median age of about 18 years. Furthermore, several generations of Afghan boys and girls have grown into adults knowing and seeing nothing but continuous war (Frank, 2002, p. 82). While universal education is a legal requirement, due to economic realities, only a small percentage of the population is literate (Mujtaba, 2007). For several decades, Afghanistan has become dependent on the international community for assistance in all matters. "As a result of this long-term foreign assistance and dependence, Afghanistan has regressed" (Kaifi, 2008, p. 17).

No accurate population census has been conducted since 1979 in Afghanistan due to more than three decades of war and conflict. Furthermore, in 2023 the Pakistani government ordered the expulsion of all undocumented people from within its borders, including over 1 million Afghans. The government of Iran also made a similar request. This explains why the population of Afghanistan is in the range of 30 - 41 million. However, according to data retrieved from the *Center for Afghanistan Studies* at the University of Nebraska (2024), the literacy rate in Afghanistan is about 36% - 37% and the population is about 36 million.

Table 1: Benchmarking of Country Profiles

Country	Population (millions)	Infant Mortality Rate (per 1,000 live births)	Population Under 15 Years of Age (%)	Life Expectancy (in years)	Literacy Rate (%)	Per Capita GDP ($USD)
AFG	36	44	42	65	37	370
US	331	5	17	77	79	70,000
BRAZIL	214	11	19	74	94	7,507
CAN	38	4	15	81	99	52,000
MEX	126	12	31	70	99	10,045

Afghanistan's profile confirms the fact that this largely rural, poor population embodies the characteristics of a collective culture that remains close to its tribal and village-based lifestyle. According to one study, "The schools generally requested help from students' fathers for renovations and improvements to classrooms and schools, which accorded with traditional gender roles and expertise" (Hoodfar, 2007, p. 280). Furthermore, school teachers and educational officials in rural parts of the country tend to rely more on tribal and community leaders to educate their students. Obviously, women play a critical role in the education and wellbeing of their children; however, due to years of cultural norms, it is customary to address all official requests to the fathers or the oldest males in the family. While women might show more empathy toward people and lead with a care orientation, it is evident from modern research that males and females will be equally effective in leadership roles (Jones & George, 2009). Unfortunately, since Afghanistan has been economically depressed due to decades of intense and destructive war and violence, fewer women have had educational opportunities which would qualify them to reach higher ranks of management and leadership positions (Mujtaba, 2007). As such, Afghan leaders and government officials should strategize to provide more educational and management development opportunities to this underrepresented group. In Afghanistan, there was a transformational and visionary leader, King Amanullah, who embraced the importance of independence, modernization, education, and equality.

Afghanistan's King Amanullah and Independence

A visionary leader named King Amanullah who reigned from 1919-1929, was the son of King Habibullah (reigned during 1901-1919) and the grandson of King Abdur Rahman (reigned during 1880-1901), had a dream for Afghanistan to progress.

As documented in history, "On February 27, 1919, Amanullah was formally crowned" (Ewans, 2002, p. 87). King Amanullah and his soldiers defeated the British in a month-long war and gained complete independence of Afghanistan during the third Anglo-Afghan war, and he soon after became a national hero.

King Amanullah was a strategic forward-thinker and an agent of change, and he was able to properly evolve the country into a modernized society.

Following in his father's footsteps, King Amanullah helped Afghanistan flourish into an independent nation that focused on enhancing human rights, education, and promoting modernization. He understood the inequalities faced by women in Afghanistan and quickly worked toward granting them equal rights. The King's ability to enhance the quality of life in Afghan society will always be commendable and admirable. "For the first time [in Afghan history], a written constitution was written up, implemented, and promulgated" (Ewans, 2002, p. 93). The public was both astonished and surprised by his bold endeavors to make positive changes. According to Faiz (2013):

> In spring of 1919, having won the stunning political victory and securing Afghanistan's recognition as a fully-sovereign and independent state abroad, King Amān-Allāh did not rest on his laurels. Similar to his grandfather, King AbdurRaḥmān, he turned his attention inward towards the *administration* of the country. He reorganized the royal cabinet into an expansive government bureaucracy that included the establishments of brand-new ministries in Kabul, including Ministries of the Interior, Foreign Affairs, Education, Finance, Justice, Trade, Public Works, Public Health, and a Postal and Telegraph Office (p. 498).
>
> The mullahs preached from their pulpits the next Friday against plays which showed religion in disrespect. Finally, King Amān-Allāh found some

mullahs so openly hostile to all his policies that he put several under arrest. These had two chief complaints: the education of the young by Europeans who might fatally flaw their religious natures, and the tendency to give undue freedom to women (p. 549).

In the 1920s, Turkey played a major role in the development of Afghanistan's educational institutions, sending a number of teachers to Afghanistan to open schools and provide educational services. Historians of Turco-Afghan relations often begin their histories with the Amān-Allāh Khan era, such as Özlem Korkmaz, who writes, "Turkey's technical and educational assistance to Afghanistan began in the era of Emanullah Han (p. 651).

Within a year of his rise to power, King Amān-Allāh Khan commissioned an elite team of Afghan, Ottoman Turkish, and Indian Muslim jurists with a singular mandate: to lay the juridical foundations for a modern state. By 1923, King Amān-Allāh had promulgated not only Afghanistan's first constitution, but a total of seventy-eight codes known collectively as the Niẓāmnāmā, or "Regulations." In addition to civil, criminal, and commercial law statutes, the Niẓāmnāmā incorporated sweeping plans for a centralized network of courts with newly trained judges salaried by Kabul, a national army raised through conscription, and an individuated tax system that abolished exemptions for powerful Pashtun tribes. The Niẓāmnāmā also mandated universal primary education, including schools for girls and young women (p. 655).

King Amanullah went on a grand tour with his wife Queen Soraya where he spent time in India, Egypt, France, Germany, Britain, the former Soviet Union, Turkey, and Iran. This notorious tour allowed him to be exposed to different cultures, lifestyles, and ideologies. Being a charismatic and visionary leader allowed him to accept, adapt, and enjoy the differences that he and his wife encountered.

King Amanullah understood the importance of education and the positive impact education has on a society. He established a number of schools, including some for girls, with the help of Queen Soraya, and started to "send young Afghans abroad for higher studies" (Ewans, 2002, p. 93). In 1922, he elevated the Department of Education to the status of the Ministry of Education, allocating a substantial budget to it, making it the third-largest ministry in terms of funding. Suddenly, Afghans were immersed in their studies and worked hard to receive scholarships to study abroad. Many Afghans traveled to the west during his time, received advanced degrees, and returned to Afghanistan to help with the development process. King Amanullah influenced the people of Afghanistan by empowering them to be visionary, proactive, and an active part of the global community. Unfortunately, after King Amanullah's reign ended in 1929, all of his successors neglected his progressive reforms and instead, were manipulated and influenced by foreign powers and became dependent on foreign resources, support, and aid.

Many countries received their independence after Afghanistan and are thriving. For example, South Korea gained independence on August 15, 1948. South Korea has experienced one of the largest economic transformations of the past 60 years. It started as an agriculture-based economy in the 1960s, and it became the 11th largest economy in the world in terms of gross domestic product (GDP) in 2016. Interestingly, South Korea is one of the top-performing OECD (Organization for Economic Cooperation and Development) countries in reading, literacy, mathematics and sciences with the average student scoring about 519, compared with the OECD average of 493- this ranks Korean education at ninth place in the world. Within a single generation, South Korea has moved from starvation to prosperity: it is now the home of Samsung Galaxy phones, world-class internet speeds and Hyundai. Just half a century ago, the country was one of the world's poorest, faring worse than that of its archenemy North Korea.

A different country that gained its independence after Afghanistan is Pakistan, which gained its independence in 1947 and became a nuclear power in 1998. Furthermore, a few Middle Eastern countries (e.g., Iran, Egypt, Turkey, Iraq, and Saudi Arabia) achieved their independence in the 1920s and 1930s. A common trend is that the countries mentioned above have significantly higher literacy rates when compared to Afghanistan. In many of the book markets throughout Iraq, books remain in the street at night because the people of Iraq believe that, "*the reader does not steal and the thief does not read.*"

Literacy Rates and Implications for Afghanistan

Afghanistan, a country marked by decades of conflict and economic challenges, has long faced issues concerning its literacy rates. According to Dr. Saif Rahman Samadi (2014) who in the 1960s served as the President of the Department of Vocational Education and Teacher Training, Associate Professor (Faculty of Science) at Kabul University, and Deputy Minister of Education in Afghanistan:

> Adult literacy has been a major problem in Afghan society. The main reasons are limitation of resources for an effective literacy program and lack of schooling for a significant portion of the school age population. In order to improve the situation, it is necessary to undertake a national campaign for adult literacy with appropriate strategies and adequate resources, and continue efforts for

achievement of basic education of all children. Substantial private and public resources will have to be mobilized, large number of teachers from the formal and non-formal education systems and volunteers including university students should be trained and innovative methods and relevant materials developed for functional literacy.

This section delves into the literacy landscape of Afghanistan, drawing insights from a recent World Bank research study. The historical backdrop of Afghanistan, characterized by political instability and conflict, has significantly impacted its education system. The destruction of infrastructure, displacement of populations, and societal norms have contributed to a complex environment for educational development.

According to the latest *World Bank* research, Afghanistan's literacy rate remains a concern. Literacy is defined as the percentage of people ages 15 and above who can both read and write a short simple statement about their everyday life. While the country has made some progress in improving access to education, challenges persist. The following statistics underscore the disparities between urban and rural areas, as well as gender disparities, with women facing additional barriers to literacy. Here are some thought-provoking statistics:

- **Adult literacy in Afghanistan is lower among women than among men (2021)**

  The gap in adult literacy between men (52.1%) and women (22.6%), is larger (29.5) than the gap of the South Asia aggregate, 15.7.

- **83 of every 1,000 girls ages 15-19 gave birth in Afghanistan in 2021**

  In Afghanistan, the rate of adolescent fertility has decreased since 2010. The rate in 2021 was lower than the average rate in its income group.

- **43.1% of girls and 72.7% of boys complete lower secondary school in Afghanistan as of 2019 data**

  The gap in lower secondary completion rate between boys and girls, 29.6, is larger than the gap of the South Asia aggregate, 2.8. Lower secondary education completion rate measures how many children have completed the last grade of lower secondary education regardless of age completed.

- **In Afghanistan, the labor force participation rate among females is 16.5% and among males is 66.7% for 2020**

  The labor force participation rate is the proportion of the population ages 15 and older that is economically active. Since 1990, female labor force participation has remained roughly the same. Compared with labor force participation in the low-income group of nations, the gap between men and women is higher in Afghanistan.

- **32.6% of women participated in making major decisions in the household in 2015**

  Women participating in making major decisions is the percentage of currently married women ages 15-49 who say that they alone or jointly have the final say in (i) making major household purchases, (ii) decisions about their own healthcare, and (iii) visits to family, relatives, and friends.

Several factors contribute to Afghanistan's literacy challenges. Ongoing conflict disrupts educational institutions, limiting opportunities for learning. Economic hardships may force families to prioritize survival over education, exacerbating the cycle of illiteracy. Furthermore, cultural norms in certain provinces may impede girls' access to education. According to Samady (2001), in 1950, an adult literacy course was created as well as a periodical for new adult readers. Over the next decade, many Ministries focused on conducting literacy courses in hopes of eradicating illiteracy.

Challenges persist despite efforts to improve literacy rates. Security concerns may hinder the implementation of education programs in certain areas. Economic stability and political reforms are integral to creating an environment conducive to sustained educational development.

Afghanistan's literacy rate is a multifaceted issue influenced by historical, cultural, and economic factors. While progress has been made, persistent challenges require a comprehensive and collaborative approach. The World Bank's research sheds light on the current state of literacy in Afghanistan, emphasizing the need for sustained efforts to promote education and alleviate barriers hindering literacy development.

Phonics

Phonics instruction teaches the relationships between the letters of written language and the sounds of spoken language. Phonemic awareness is the ability to hear, identify, and manipulate individual sounds—phonemes— in spoken words. Phonemic awareness is important because it improves children's word reading and reading comprehension and also helps children learn to spell. Phonemic awareness can be developed through a number of activities, including asking children to identify phonemes, categorize phonemes, and blend phonemes to form words.

Phonemic awareness instruction is most effective when children are taught to manipulate phonemes by using the letters of the alphabet and when instruction focuses on only one or two rather than several types of phoneme manipulation. Phonics instruction helps children learn the relationships between the letters of written language and the sounds of spoken language. Phonics instruction is important because it leads to an understanding of the alphabetic principle—the systematic and predictable relationships between written letters and spoken sounds.

Programs of phonics instruction are effective when they are systematic—the plan of instruction includes a carefully selected set of letter-sound relationships that are organized into a logical sequence—and explicit—the programs provide teachers with precise directions for the teaching of these relationships. Effective phonics programs provide ample opportunities

for children to apply what they are learning about letters
and sounds to the reading of words, sentences, and
stories. Systematic and explicit phonics instruction
significantly improves children's word recognition,
spelling, and reading comprehension and is most
effective when it begins in kindergarten or first grade.

**A Conversation with Mashal Hamidi - Regional
Director of *Read to Lead Afghanistan***

Mashal Hamidi is the Regional Director of Read to Lead
(R2L) Afghanistan. Mashal earned her degree in
Sociology at Adelphi University and graduated with
honors as a Levermore Global Scholar. She has been
working with R2L since its inception in 2017 and prior
to that, she was involved in challenging humanitarian
work. Her mother (Shakila Zadran Hamidi) is the
Executive Director and the brains and magic behind
R2L. The entire interview can be found in Appendix A.

**Authors: Please explain what *Read to Lead
Afghanistan* is all about.**

> **MH:** Read to Lead (R2L) Afghanistan was
> founded in 2017 and began as a grassroots
> organization based in Kabul, Afghanistan. R2L
> works one on one with child workers in Kabul in
> ensuring school enrollment through sports,
> literacy, art and mentorship programs. The idea
> behind R2L was primarily based on the
> importance of books. During one of our trips to
> Afghanistan, we realized that a book per child will
> save the future. R2L provides the children with
> sports uniforms, coaches, mentors, books, school

supplies, winter clothes and other necessities. Our children are often the main breadwinners of their family, making approximately 100-200 AFG a day (1.50 to 2.50 dollars). Most are exposed to drug and substance abuse through their parents which create a vulnerable and unstable environment and force them to work. Read to Lead Afghanistan is committed to supporting children who are exploited as child workers in Kabul. We not only work with children but their families as well in ensuring access to healthcare, financial opportunities, and sustainability. Currently, with the restrictions placed by the new regime, we've pivoted our efforts more towards sustainable aid and emergency relief.

Authors: What is the goal of Read to Lead Afghanistan?

MH: The goal is to ensure children are no longer working on the streets at risk to vulnerable situations. Our Streets to School initiative consists of recreational, art and sponsorship programs. Essentially, we aim to create as many literacy opportunities as possible through the establishment of schools and courses. Sustainability is vital in all of our projects and we try to work within the parameters the current government permits us to.

Authors: Discuss the "Read With Me" Program.

MH: "Read With Me" also known as با من بخوان encourages peer to peer collaboration in encouraging each other to read. Read With Me is

a storytelling program where children are required
to read and discuss books taken out from our
library. The goal is to enhance their literacy and
speaking skills through engagement with their
peers and mentors.

Through "Read With Me" we encourage school
attendance by providing school supplies, school
uniforms and books to educational facilities to
ease the financial burden of families. Within the
past year, Read to Lead provided over 1,300
children with either uniforms, school supplies or
books through Read to Me. Our in-house library
is open to our participants even when school is
not in session. We aim to promote life-long
learning and tackle inequality through the passion
for books.

**Authors: From your perspective, why do you believe
reading is so important for Afghan children?**

MH: We believe that the greatest friend one can
have is a book. The ability to read from a tender
age as a child encourages ambition and can
prevent the growing population of child laborers.
Reading enriches emotional awareness and fosters
development in youth. Children are not meant to
be on the streets making a dollar a day. They
belong in classrooms where they are able to focus
on enhancing their cognitive development via
reading and education.

Implications of Illiteracy in the US

American politicians often claim that prison planners use third grade reading scores to predict the number of future prison beds needed. Although this claim cannot be proved, there is an undeniable connection between literacy skills and incarceration rates. The Literacy Project Foundation found that three out of five people in U.S. prisons can't read and 85 percent of juvenile offenders have trouble reading. Other research has estimated that illiteracy rates in prisons are as high as 75 percent of the prison population. Below are some interesting facts to be taken into consideration:

- 85 percent of all juveniles who interface with the juvenile court system are functionally low literate.
- Juvenile incarceration reduces the probability of high school completion and increases the probability of incarceration later in life.
- High school dropouts are 3.5 times more likely than high school graduates to be arrested in their lifetime.
- High school dropouts are 63% more likely to be incarcerated than their peers with four-year college degrees.
- Mississippi has the second highest incarceration rate in the nation. The average adult inmate reads on a sixth-grade level when admitted. Half of the state's inmates never finished high school.

Reading on grade-level by the end of third grade is one of the most critical milestones in education. A 2009 study by Northeastern University shows that 74% of 3rd graders who read poorly still struggle in ninth grade, and third grade reading scores can predict a student's likelihood to graduate high school. Donald Hernandez (2011) reported in *Double Jeopardy*, children who do not read proficiently by the end of third grade are four times more likely to leave school without a diploma than proficient readers. While those with the lowest reading scores account for only a third of students, this group accounts for more than 63% of all children who do not graduate from high school.

Helping someone to read and write effectively or acquire the basic math skills so many of us take for granted, improves the future of everyone in society. Literacy is critical to economic development as well as individual and community well-being. An economy is enhanced when learners have higher literacy levels.

Instruction in English

The business language of the world is English. Therefore, the schools in Afghanistan need to implement policies where English becomes a significant part of the curriculum. According to Samady (2014):

> Afghan students should learn English to be able to study English texts and communicate with fluency in this international language. It would be very useful and efficient in terms of quality if science and technology subjects and business courses could be taught in English. However, the teaching of all subjects in English is neither doable nor advisable. In India and Pakistan, the English language as the medium of instruction in colleges is part of their colonial heritage. The great majority of Afghan students and faculty will

not be able to use English as a means of instruction and learning effectively. It would be highly desirable to be able to make use of available English textbooks, references and resource materials. They should also be able to study abroad when the opportunity comes up. In this perspective, efforts should be made to provide intensive English language training to university students.

Throughout primary school, Afghan students should learn English as a second language. In secondary school, English should become the mode of instruction in at least 25% of the curriculum or courses. At the university or post-secondary level, English should become the mode of instruction in at least 50% of the courses. The goal is for Afghans to become multilingual (English, Farsi, Pashto, and Coding/Programming) so that they have more opportunities when they graduate. Currently, in the Netherlands, about 17 schools are piloting official bilingual schools where they teach in English 50% of the time. If the results are positive, then there will be more bilingual schools in the Netherlands in the future. By learning to speak and write in English, Afghan students will have more employment and educational opportunities upon graduation—this will be discussed in future chapters.

Coding and Programming

Although "coding/programming" is not an official language, it is considered a programming language. As such, students should learn how to code and program at a very young age and continuously develop their skills throughout primary and secondary schools. Typically, coding is done using a programming or scripting language—like HTML, Python, or JavaScript—which the coder uses to translate his or her ideas into words, phrases, and syntax that the computer understands. These instructions are also called "commands."

In primary school, students should start learning how to code. Coding is the process of writing out steps for a computer to follow to achieve a goal or perform a task. In Secondary school, students should start learning how to program. Computer programming is the larger process: It involves identifying a problem or challenge, considering potential solutions, writing code that can enact those solutions, and then testing and revising the code to achieve the desired results. In the US and many other countries, some form of computer science standards are being added as a part of the curriculum at the primary and secondary levels.

> **"Everybody should learn to program a computer because it teaches you how to think."**
>
> -Steve Jobs

Islamic Education

Many countries around the world have large populations of Muslims. In Afghanistan, over 99% of the population is Muslim. Among the Muslim countries, Indonesia has the largest Muslim population in the world and their school curriculum has aspects of religious teachings. According to Daulay (2017), "In Indonesian schools, general subjects such as natural science, social science, English, and geography are the main program, while religious subjects are supporting the program" (p. 295). As such, about 10% of the primary school curriculum in Afghanistan should focus on the basics of Islam. Also, the basics of Islam should be taught at home. About 10% of the secondary school curriculum should focus on embedding the application of Islam into curriculum and also teaching how Muslims contributed to the world. For example, "Islamic contributions to mathematics began around AD 825, when the Baghdad mathematician Muḥammad ibn Mūsā al-Khwārizmī wrote his famous treatise al-Kitāb al-mukhtaṣar fī ḥisāb al-jabr wa'l-muqābala (i.e., The Compendious Book on Calculation by Completion and Balancing) translated into Latin in the 12th century as Algebra et Almucabal, from which the modern term algebra is derived." Afghan students who would like to become a Hafiz (a person who has memorized the Qur'an) should go to a specialized Madrassa. However, the "Madrassification" of all schools is not necessary.

Islam, Women, and Education

Many individuals have a misguided judgment about Islam; in part, this is due to the influence of cultural norms, and it is also due to the media, which generally shares a tainted image of the religion (Kaifi, 2009). Over 99% of the people in Afghanistan follow the religion of Islam. According to Samady (2001), "In the late 1950s, some of Afghanistan's primary schools became co-educational; secondary schools remained segregated" (p. 591). There are many Muslim women who are educated and who did not have to fight for their right to an education (Sadat, 2004). There have been several female Muslim leaders throughout the Muslim countries; for example, Benazir Bhutto (1993-1996) was the Prime Minister of Pakistan and Sima Samar (2001-2003) was the Minister of Women's Affairs of Afghanistan. Furthermore, Megawati Sukarnoputri (2001-2004) served as the president of Indonesia. As a final example, Hasina Shaikh is the current Prime Minister of Bangladesh.

Today, however, many women in numerous Islamic countries are forbidden to go to school, and many Muslim women have to fight for their right to an education. In Afghanistan, parents may be reluctant to send their daughters to school. According to Emadi (2005), some Afghans condemned and strongly opposed the transformation of Afghan schools that allowed female students to attend classes.

Traditionally, in Afghanistan, the girls who were encouraged to go to college were allowed to obtain vocational training to become a nurse or midwife, for example, in order to better serve other women in the country (Emadi, 2005). Due to their pride and honor, Afghan men did not want their wives to be seen by a male physician without a female chaperone; therefore, female nurses were preferred, and this was an acceptable career for Afghan women (Emadi, 2005).

Therefore, it is not the religion, but the Afghan culture that has brought on the oppression of women (Entezar, 2007). Oppressing women and depriving them of human rights are not supported by the Qur'an or by Islam; as a matter of fact, Islam was one of the first religions to give equal rights to women (Emadi, 2005; Kaifi, 2009; Younos, 2002).

Furthermore, Godlas (2003) stated that the *hadiths* are the sayings and the traditions of Prophet Muhammad (PBUH) or a report from others about something the Prophet did. According to the hadiths, men and women are considered equal (Younos, 2002). Younos (2002) also claimed that "knowledge lays the foundation of learning and education in Islam for both sexes" (p. 20). Verse 20:114 of the Qur'an reads, *"Exalted is God, the true ruler. Do not rush with Recital before its revelation to you is concluded; but say, "My Lord, increase me in knowledge," (Taha – 20:114).* The above quote can be interpreted to demonstrate that God asks all Muslims (men and women) to pray for knowledge. Furthermore, Younos (2002) cited Al-Bukhari (1981) who claimed that the hadiths stated, "Seek knowledge from cradle to grave" (p. 22). This is not gender specific and is believed to speak to both men and women. Consequently, the overall message of the hadiths relating to education is that learning is an obligation for both men and women (Younos, 2002). According to Tabari (as cited in Younos, 2002), in Islam, the first object God created was the pen and the first words that were revealed to the Prophet was *iqra* (read). The Qur'an states, "Read, in the name of your Lord, who created; Read, for your Lord is most generous, the one who taught the use of the pen, taught man what he did not know" (Al'-Alaq - 96: 1, 3, 4, 5; translated by Cleary, 2004, p. 298). These texts imply that Islam supports learning and education for all people. Weatherby et al. (2009) emphasize the importance of education for women within a society:

> Females who are educated tend to marry as adults rather than as adolescents. They have fewer children, they have access to important

information on health and nutrition, and they have greater opportunities for better wages in the marketplace (p. 91).

When women cannot find jobs, they turn to earning wages by domestic labor or prostitution to survive. Apart from traditional families and clan protection, women become even more vulnerable to violence, disease, and isolation (p. 88).

Income is related to life expectancy. In high-income countries, 90 percent of women live to age 65. In low-income countries, the percent falls to 42. In Zimbabwe, for example, only 8 percent live to 65; the remainder perishes at an earlier age (p. 91).

Education is the key to the development of a country and its capacity to develop infrastructure. According to Fereshteh Forough, the Founder and Executive Director of *Inspire to Code*, "The women and girls of Afghanistan are invaluable treasures. By investing in their education, you are investing in the foundation of peace and prosperity for an entire nation." As such, administrators and officials in Afghanistan must do what they can to provide an environment where people are encouraged and supported to complete their educational dreams (Mujtaba & Scharff, 2007). Unfortunately, the past and current Taliban regime in Afghanistan has banned girls from studying after the 6th grade and women are unable to attend university. Moreover, professional opportunities for women have been severely restricted.

Women and Education in Islam - A Conversation with Dr. Farid Younos

Dr. Farid Younos is a retired Professor of Cultural Anthropology and Islamic Philosophy at California State University, East Bay. Dr. Younos completed his doctoral degree in Education (International and Multicultural Education) from the University of San Francisco. The entire interview can be found in Appendix A.

Authors: Are you hopeful that women's rights in Afghanistan will take a turn for the better in the future? In recent years, Saudi Arabia has made some progress with women's rights.

> **FY**: Women and men in Islam have equal civic rights in Islam. I don't think the Taliban will change. This is because the Taliban came to power based upon their own ideology. Those who possess an ideology don't change.

Authors: Based upon your many years of research and understanding of Islam, what does Islam teach about education and women's rights?

> **FY**: The foundation of Islam is knowledge. The first aya (verse) revealed was "to read". Later the Prophet (peace be upon him) said that the first thing God created was the pen. Hence the foundation of this Deen is learning for both genders. The Quran says: "*Oh my Lord advance me in knowledge*" in surah Ta-Ha; 20:114. This verse is very much universal and applies to both men and women. Fatima al-Fihri was a Muslim woman

from Tunisia who founded the first known university more than 1,000 years ago: the University of al-Qarawiyyin in Fez, Morocco.

Education is a Human Right

According to the United Nations, the *Universal Declaration of Human Rights* affirms that education is a fundamental human right for everyone, and this right was further detailed in the Convention against Discrimination in Education. What exactly does that mean? Why is education a fundamental human right?

The right to education is a human right and indispensable for the exercise of other human rights. Quality education aims to ensure the development of a fully-rounded human being. It is one of the most powerful tools in lifting socially excluded children and adults out of poverty and into society. UNESCO data shows that if all adults completed secondary education, globally the number of poor people could be reduced by more than half. It narrows the gender gap for girls and women. A UN study showed that each year of schooling reduces the probability of infant mortality by 5 to 10 per cent. For this human right to work there must be equality of opportunity, universal access, and enforceable and monitored quality standards.

Article 26 of the Universal Declaration of Human Rights

1. Everyone has the right to education. Education shall be free, at least in the elementary and fundamental stages. Elementary education shall be compulsory. Technical and professional education shall be made generally available and

higher education shall be equally accessible to all on the basis of merit.
2. Education shall be directed to the full development of the human personality and to the strengthening of respect for human rights and fundamental freedoms. It shall promote understanding, tolerance and friendship among all nations, racial or religious groups, and shall further the activities of the United Nations for the maintenance of peace.
3. Parents have a prior right to choose the kind of education that shall be given to their children.

Fragile States Index (FSI)

The Fragile States Index is an annual report mainly published and supported by the United States think tank, the Fund for Peace. The Fragile States Index is based on a conflict assessment framework – known as "CAST" (Conflict Assessment System Tool) – that was developed by Fund for Peace nearly a quarter-century ago for assessing the vulnerability of states to collapse. The Fund for Peace methodology triangulates data from three primary sources and subjects them to critical review to obtain final scores for the Fragile States Index. The main data collection methods are: Content analysis (electronic scanning), Quantitative data, and Qualitative input. The maximum score that a country can receive for being in danger of complete state collapse is 120. There are three groupings: social, economic and political with twelve overall indicators worth 10 points each.

Social Indicators:

- Demographic pressures
- Refugees or internally displaced persons
- Group grievance
- Human flight and brain drain

Economic Indicators:

- Uneven economic development
- Poverty and economic decline

Political and Military Indicators:

- State legitimacy
- Public services
- Human rights and rule of law
- Security apparatus
- Factionalized elites
- External intervention

Table 2: Fragile States Index Scores

Country	FSI
Afghanistan	106.6
US	45.3
Bangladesh	85.2
Australia	22
Pakistan	89.9
China	65.1
Brazil	74.5
India	74.1
Russia	80.7
Zimbabwe	96.9

Human Development Index (HDI)

In 1990 the first Human Development Report introduced a new approach for advancing human well-being. Human development – or the human development approach – is about expanding the richness of human life, rather than simply the richness of the economy in which human beings live. It is an approach that is focused on people and their opportunities and choices.

The human development approach, developed by the economist Mahbub Ul Haq, is anchored in the Nobel laureate Amartya Sen's work on human capabilities, often framed in terms of whether people are able to "be" and "do" desirable things in life.

Ideas on the links between economic growth and development during the second half of the 20th century also had a formative influence. Gross Domestic Product (GDP) and economic growth emerged as leading indicators of national progress in many countries, yet GDP was never intended to be used as a measure of wellbeing. In the 1970s and 80s the development debate considered using alternative focuses to go beyond GDP, including putting greater emphasis on employment, followed by redistribution with growth, and then whether people had their basic needs met. These ideas-both the approach and its measurement- helped pave the way for human development.

People: human development focuses on improving the lives people lead rather than assuming that economic growth will lead, automatically, to greater well-being for all. Income growth is seen as a means to development, rather than an end in itself.

Opportunities: human development is about giving people more freedom to live lives they value. In effect this means developing people's abilities and giving them a chance to use them. For example, educating a girl would build her skills, but it is of little use if she is denied access to jobs, or does not have the right skills for the local labor market. Three foundations for human development are to live a long, healthy and creative life, to be knowledgeable, and to have access to resources needed for a decent standard of living. Many other things are important too, especially in helping to create the right conditions for human development, and some of these are in the table below. Once the basics of human development are achieved, they open up opportunities for progress in other aspects of life.

Choice: human development is, fundamentally, about more choice. It is about providing people with opportunities, not insisting that they make use of them. No one can guarantee human happiness, and the choices people make are their own concern. The process of development - human development - should at least create an environment for people, individually and collectively, to develop to their full potential and to have a reasonable chance of leading productive and creative lives that they value.

As the international community moves toward implementing and monitoring the 2030 agenda, the human development approach remains useful to articulating the objectives of development and improving people's well-being by ensuring an equitable, sustainable and stable planet.

One of the more important achievements of the human development approach, as embodied in successive HDRs, has been to ensure a growing acceptance of the fact that monetary measures, such as GDP per capita, are inadequate proxies of development. The first Human Development Report introduced the Human Development Index (HDI) as a measure of achievement in the basic dimensions of human development across countries. The Table below provides a snapshot of six countries and how they rank against each other from the 2021/2022 Human Development Report.

Table 3: Human Development Index Scores

Country	Rank
Afghanistan	180 out of 191
US	21 out of 191
UK	18 out of 191
South Sedan	191 out of 191
Qatar	42 out of 191
Russia	52 out of 191

Freedom House Index (FHI)

Freedom in the World is an annual global report on political rights and civil liberties, composed of numerical ratings and descriptive texts for each country and a select group of territories. The 2023 edition covers developments in 195 countries and 15 territories from January 1, 2022, through December 31, 2022.

The report's methodology is derived in large measure from the Universal Declaration of Human Rights, adopted by the UN General Assembly in 1948. Freedom in the World is based on the premise that these standards apply to all countries and territories, irrespective of geographical location, ethnic or religious composition, or level of economic development. Freedom in the World operates from the assumption that freedom for all people is best achieved in liberal democratic societies.

Freedom in the World assesses the real-world rights and freedoms enjoyed by individuals, rather than governments or government performance per se. Political rights and civil liberties can be affected by both state and nonstate actors, including insurgents and other armed groups. Afghanistan has a Global Freedom Score of 8 out of 100.

Table 4: Freedom House Index Scores

Country	Scores	Totals
Afghanistan		
Political Rights	1/40	**8/100**
Civil Liberties	7/60	
United States		
Political Rights	32/40	**83/100**
Civil Liberties	51/60	
Finland		
Political Rights	40/40	**100/100**
Civil Liberties	60/60	

Global Hunger Index (GHI)

In the 2023 Global Hunger Index, Afghanistan ranks 114th out of the 125 countries with sufficient data to calculate 2023 GHI scores. With a score of 30.6 in the 2023 Global Hunger Index, Afghanistan has a level of hunger that is serious. The Global Hunger Index (GHI) is a tool for comprehensively measuring and tracking hunger at global, regional, and national levels. GHI scores are based on the values of four component indicators:

> **Undernourishment:** the share of the population with insufficient caloric intake.

> **Child stunting:** the share of children under age five who have low height for their age, reflecting chronic undernutrition.

> **Child wasting:** the share of children under age five who have low weight for their height, reflecting acute undernutrition.

> **Child mortality:** the share of children who die before their fifth birthday, partly reflecting the fatal mix of inadequate nutrition and unhealthy environments.

Based on the values of the four indicators, a GHI score is calculated on a 100-point scale reflecting the severity of hunger, where 0 is the best possible score (no hunger) and 100 is the worst. Each country's GHI score is classified by severity, from low to extremely alarming.

≤ 9.9	10.0 - 19.9	20.0 - 34.9	35.0 - 49.9	≥ 50.0
Low	Moderate	Serious	Alarming	Extremely Alarming

SABER SD

The *Systems Approach for Better Education Results Service Delivery* (SABER SD) tool was developed in 2016 in the Global Engagement and Knowledge Unit of the Education Global Practice (GP) at the *World Bank*, as an initiative to uncover bottlenecks that inhibit student learning in low and middle-income countries and to better understand the quality of education. In addition, SABER SD:

- Provides policy-makers with a quick, comprehensive overview of how their education system is currently functioning;
- Complements existing SABER domain research to deepen the knowledge and understanding of education systems;
- Identifies breakdowns in policy implementation at various levels of government;
- Provides metrics to assess the quality of education service delivery in a country;
- Links gaps in policy and policy implementation to real consequences in the classroom;
- Offers information and accountability for the education system as a whole;
- Provides data which could help bridge dialogue among financiers, policy-makers, and frontline education service providers; and
- Generates information on the implementation of country policies benchmarked by SABER.

The Afghanistan SABER SD survey was implemented across 21 provinces in Afghanistan in 200 primary schools, of which 170 are public schools and the remaining 30 are Community Based Education (CBE) schools. The sample of 170 public schools is nationally representative, to the extent possible, of the places in Afghanistan that were secure enough for the teams to visit. Since it was not possible to obtain the sample frame from the universe of CBE schools, the sample of 30 CBE schools is not representative of the universe of CBE schools, but only of on-budget CBE schools. The Afghanistan SABER SD survey covered the following 21 provinces: Balkh, Faryab, Ghazni, Ghor, Hilmand, Hirat, Jawzjan, Kabul City, Kabul Province, Kandahar, Khost, Kunar, Logar, Nangarhar, Nuristan, Paktia, Parwan, Sar-i-Pul, Sarepul, Takhar and Wardak.

The World Bank conducted a comprehensive study from April to August 2017, and the results are alarming:

- Schooling is not learning. Although access to schooling has improved significantly in the last decade, Afghan students are not learning. After spending 4 years in primary (elementary) school, around 65% of Afghan students have only fully mastered Grade 1 Language curriculum and less than half of them mastered Grade 1 Mathematics curriculum.

- Data collected from the SABER SD survey show that Afghan students could correctly answer only 30% of the questions on the Language test, on average. In particular, one- third could not identify a picture from a given word, three-quarters could not form a sentence with the verb "went" or the verb "is cooking", and less than 15% could comprehend a simple paragraph.

- Their performance in Mathematics is even more worrisome; Afghan students scored an average of only 25% on the Mathematics test. Although most Afghan students could add single and double digit numbers and subtract single digit numbers, they were unable to subtract double digit numbers or complete triple digit equations.

- Most students lack both multiplication and division skills, and almost none could solve word problems, compute fractions, identify shapes, or calculate an area. In other words, even though a Grade 4 student has been in the system for 4 years, they only display the knowledge of a Grade 1 student.

- More specifically, just 65% of the Grade 4 students have mastered the Language curriculum for Grade 1 and only 15% could perform Grade 4 Language questions. Similarly, in Mathematics, less than half the students have mastered the Grade 1 mathematics curriculum. Moreover, less than 3% of students could solve Grade 4 Mathematics questions.

"Extreme poverty anywhere is a threat to human security everywhere."

— Kofi Annan, Former Secretary-General of the United Nations

From Brain-Drain to Brain-Gain

Educational opportunities for the local community as well as programs to encourage the return of Afghan expatriates will alleviate the brain-drain challenges facing the country. Many educated Afghan-Americans are hopeful that a stable and secure Afghanistan will emerge so they can return to Afghanistan to assist with the development process. In a qualitative research project by Kaifi (2010), the following two Afghan-American female professionals conveyed the following:

> The Afghan female physician stated the following: "My grandmother was a strong woman. 'I'm from the mountains', she would say when questioned about her ability to remain steadfast through war in Afghanistan, refugee status in India, and poverty in America. However, I witnessed her strength falter for the first time when news arrived from Kabul announcing the death of her niece during childbirth, leaving a husband widowed and young children motherless. My grandmother quickly regained her composure, but those

fleeting moments of weakness were unsettling. I would soon learn that these tragedies were not uncommon for Afghans and that, in fact, Afghanistan endured one of the highest maternal mortality rates in the world. Although I was born and raised in America, my grandmother had instilled in me the desire to help the women of Afghanistan" (Kaifi, 2010, p. 98).

The Afghan female civil engineer stated the following: "Initially, I had entered college as a computer engineering major, but after 9/11 and the ensuing war on Afghanistan; I saw the ousting of the Taliban as a potential opportunity for a democratic Afghanistan. I figured a time would come where there would be more stability in Afghanistan and I could go back and help rebuild. I felt I would be better able to contribute to the rebuilding efforts in Afghanistan as a civil engineer, and so I changed my major halfway through my college career to civil engineering" (Kaifi, 2010, p. 103).

According to Mujtaba and Kaifi (2010), "Afghanistan, however, lacks sufficient human capital that can develop the next generation of workers in a speedy manner. The Afghan workforce needs to be educated and trained so they can create a peaceful environment for themselves and effectively compete with their neighbors in the marketplace" (p. 43). High literacy rates, continuous education, vocational training, and equipping the workforce with the right skills to become industrialized are critical elements to Afghanistan's progressive development and growth (Mujtaba, 2007). Such workforce training efforts can accelerate economic development and reduce Afghanistan's heavy dependence on foreign aid. Therefore, Afghan elders and war veterans should encourage the youth to seek knowledge and to become more competitive both locally and globally. However, there might be cases when Afghan elders, as effective situational leaders, may have to humbly and voluntarily step aside to let the most knowledgeable person lead. Educational qualifications and relevant experience should be the criteria for choosing who will be best suited to make the people, the department, and the country of Afghanistan more economically competitive (Mujtaba, 2005; Mujtaba, 2007; Kaifi, 2013).

Summary

This chapter provided context regarding the socio-political and humanitarian crises that the fragile education system in Afghanistan faces. By acknowledging these shortcomings, future Afghan leaders can focus on educational reform. Education reform is the process of constantly renegotiating and restructuring the academic standards to reflect the ever-evolving contemporary ideals of social, economic, and political culture. Reforms can be based on bringing education into alignment with the standards of the global society. There is clearly a moral imperative to educate all students in Afghanistan.

Chapter One Discussion Questions

1) Based upon the data presented throughout this chapter, what is the most alarming and why?

2) What did you learn about King Amanullah Khan and his vision for Afghanistan?

3) What did you learn about Islam and education?

4)What did you learn about the importance of literacy?

5) How does it help a nation if females are also educated?

6) What additional measures of development, other than GDP, can be considered when evaluating a country?

2

HIGH SCHOOL EDUCATION

"We cannot always build the future for our youth, but we can build our youth for the future."
— President Franklin D. Roosevelt (FDR)

*H*igh school years are unforgettable for many reasons and each person has different recollections of his or her experiences. According to Samady (2001), "in 1932 the first secondary school for girls was established in Kabul and in 1941, the first provincial girls' school was established in Kandahar" (p. 591). Many would agree that high school prepares individuals for the "real world" because of the competition in academics, sports, popularity, social clubs, and extracurricular activities. For the first time, students are exposed to the concept of *Social Darwinism.* However, in some developing countries, the high school experience is nonexistent. According to a recent UNICEF report, an estimated 3.7 million Afghan youth are out-of-school in Afghanistan – 60% of them are girls. Moreover, the combination of unqualified teachers and administrators, limited resources and infrastructure, and an archaic curriculum coupled with ineffective teaching practices poses many problems for students. Furthermore, the disconnect between provinces, lack of a national curriculum, and community-based education (CBE) due to living in a conflict zone all become a major threat to the validity and reliability of the educational system throughout Afghanistan.

Under these dire circumstances, instructional strategies can be learned from other countries throughout the world. For example, Hogan (2014) explains how Singapore's instructional regime and institutional arrangements include a broad commitment to a nation-building narrative of meritocratic achievement and social stratification, ethnic pluralism, collective values and social cohesion, and economic growth. The years spent in high school are truly convoluted for Afghan teenagers because of all of the different social, political, and economic factors that influence their abilities to focus on school and only school. Currently there is no education data available regarding PISA (Programme for International Student Assessment) test scores for Afghanistan. The PISA is used to assess 15-year-olds around the world.

> **"Education experts emphasize the importance of PISA scores; of reading and mathematics. It is also important how a nation educates its children to become good citizens. There is no measure for this, despite its immense value to a well-functioning democracy."**
>
> **— R. James Breiding**

This chapter will focus on the importance of high school and how high schools in Afghanistan can improve to better serve and teach the future generations of Afghanistan.

King Habibullah's 1906 Speech at Habibia High School

One of the oldest schools in Afghanistan is the Habibia High School in Kabul, which was built by the decree of King Habibullah Khan in 1903 to educate students from the nation's elite class. Below is King Habibullah Khan's translated 1906 speech on the unsatisfactory state of education at the Ḥabibia high school:

"The Habeebiya school was opened nearly three years ago, but now we observe its work retrogressing; it is the Government officers that are especially to blame.

If education be the qualification for service, as it is all over the world, then indeed out of ten Afghan officials, under the present circumstances, even two are not fit for any service in the State. They think: "We have gained the highest honour and we are well nigh the end of our lives, as education is the only path to service in the State, the educated sons of peasants will gain distinction and our children will become obscure men.

Our officials, not caring for education and keeping view for their children their inherited honour alone, wish the work of the school to come to naught."

With regard to their attitude, We say: "the ignorant sons of the Vizier went abegging before rustics. The wise (educated) children of the rustics become Viziers of the King."

And as to their sons, we cite those who take a pride merely in their ancestors who are like dogs pleasing themselves with bones. The superiority of one man over another is through knowledge and good breeding and not through wealth and high lineage.

However, when the truth is revealed falsehood is exposed [Qur'ānic verse]. Therefore, we strongly desire the progress of the school, by God's help, and we will, please God, personally give it our fullest attention.

Addressing the present staff of the school we say :--Give us a complete account of the defects of the school as it has gone on till now and of your future plan as to its progress, that we may remove its shortcomings and improve it, God willing the Habeebiya school will rise to a very high level of efficiency."

Source:
NAI FD/FRNT/B September 1906 141 ("H.H. the Amir's speech at Kabul on education in Afghanistan").

Even after approximately 120 years, the same speech is just as applicable when assessing the quality of education throughout Afghanistan. Samady (2001) provides some important information on how secondary education changed over the years in Afghanistan:

> Like primary schools, secondary schools went through a number of reforms in the twentieth-century. In 1930, secondary schooling was an eight-year cycle, with four years in middle school and four years in lycée; in 1944, secondary school was reduced to six years, with three years each in middle school and at the lycée level; the 1975 reforms reduced secondary school to a total of four years; in the 1980s, secondary school consisted of six years of study, four in middle school and two in the lycée; finally, in 1990, when primary education was again extended, secondary school was reorganized into three years of middle school and three years in the lycée (p. 594).

The constant and countless changes that were implemented in the secondary school structure illustrate the instability and inconsistencies of secondary school in Afghanistan. In 1995, Turkey recognized the need for a better education system in Afghanistan and, as a result, established the highly selective and respected Afghan-Turk schools throughout Afghanistan. According to the Afghan-Turk website,

Afghan-Turk Maarif Schools are serving for the future of the brother country Afghanistan with 25 institutions in 7 provinces across Afghanistan. Afghan-Turk Maarif Schools, which have pre-school, primary school, high school and training centers and more than 6 thousand students and more than a thousand staff, are the only official Turkish schools in Afghanistan.

Throughout Afghanistan's history, nations such as France and Germany have also attempted to improve the education system by establishing reputable high schools (e.g., *Lycée Esteqlal and Lycée Amani)*. The ongoing issue, however, is the lack of standardization with the curriculum throughout Afghanistan.

Standardization of the Curriculum

In the short-term, establishing a standard national curriculum in Afghanistan can be challenging because Afghanistan has two main languages and there are many perspectives on what the curriculum in Afghanistan should encompass. Therefore, Afghanistan can use a system that is similar to the US or Canada. There are currently no national standards for curriculum in the US - all US states have their own state standards. Content standards guide what students should learn in certain courses and grade levels. For example, in California the standards are called the Common Core State Standards (CCSS). In Texas, the standards are called the Texas Essential Knowledge and Skills (TEKS). Canada does not have a national curriculum and each province has its own ministry-established common curriculum. Similarly, Afghanistan can create an educational system for high school where each of the 34 Provinces creates its own standards that prepares students for the national Kankor exam for university admissions. An important recommendation is to stop focusing on rote learning in the classroom and instead focus on experiential learning. In order to create this classroom experience, the teachers need to be highly qualified.

Teacher Training Colleges

The history of Teacher Training Colleges (TTCs) in Afghanistan goes back to the era of Amir Habibullah Khan. The first Kabul TTC was established in 1913 (Barakat, 2014). In the early 1920s, a TTC was established in Kabul, while the students of this TTC were the primary school teacher graduates. Samady (2001) provides some historical knowledge on this topic:

> A teacher-training school was set up in Kabul in 1923 and approximately 100 young men with the equivalent of a primary education were admitted. They graduated four years later as teachers. In the 1950s, special attention was given to teacher education and, in 1956, three new teacher-training schools were established in the provinces (Herat, Kandahar and Nangarhar). The Institute of Education and the Faculty of Education were established in co-operation with Columbia University in 1955 and 1962 respectively (p. 596).

In 1964, two more TTCs were established - the first one was Darul-Malimeen-Uali (High level TTC) and is currently called Sayed Jamaludin Afghan TTC. The second one was Teacher Training Academy to train

TTCs' teachers, but they did not hire teachers through an established procedure. The procedure for students' enrollments was also not clear, however those who graduated from grade seven could continue their lessons at the TTCs (Kamgar, 2003). According to Barakat (2014), "the majority of the students in public and private TTCs are those who fail the Kankor exam." Mansory (2012) corroborates this point by stating that "the last choice of the students is TTCs when passing the Kankor." However, Samady (2001) explains that decades ago teaching was a respected profession in Afghan society and that teachers were given some special perks or incentive for teaching. For example, six years of successful teaching could replace the mandatory one to two years of military service in Afghanistan. Teachers working in villages were expected to set moral and ethical standards and were treated as community leaders.

In the US, teachers must have a Bachelor's degree and must complete a specific teaching credential program which requires the student to complete coursework, an internship for experience, and the successful completion of a state exam in the subject that they will be teaching. Teachers in Finland must have a Master's degree and spend fewer hours at school each day and less time in classrooms than American teachers. According to Muhonen (2017), "With such selective admissions — it was harder to gain entry to the University of Helsinki's teacher education program (6.8 percent acceptance rate) than the law program (8.3 percent acceptance rate) or the medical school (7.3 percent acceptance rate) in 2016 — and rigorous preparation, one might expect Finland to suffer teacher shortages." The following table (Table 5) compares the amount of education needed to teach in three countries,

the literacy rate in each country, and the Better Life
Index (i.e., quality of life) where each of the 11 topics
being assessed contribute to overall well-being.

> **"Anyone who stops learning is old, whether at twenty or eighty. Anyone who keeps learning stays young."**
>
> **— Henry Ford**

Table 5: Teaching Requirements Needed

	Afghanistan	US	Finland
Minimum Education Needed to Teach in Kindergarten - 12th Grade Education	High School Diploma (teachers in the villages or remote areas do not meet this requirement due to teacher shortages)	Bachelor's Degree plus a teaching credential	Master's Degree
Literacy Rate of the Country	36% - 37%	79%	100%
Better Life Index from OECD	Not Available	7	7.9

Samady (2001) provides some valuable historical
information on Afghan teacher training
programs/colleges in the 1960s and 1970s:

- Teacher training was organized and adapted to the Afghan situation. It evolved with the increase in expertise as well as with the availability of human and material resources. In 1975, twenty-seven teacher-education schools and institutions, with the capacity to enroll 6,000, were training teachers. There were eight basic teacher-training schools, five higher teachers' colleges at the post-secondary level, four university level institutions, eight theological schools, one arts and crafts school, and one physical education school.

Teacher education was structured as follows:

- Primary school teachers were trained in basic teacher-training schools. Secondary school graduates also had the option of one year of professional training to become teachers.

- In order to train teachers for teacher shortages in some remote areas, an emergency teacher-training project was launched in 1962 through which middle-school graduates received one year of professional teacher training. Over 5,000 teachers were trained this way between 1962 and 1970.

- In 1964, the Higher Teachers College, consisting of grades thirteen and fourteen, was established in Kabul to train middle school teachers. By 1975, four other such colleges had been established in the provinces with an annual intake of 400 students.

- Upper secondary school teachers were highly trained, specializing in areas such as national languages, foreign languages, science and mathematics, or history and geography.

- The Faculty of Theological Studies and a number of secondary level theological schools in Kabul and the provinces trained teachers for religious education, Arabic, and ethics.

- The Academy for Teacher Educators was established in 1964 to provide postgraduate training to experienced teachers who were assigned to newly established teacher-training institutions.

- The Institute of Education provided in-service training for teachers who needed qualifications in general education or professional training. The institute's courses were organized during the summer and winter school vacations. Between 1955 and 1966, over 6,000 teachers benefited from these courses and obtained the relevant qualifications. In 1967, in-service teacher education was made the responsibility of teacher-training colleges.

Based upon Afghanistan's current situation, Teacher Training Programs must have a rigorous curriculum along with student teaching (field experience) and a final national and/or provincial assessment. Teachers should have at least a bachelor's degree in the subject that they would like to teach in before starting a Teacher Training Program. One course that should be mandatory to include in the curriculum for teachers is *Trauma Informed Pedagogy*. As Marquart and Báez (2021) write, such approaches aim to address "barriers resulting from the

impacts of traumatic human experiences" in order to
"create classroom communities that promote student
wellbeing and learning" (p. 64). New teachers in
Afghanistan should also learn about Bloom's Taxonomy
and how to use this framework in the classroom so there
is less memorization by the students and more analyzing,
synthesizing, evaluating, and creating. Courses that focus
on assessment, Social Emotional Learning (SEL),
neuroscience, V.A.R.K. (visual, auditory,
reading/writing, and kinesthetic) learning styles,
experiential learning, and classroom management are
also some of the important topics to include in Teacher
Training Programs. It is always important to remember
what Mustafa Kemal Atatürk, the first president of the
Republic of Turkey, once said: *Teachers are the one and
only people who save nations.*

مصطفی کمال اتاترک، اولین رئیس جمهور ترکیه زمان گفته بود، «معلمان یگانه افرادی هستند که ملت ها را نجات می دهند.»

د ترکیی لومړي ولسمشر مصطفی اتاترک یو ځل ویلي و: ښوونکي یواځني خلک دي، چی ملتونه ژغوري.

Ideally, the best students in Afghanistan should become
teachers so that they can give back to their country and
as a result, they should receive the same respect, status,
and compensation as medical doctors. According to
Walker (2018), "In China and Malaysia, the teaching
profession is often placed on par with doctors." Other
incentives such as early retirement, affordable housing,
paying less taxes, and waiving military service should be
considered for Afghan teachers.

PISA and the Organization for Economic Cooperation and Development (OECD)

The Programme for International Student Assessment (PISA) is a worldwide study by the Organisation for Economic Co-operation and Development in member and non-member nations intended to evaluate educational systems by measuring 15-year-old school pupils' scholastic performance in mathematics, science, and reading. The following table provides some data on the 2022 PISA assessment results for three nations. Unfortunately, there is no education data available for the PISA test scores for Afghanistan.

Table 6: PISA Benchmarking

US	Mexico	UK
In mathematics, the main topic of PISA 2022, 15-year-olds scored 465 points compared to an average of 472 points in OECD countries.	In mathematics, the main topic of PISA 2022, 15-year-olds scored 395 points compared to an average of 472 points in OECD countries.	In mathematics, the main topic of PISA 2022, 15-year-olds scored 489 points compared to an average of 472 points in OECD countries.
On average, 15-year-olds scored 504 points in reading compared to an average of 476 points in OECD countries.	On average, 15-year-olds scored 415 points in reading compared to an average of 476 points in OECD countries.	On average, 15-year-olds scored 494 points in reading compared to an average of 476 points in OECD countries.
The average performance of 15-year-olds in science is 499 points, compared to an average of 485 points in OECD countries.	The average performance of 15-year-olds in science is 410 points, compared to an average of 485 points in OECD countries.	The average performance of 15-year-olds in science is 500 points, compared to an average of 485 points in OECD countries.

Average 2022 results were down compared to 2018 in mathematics, and about the same as in 2018 in reading and science.	Average 2022 results were down compared to 2018 in mathematics and science, and about the same as in 2018 in reading.	Average 2022 results were down compared to 2018 in mathematics and reading, and about the same as in 2018 in science.
The 2022 results are among the lowest ever measured by PISA in mathematics. In reading and science, however, results confirm a long-term stability in results.	Almost no students were top performers in mathematics.	11% of students were top performers in mathematics

Afghan leaders must strive for the youth of Afghanistan to be included in this important assessment for benchmarking purposes so continuous improvements can be made with the overall curriculum.

High School GPA

In most countries, GPA (Grade Point Average) is very important as it has the potential to open up many tangible and intangible opportunities, which is precisely why high school becomes so competitive. Most students in high school have an average IQ (intelligence quotient) level of about 100. Albert Einstein had an IQ of 150, and there are many people in the world who have an IQ of 190 or higher. There are some students who are able to learn new and abstract material based upon their high IQ without much studying while others have to work strenuously to learn the same material. Like everything else in life (hair color, eye color, and height), IQ is hereditary to a certain extent. This does not, however, mean that someone with a low IQ cannot have a high

GPA. As mentioned above, it is the time that is invested in a specific task that determines the level of success one will have. For example, a person with a lower IQ may have to work harder at learning new material but may actually learn more during the process. The information below highlights the importance of high school GPA for students considering higher education.

Example of GPA Requirements for University of California (UC) Admissions

- You must earn a GPA of 3.0 or higher if you are a California resident, or you must earn a GPA of 3.4 or higher if you're a nonresident.

- Furthermore, you may not score lower than a C in any of your courses. GPA is calculated using specific courses (History, English, Mathematics, Science, Language other than English, Visual and Performing Arts, and College Preparatory Electives).

- The UC school system has a specific way to calculate GPA, so the GPA your school gives you may not be the same as how a UC school would calculate it.

In the US, colleges and universities seek students who have high GPAs because in their eyes, high GPAs reflect an ability to strive for excellence. In Afghanistan, a student's GPA is insignificant when applying to a public university. As a matter of fact, a student does not even report their GPA in high school when applying to a public university. This raises an important issue: the motivation for a student to perform well in high school if grades are not helpful when applying to a public university. Furthermore, what are teachers teaching in the classroom? Considering that there is no national uniform curriculum in Afghanistan, no rigorous teaching credentialing program for teachers, and a lack of meaningful oversight, how are students being prepared for post-secondary education? The only admissions criterion that is used for admitting a student into post-secondary education at a public university in Afghanistan is the controversial Kankor exam. Basically, one exam determines your future.

The Emergence of the Kankor Exam in Afghanistan

In Afghanistan, the entrance exam for university admissions is considered a significant event. According to the Afghan National Examination Authority (NExA) website and archives, "In 1960, Kabul University started conducting [some] entrance exams for students" aiming to fulfill their aspirations and facilitate their admission to universities. Perhaps the NExA used a staggered approach with administering the Kankor exam to different colleges within Kabul University. As a case in point, Dr. Abdul Qayum Safi graduated from a high school in Kabul in the 1960s. He did not take the Kankor exam in order to start his studies at Kabul University. Dr. Safi mentioned the following,

> *The year I graduated from high school in Kabul and was admitted to the College of Education at Kabul University, the Kankor examination was probably not a requirement.*

After many years of hard-work and dedication, Dr. Safi traveled to the US and earned a doctoral degree in Education from Columbia University - a highly respected Ivy League university - in 1978. Thus, the exact date when *all* Afghan students were required to take the Kankor exam is not clear at this time.

Initially, the Kankor exam was conducted in a simplified manner, but it paved the way for conducting an entrance exam for talented students in subsequent years. A committee was formed for the exam, and a specific location within the central library of Kabul University was designated for this purpose, where the committee members conducted interviews and assessed candidates' qualifications. The word *"Kankor"* originates from the word *"Concours"* which means "competition" in French because students and schools compete against one another on this exam. In France, the Concours Général is the most prestigious academic competition held every year between students of Première (11th grade) and Terminale (12th and final grade) in almost all subjects taught in both general, technological, and professional high schools. According to Egéa-Kuehne (1999), the National French Contest (NFC) was first given in 1935.

According to Farrokhi-Khajeh-Pasha et al. (2012), "in Iran, the *Konkoor* was first conducted 46 years ago [in 1966 based upon when this article was published], in an attempt to introduce a single, common test for the entire pool of national candidates for higher education. Through its relatively long history, the Konkoor has not undergone any significant revisions" (p. 1). While the Kankor exam might be appropriate for some countries, Afghanistan may want to reevaluate the fairness and objective of this exam – especially after 40+ years of war and conflict. It should be mentioned that many universities in the US are no longer requiring students to take the SAT exam for university admissions because the exam is considered unfair.

Afghanistan's Kankor Exam

For the longest time in the US, taking the SAT (Scholastic Aptitude Test) or ACT (American College Testing) was a critical requirement during high school for those who were interested in attending a four-year university. After years of debates, many universities in the US no longer require the SAT or ACT. The SAT is comprised of two sections: Evidence-Based Reading and Writing, and Math. The ACT contains four multiple-choice tests—English, mathematics, reading, and science—and an optional writing test. According to Beall (2022), "In March 2022, the California State University Board of Trustees approved the removal of the SAT and ACT standardized tests from undergraduate admissions processes. The decision followed the nearly two years during the COVID-19 pandemic when submitting those test scores was not required for CSU applicants." The CSU system decided to eliminate a high-stakes test that can cause great stress on students and their families as it does not add any additional predictive value over high school GPA. As a result of this decision, the CSU system believes that being test-free will better meet the needs of their future students.

As a different example, UC Berkeley is a "Test Free" school, meaning it does not use SAT/ACT test scores in any part of its application process. According to Hubler (2021), "In the last decade or so, more than 1,230 colleges and universities have made the SAT and

ACT optional for admission, according to FairTest, a group that has pushed to end testing requirements." Opponents of the SAT contend that injustice emerges because wealthier families have the money and effort to invest in test practice tools and services. On the other hand, some universities in the US do require a student's scores on the SAT or ACT when applying for admissions. For example, at the University of Florida, all applicants must submit test scores from the SAT or ACT along with the other components of the application process.

In the US, critics of standardized assessments claim that the tests put less wealthy students at a disadvantage. More specifically, the tests are too easily gamed by students who can pay thousands of dollars for private coaching and test prep. The same is true for students in Afghanistan who are interested in furthering their education at one of Afghanistan's free public universities.

According to Sherzad (2016), "In Afghanistan, high school graduates, in order to continue higher education, need to pass the National University Entrance Exam known as the Kankor (from the French word "Concours" which means "*Contest*")." The author further states, "Kankor is very important and requires further research and studies as it is used as the only means and tools to identify the participant's competence and skills" (p. 1).

According to Bamik (2019),

> All students from across Afghanistan at the end of their secondary school who wish to enter public universities, free of cost, are required to

take the Kankor examination. Every year, on average 200,000 students from 34 provinces of Afghanistan attend the Kankor examination between February and April. In Afghanistan, the Kankor examination is the only way through which the Ministry of Higher Education (MoHE), the responsible entity for administering Kankor examination, can evaluate secondary school graduates to determine whether they are capable of undertaking undergraduate courses at higher education institutions (p. 12).

As of 2024, students are able to take the Kankor exam in July and August. Furthermore, the Kankor exam is no longer administered by the Ministry of Higher Education. The Kankor exam is currently administered by the Independent Directorate which is responsible for all governmental exams.

According to Sakhi and Nabizadah (2015), "Kankor is held every year, mainly in the capital and large provinces, usually between December and the end of February. Since 2006 the Kankor examination process was computerized. Prior to 2006, usually six months were required in order to finish Kankor – from registering for the exam until announcing the final results" (p. 9). Kankor questions are provided both in Pashto and Dari (MoHE, 2011, pp. 45–56). "All the questions are multiple choice, and generally, the participants have two to three hours to answer and choose the proper options. Usually, correct answers are worth one to three points. The maximum number of points is between 320 and 370, but more important is the minimum number of points needed to qualify for a university slot" (Sherzad, 2016, p. 3).

According to Bamik (2019), "The National Kankor Examination in Afghanistan contains 160 questions. All the questions are from the subjects taught during secondary school particularly in grades 10 to 12. The applicants have two to three hours to answer 160 questions. The weights of the questions are different, which means that some questions have more values while some questions have less value" (pp. 14-15). According to Bamik (2019), "science and math subjects form 50% of the Kankor examination questions, and the next 50% is from social subjects including languages, geography, history, Islamic studies, and so on. Apart from that, science questions have more values than social science questions on the Kankor examination. So, students who are not good at science subjects are easily failed on the Kankor examination because of their poor performance in the science section. This issue resonates a lot with those students who are not interested in studying science disciplines" (p. 16). Researchers have started analyzing the reliability and validity of the Kankor Exam in Afghanistan.

> **"Success is not final; failure is not fatal.
> It is the courage to continue that counts."**
>
> **— Winston Churchill**

The following table highlights some of the flaws that have been identified by Sherzad (2016) and Bamik (2019) regarding the Kankor exam:

Table 7: Kankor Exam Flaws

Flaw	Research
Student Unfamiliarity With the Exam Structure	Sherzad (2016) mentions that "the data indicate that more than 70% of participants severely lack a proper understanding of the structure, methods and overall procedures for the Kankor test. More than 80% believe unfamiliarity with the Kankor test and lack of preparation for Kankor are two of the main reasons participants fail in the Kankor" (p. 2).
Inappropriate Medium to Identify Student Knowledge	Sherzad (2016) points out one major flaw of the Kankor by stating that the "Kankor, as a standardized test, is found not to be the appropriate medium to identify the level and extent of participants' knowledge. While 50% of the questions focus on mathematics and science, the other 50% is allocated to the rest of areas of study including languages, geography, history, theology, etc. For example, some participants who are interested in pursuing a degree in Fine Arts fail to pass the Kankor exam because the questions related to mathematics and science have higher scoring values" (p. 2). Bamik (2019) correctly proposes that all Kankor

	candidates should answer specific questions related to the field of study that they are interested in, and then for the shared section questions (for all students) to ask questions that focus on English language skills and mathematics. The English component of the proposed Kankor exam is necessary for students to compete on a global level.
Generic Assessment With a Focus on Math and Science	According to Bamik (2019), "the current university entrance examination system in Afghanistan does not help students get into their desired disciplines" (p. 16). This means that a student must first pass the exam with a minimum score and then based upon their actual score, they are placed into a major based upon the score cut-off for each program. According to Bamik (2019), "The exam is not specialized, and this is viewed as a big challenge of the current Kankor examination" (p. 13). According to Sherzad (2016), "It is wise to revise the Kankor scoring system based on the candidate's choice of field of study. For example, fields of study relevant to science require a strong understanding of mathematics and science subjects. While theology and

	similar fields of study do not. This will be a pioneering step leading toward offering a specialized Kankor exam (p. 14).
Unrealistic Competition	According to Sherzad (2016), "It is very challenging to get admitted into the desired higher education institutions when more than 250,000 high school graduates are applying for about 55,000 slots" (p. 3).
Outdated Questions and Exam Ambiguity	According to Bamik (2019), "The history of the current Kankor examination dates back to 80 years ago – prior to the establishment of Kabul University. But unfortunately, its contents, and even in some cases its questions, have not been changed. While ways of learning, performance measurement and evaluation methods, effectiveness and efficiency indicators are constantly changing in the world. But the Kankor examination methods are still outdated and replete with flaws" (p. 15).
Lack of Triangulation	Data triangulation uses multiple pieces of data (three or more) to examine the same phenomenon (e.g., student achievement or student ability).
Lack of Feedback and Transparency of Results	Standardized tests don't provide any feedback on how to perform better. Results aren't given back to the

	students until months later, and there are no specific instructions provided to high school teachers for better preparing students in the future.

Students who live in rural provinces do not have the same opportunities as students who live in urban and more developed cities. This does not constitute a level playing field because standardized tests favor those who have socio-economic advantages. Consider the following two students in Afghanistan and their respective situations:

- *Student "X" grew up in Kabul, has had better trained teachers with more education, attended better schools with actual infrastructure and textbooks, and both parents have extra money for a Kankor prep tutor to assist their child.*

- *Student "Y" grew up in a remote village in the mountains of Badakhshan without electricity, with unprepared teachers and no infrastructure, has one surviving parent, and no extra money for extra tutoring for the Kankor exam. Also, the student has to work before school and after school to help feed his family of 8.*

Unfortunately, the second example is the norm for over 50% of the population in Afghanistan. Consequently, it is unfair and unjust when making university admission decisions based upon only the Kankor assessment which requires significant travel for many students. To make matters more complicated, there have been reports of corruption and cheating on the Kankor exam. For example, in March 2013, Azizullah Ludin, then head of the High Commission of Oversight and Anti-Corruption, demanded the abolition of the Kankor altogether as "half of the corruption in the Ministry of Higher Education is linked to it." As a different example, officials in Herat had found out that teachers from the Ustad Reyaz School in the province's capital had somehow obtained the right answers to the test and given them to students beforehand (Ali, 2014).

How can students be expected to pass a standardized national exam for admissions when there is no uniform curriculum throughout the country, the qualifications of teachers differ significantly by Province, resources are not the same, some students are able to bribe officials, and the socio-economic backgrounds of the students are not the same? This is a recipe for disaster which has been the case of education in Afghanistan since its inception.

There is no simple solution to this predicament. However, it is important to keep in mind that policies and procedures for standardized testing may change in the near or distant future in many countries. More specifically and based upon historical facts, it is clear that American universities will not base their admissions decisions based upon only one standardized assessment like in the case of Afghanistan. There are other components to an application that need to be taken into consideration. A more comprehensive and humanistic approach for admissions may be necessary in Afghanistan to end the cycle of poverty for so many students considering that the country has been dealing with decades of war and instability.

Implementing an Index Score for Afghan University Admissions

The current Independent Directorate responsible for administering the Kankor exam may want to take into consideration that most developed countries do not rely upon only one criterion for university admissions. Even the best universities in the world do not have such a stringent requirement. As such, what is the rationale for making university admissions so challenging for Afghan students?

One researcher proposed the following regarding the Kankor exam: "students who are interested in studying a social science major should answer more questions related to the field of social sciences and those who are interested in majoring in a science related field should answer more questions related to the field of science" (Bamik, 2019, p. 20).

Proponents of a change to standardized assessments believe that it is fairer to judge students by other measures, such as teacher recommendations. Some studies have suggested that high school grades better measure a student's likelihood of graduation and cumulative performance in college. At the absolute minimum, the Ministry of Education in Afghanistan, the Ministry of Higher Education in Afghanistan, and the public universities in Afghanistan should use an Index Score that consists of a student's Grade Point Average (GPA) and Kankor exam score; however, it is highly recommended to use a more holistic and comprehensive approach with multiple factors being evaluated for university admissions. With advancements in technology, a portal (e.g., *Naviance* is one of the many portals used in the US) can easily be used for students to upload their scores, transcripts, and documents.

In the US, universities use different quantitative formulas when reviewing applications of potential students. For example, one university uses an index score methodology for students who are interested in their MBA program, where potential students must have a 1,200 index score or higher in order to even be considered for admissions. The index score is calculated by multiplying a GPA by 200 plus the GMAT score. If a person has an overall undergraduate GPA of 3.0 and a GMAT score of 600, he or she would have a 1,200 index score or as a different example, a different student may have a GPA of 3.5 and a GMAT score of 500 which also equates to a 1,200 index score. The formula is:

GPA x 200 + GMAT score = *Index Score*

In the case of Afghanistan, the Ministry of Education and the Ministry of Higher Education must figure out a better system for calculating grade point averages that is consistent with the rest of the world. This will help with transferring from one university to another, earning a graduate degree abroad, and creating reliability and validity throughout the educational system. Once this has been established, then the academic departments at public universities could use a *similar* index score methodology and can determine the threshold based upon how grades are allocated throughout high schools in Afghanistan. For example, the following formula can be used:

GPA x 200 + Kankor score = *Index Score*

Each academic department within public universities in Afghanistan should collaborate and have their own method of determining who is eligible for admissions based upon at least two different components. Ideally, several data points should be used for making a more informed decision about each student. More specifically, there are several other components that should be taken into consideration when reviewing a student's application for university admissions such as: class rank, personal statement, letter of recommendations, TOEFL score, sports, school clubs, extracurricular activities, creativity, and/or conducting student interviews.

Class Rank

In the US, there has been some controversy over class rank and its relevance when applying to universities nationally. As a matter of fact, some high schools stopped ranking their students. The schools that still use this method to determine how students rank with their peers help universities determine the overall ability of students to thrive in a competitive atmosphere. Competition is unavoidable and as individuals get older and step into the "real world" the competition only gets more rigorous. In Afghanistan, the class rank system is widely used at all high schools. However, a student's class rank is neither used nor significant when applying to a public university. According to Wood (2022), in the US class rank is a ranking of all the students in a high school class from highest to lowest GPA, with the student with the highest GPA being ranked No. 1. Class rank may be based on an unweighted GPA, which calculates a student's average grade out of a 4.0 scale, or a weighted GPA, which uses a 5.0 scale to take coursework difficulty into account. High schools typically report class rank on students' report cards and submit this information in college application materials. Some schools also report what percentile students are in their class, based on their ranking number and the total number of students in the class.

TOEFL Exam Scores

The Test of English as a Foreign Language (TOEFL) exam may also be a helpful indicator of success at a university in Afghanistan if and when instruction is in the English language for at least 50% of the curriculum. The TOEFL is a standardized test to measure the English language ability of non-native speakers wishing to enroll in English-speaking universities. The test is accepted by more than 10,000 universities and other institutions in over 180 countries and territories. The TOEFL exam is also used for students interested in earning a Fulbright Scholarship to study in the US.

Personal Statement

A personal statement is how universities find out more about who you are as a person. They're looking to learn a few specific things about you, such as how you think, approach problems, and network with others. A simple anecdote or description of a passion can say quite a bit about how you approach and view the world. Students should be able to indicate what their overall objective is and what they will be doing with a specific degree upon graduation. It is important to keep in mind that thousands of other students will be applying to the same university and each student should be able to differentiate himself or herself from other applicants in a limiting two or three pages. When writing an essay, many recommend brainstorming with parents and peers, then preparing an outline, and finally working on the essay. The sooner a student starts on the essay, the more time he or she will have for others to proof-read and evaluate each draft.

As a student, it is important to have several people analyze the essay because others will be able to enhance the essay based upon their feedback and suggestions. Teachers can be involved in the application process by reading and evaluating drafts of the personal statements and writing letters of recommendations.

The personal statement seems like an easy step that can be taken care of a couple of days before the application is due, but this mentality has proven to be incorrect and many regret not starting on the essay much earlier. What most people forget is that it is easy to write about others but can be difficult to write about oneself. For many universities, this essay tells the admissions team what a student's personality is like, what makes him or her unique, and how the student will complement their university. A personal statement gives a potential student the opportunity to explain and justify certain areas of the application that are sub-optimal, but it is important to turn negatives into positives. For example, a student named Adam shared the following excerpt from his personal statement essay:

> I am the first sibling in my family to obtain a college degree with all of the obstacles faced by my immigrant experiences. I started working at

the age of fourteen and continued working
throughout high school to help my parents with
their finances. I can recall being in high school
and waiting for the final bell to ring so I could
rush to work. This experience helped me become
more independent and resourceful and has helped
me excel in every aspect of life. This experience
has also contributed to my success in time
management, entrepreneurship, and has taught
me responsibility and accountability.

This person is able to show that he is a hard-worker, is
able to turn negatives into positives, and understands the
importance of priorities. The personal statement is not a
time to vent, complain, or whine about life experiences
because everyone faces trials and obstacles. As a
different option during the application process, students
can be required to obtain letters of recommendation
from teachers and administrators who can provide
valuable insights into a student's potential.

Letters of Recommendation

Most universities in the US require that students
submit three letters of recommendations with their
application because they give a student credibility,
confirm a student's academic performance, and are
written by professionals who are able to validate that a
student will be successful. For some, getting a letter of
recommendation is very difficult because they do not
feel comfortable asking a teacher to write a letter for
them even though they have the highest grade in the
class. This requires a paradigm shift by the students, or
changing their mindsets because teachers and counselors

are expected to write letters of recommendations for students who are applying to college. Also, it should be mentioned that teachers were required to get letters of recommendations when they applied to go to a university, again in their credential programs, and lastly by their employer when they were being interviewed. Because of this, they know the process very well and they understand the importance of obtaining letters of recommendation. This phenomenon is not new and will always be significant throughout a student's educational and professional career.

When asking for letters of recommendation, it should be emphasized that students must ask someone who knows their strengths and who can write a strong letter of recommendation that will validate their abilities. When applying to a university, the admissions team seeks solid letters from high school counselors, teachers, coaches, and principals.

If teachers recognize a student's abilities and strengths, they will gladly write a letter of recommendation that will increase the student's chances of getting into the university of his or her choice. Students should send a thank you card or email to all of their teachers who took time out of their busy schedule to write a letter of recommendation. The final step in reviewing a student's application includes nonacademic and personal factors.

Sports and School Clubs

Playing sports in high school is recommended by many athletes, adults, professionals, and colleges throughout the U.S. Those who are able to play sports engage in a competitive environment where teamwork is rewarded, leadership emerges, and confidence is built. The memories last a lifetime and more importantly, playing sports in high school makes a student more competitive when he or she is applying to different universities.

A college's admissions team looks for well-rounded individuals who are smart, athletic, and are natural leaders. A different nonacademic factor that may help an individual become more competitive is joining a school club on campus such as the chess club, math club, science club, reading club, or even the drama club. School clubs are a great way to meet new people, brainstorm ideas with peers who have the same interests, and learn new talents and skills. The last criteria that can potentially help a student get into the university of his or her choice is an individual's participation in extracurricular activities.

Extracurricular Activities

High school is a time of exploring and figuring out how to live a comfortable life with many responsibilities. Many students have a lot on their plate during high school years because they are juggling sports, projects, exams, and a versatile social life. Those who are successful are able to prioritize accordingly. When applying to colleges, it is imperative for each individual to be competitive (as mentioned above) which is why some students start gaining experience in their field by "job shadowing" at an early age. It is always important to remember that when a student is job shadowing, he or she will work for free (*pro-bono*) but will learn and gain experience. Furthermore, by having this experience, an admissions team will know that the student is sincere about his or major and has done some research. Some students are able to find time in their busy schedules for community service—many universities seek students who find extra time for community service because it's a service that is provided pro-bono. Most university applications ask if the student has performed any type of community service, so those who have that experience will once again have an advantage. A different option that may help a student out when applying to universities is tutoring. Being a tutor is not an easy job and takes a lot of patience and creativity. Students who want to stand out in the application process should be able to prove that they are willing to help those in need or work for free to gain practical experience that will help them in the long run. Thus, high school is a world full of opportunities that can become reality. Those who have their priorities straight and have a game plan will be successful. There are different avenues that can be taken in high school that will help a student when applying to universities. Even with all of the advice in the world, high school still remains the most challenging time for many students because of the external social issues that interfere and create barriers.

Creativity

A student can address what creativity means to them and provide examples of how they are creative. Being creative is a talent that can help an individual throughout life because of its importance and relevance in educational settings, the workforce, and society. "Sometimes a problem requires coming up with entirely new ways of looking at the problem or unusual, inventive solutions. This kind of thinking is called *creativity*: solving problems by combining ideas or behaviors in new ways" (Ciccarelli & Meyer, 2006, p. 304). Being creative means to challenge the status quo by developing new and abstract ideas or methods. It is important to be able to think outside of the box and figure out new ways of getting things done which requires using imagination. Employers are always looking for *innovative* individuals who can help an organization develop new competitive advantages. In the academic world, being innovative is important when conducting research because of its real-world applications.

Those who are creative usually stand out in a crowd because of their ability to shine. It is no myth that universities and employers look for creativity in interviews and personal statements. At times, being creative also means being persistent and even aggressive in the job hunt process. An example is how a small percentage of people send their resumes to potential employers even when there is not an immediate opening, followed by an email to the hiring manager to schedule an informational meeting to discuss future employment possibilities. When comparing this creative strategy to the conventional method of waiting for an opening and then sending a resume to the human resources department (which may never be sent to the hiring manager), this illuminates the importance of being creative, persistent, proactive, and aggressive in all aspects of life. Being creative also means accepting rejection and being able to find new ways of being marketable.

> **"Creativity is seeing what others see and thinking what no one else ever thought."**
> **– Albert Einstein**

Student Interviews for University Admissions

Conducting student interviews for university admissions is crucial as it offers a holistic perspective beyond academic achievements and standardized test scores. Interviews provide a platform for applicants to showcase their personality, interpersonal skills, and passion for their chosen field. Admissions officers gain valuable insights into an applicant's character, motivation, and potential contributions to the campus community, helping them make more informed decisions.

Furthermore, student interviews serve as a two-way communication channel. They allow applicants to learn more about the college culture, programs, and resources, helping them make informed decisions about their educational journey. This interaction fosters a connection between the prospective student and the institution, contributing to a better mutual understanding. This personalized approach aids in creating a diverse and vibrant student body, enhancing the overall college experience for everyone involved. Those who will be successful in life should have both *analytical intelligence* (book smarts) and also *practical intelligence* (street smarts). Psychologist Robert Sternberg (2013) explains how practical intelligence is understanding what to say to whom, knowing when to say it, and knowing how to say it for maximum effect.

In addition, interviews help identify intangible qualities such as resilience, adaptability, and leadership potential, which are essential for success in both academic and extracurricular pursuits. By delving into an applicant's experiences, aspirations, and values, colleges can select candidates who not only excel academically but also align with the institution's mission and values. In essence, student interviews enhance the admissions process by providing a more comprehensive evaluation of applicants, fostering a dynamic and enriching educational environment.

Affirmative Action in Afghanistan

Affirmative action in education refers to policies and practices aimed at increasing opportunities for historically underrepresented groups, often in the context of university admissions. Finland has focused on being mindful of equity in education. As a result, a Finnish child has the same opportunity at getting the same quality education regardless of whether he or she lives in a rural village or an urban city. The differences between the weakest and strongest Finnish students are the smallest in the world, according to the most recent survey by the Organization for Economic Co-operation and Development (OECD). Supporters argue that it addresses historical and systemic inequalities, promoting diversity and ensuring a more equitable distribution of educational resources. By considering factors such as race, ethnicity, and/or gender in admissions, institutions aim to create a more representative student body that reflects the broader diversity of society. Psychologist Beverly Tatum (1997) explains,

> Affirmative action can be defined as attempts to make progress toward actual, rather than hypothetical, equality of opportunity for those groups which are currently underrepresented in significant positions in society by explicitly taking into account the defining characteristics—sex or

race, for example—that have been the basis for discrimination (p. 117).

However, affirmative action has been a topic of debate and controversy. Critics argue that it may lead to reverse discrimination, disadvantaging certain individuals based on their race or ethnicity. Additionally, some argue that it doesn't address the root causes of educational disparities and may inadvertently perpetuate stereotypes. The debate around affirmative action underscores the complex challenges in achieving a fair and inclusive educational system that both acknowledges historical injustices and promotes equal opportunities for all.

As the discussion continues, finding a balance between fostering diversity and ensuring fairness in the admissions process remains a significant challenge. Policymakers, educators, and the public grapple with how to create an educational environment that is truly inclusive, providing equal chances for success to students from all backgrounds.

Magnet Schools

In the US, magnet schools began in the late 1960s and early 1970s as a tool to further academic desegregation in large urban school districts. These schools were intended to attract students from across different school zones. To accomplish this, magnet schools had to do two things. First, they had to open their enrollment to students outside their traditional school zones. Second, they had to provide an environment or experience that would attract students and families from other school zones. By encouraging enrollment rather than forcing enrollment, the hope was that families would voluntarily desegregate their children in lieu of being forcibly desegregated through busing.

According to the Magnet Schools of America, the unique quality of a magnet school is that they usually have a special curricular focus. Common themes include STEM (Science, Technology, Engineering, and Math), the arts, and vocational or career paths. There are many possible themes, however. According to Samady (2014):

> Science and technology play an important role in economic development and improvement of the standard of living. The application of science and technology, development of scientific infrastructure, education and training are essential for sustainable development and progress in modern societies. The teaching of science and technology to children and young people, training of engineers and scientists, and promotion of public understanding of science and technology facilitate the application of science and technology to development. During the last decade some efforts have been made in developing science and technology education and training in the country. However, greater resources and efforts are needed to promote the application of science and technology not only in education and training but also in all sectors of the economy. I have advocated the development of a national policy and long-term strategic plan for science and technology. Special attention needs to be given to applied research and development of appropriate infrastructure and mechanisms such as a National Council for Science and Technology. The promotion of

scientific literacy and public understanding of
science and technology will contribute to
modernization and development of Afghanistan.

The important point is that magnet schools are schools
of choice – children are enrolled based on their interest
in the school's theme, not on where they live. While
schools may have a general theme, students still study
various subjects. Each subject is aligned to local, state, or
national learning standards (e.g., Common Core), but
each subject is taught within the school's theme. More
often than not, magnet schools involve hands-on
learning that is both inquiry and performance-based.

School Administrators

In a comprehensive 2018 report published by the
World Bank titled *The Learning Crisis in Afghanistan*, the
authors evaluated 200 schools in Afghanistan and
mentioned that although Afghan principals work long
hours and have low absence rates, they are unaware of
basic performance indicators, such as percentage of
students in Grade 4 that can add double digit numbers
or their own teachers' content knowledge. This could in
part be explained by inadequate administrative
preparation and lack of financial support for leading the
school.

The majority of primary school principals (83%)
reported receiving school management training on
administrative skills; however, almost none received
training on helping teachers improve instruction. The
largest proportion of their time, which is a little less than
8 hours, is used to perform school management activities
such as managing teachers, managing the school

administration, and managing assets. In addition to completing their duties as principal, they use 17% of their time to teach. This is equivalent to around 1 hour and a half of teaching per week. In sum, Afghan principals are not equipped to provide any pedagogical support and coaching to teachers.

Most Afghan principals (97%) were not knowledgeable of their schools' performance, in terms of teacher absence, teacher content knowledge, and learning outcomes. In particular, nearly all Afghan principals thought the majority of their grade 4 students could solve a single digit addition problem; only 41% of principals correctly predicted the ability of their students. Similarly, almost all Afghan principals thought most of their teachers could solve a double digit subtraction problem; only 35% of principals correctly predicted the ability of their teachers.

Only 13% of Afghan principals follow good practices of teacher evaluation, which include meeting with teachers to evaluate their performance, using information from student assessments and classroom observations to assess performance, and providing regular feedback to teachers. Even with proper teacher evaluation, principals do not have the proper training to provide pedagogical support for teachers as principals' professional development focuses on administrative skills. Almost all principals in Afghanistan reported that teachers' most important responsibility is being on time to school (88%), followed by maintaining strict discipline in the classroom (7%), and lastly teaching students to be good citizens (5%). Surprisingly, none of the principals considered improving students' learning and curriculum to be the primary focus of teachers' duties.

Principals in Afghanistan lack the knowledge, skills, and abilities for their demanding jobs. When they do have some autonomy, they don't have the skills to make good decisions. For example, Afghan principals report having a lot of decision-making power when appointing a teacher to participate in training, but less than half of the principals have taken the necessary training(s) that would allow them to make a good decision about which training(s) teachers can benefit from.

> کوه هر قدر بلند باشد، سر خود راه دارد
>
> "Even the highest of mountains has a path to the top."

A Conversation with Samir Noor - Assistant Principal at a High School in the US

Samir Noor serves as a high school Assistant Principal in Northern California, bringing over a decade of valuable experience in education. His journey includes roles as an elementary school teacher, Pearson EdTPA scorer, middle school vice principal, and now, a high school Assistant Principal. Samir is pursuing his doctoral degree in Education from the University of California, Davis. The entire interview can be found in Appendix A.

Authors: As an Afghan American with significant experience in education, what are your thoughts, suggestions, or recommendations when you see the following stats regarding Afghanistan. An estimated 3.7

million children are out-of-school in Afghanistan – 60% of them are girls (UNICEF, 2023).

> **SN:** In short, it is heartbreaking that 3.7 million children are not in school. As a first generation Afghan American, education has been a big part of my life. Receiving an education has opened so many doors of opportunity for me and my family. My simple suggestion would be to open schools for all children. Boys and girls should have access to an appropriate education. Basic needs like shelter, food, and water should be a top priority and education should follow that. The government should ensure that all children receive their foundational education. Ideally, education should empower students to be able to critically think and communicate effectively. It begins with acknowledging that there is an issue. From there, creating a team to specifically address these issues is key to making a change.

Authors: In Afghanistan, the gap in adult literacy between men (52.1%) and women (22.6%), is larger (29.5) than the gap of the South Asia aggregate, 15.7. Adult literacy rate is the percentage of people ages 15 and above who can both read and write with understanding a short simple statement about their everyday life.

> **SN:** I would recommend gathering disaggregated data to identify specific regions that have higher literacy rates among adults. Reviewing programs and the education structure in those areas can assist with how to address the alarming low adult

literacy rates in other areas. I strongly recommend a team of individuals to focus on the low literacy rates and to create a comprehensive plan to address this issue because it will take a lot of time and resources to tackle this problem. Collaboration with neighboring countries that have literacy rates of 70% or higher is another way to address this. The literacy rate for women is substantially lower than men; the access and use of the internet to provide instruction (self-paced or live instruction virtually) can be another way to address this. I would also recommend building and/or expanding an adult school program in different regions in Afghanistan to help increase the literacy rate. Some jobs in specific areas in Afghanistan may not require being literate, but being able to read and write will empower those that cannot.

Authors: After spending 4 years in primary school (elementary school), around 65% of Afghan students have only fully mastered Grade 1 Language curriculum and less than half of them mastered Grade 1 Mathematics curriculum.

> **SN:** When I see this statistic, I think of the grade level teaching standards and strategies that can help guide quality and effectiveness of instruction. I am curious as to who is reviewing this data and what standards are being followed, if any. It is a good practice for teachers to continue reflecting on their teaching strategies. Effective teachers do this regularly. My suggestion here would be to assign a team of

instructional leaders (coaches) to work with grade levels that focus on data collection and assessing what the areas of strength and weakness are in each department. After gathering data and reviewing it as a collaborative team, I would recommend creating an action plan that focuses on key language and mathematical skills for each grade level. Formative assessments should be designed to regularly check for student understanding and adjusting instruction as needed. As mentioned above, the assessments should tie to a set of standards that are grade level specific.

Authors: Most Afghan principals (97%) were not knowledgeable of their schools' performance, in terms of teacher absence, teacher content knowledge, and learning outcomes.

SN: It is imperative that principals are informed of their schools' performance, especially information that directly affects student achievement. Teacher content knowledge and learning outcomes can be observed by the principal as they are the instructional leaders on campus. I would recommend the principal makes weekly visits to classrooms to observe lessons. In addition to the regular classroom visits, I also recommend collecting data to track progress and address areas of need with the teachers.

Authors: In the US, a student's high school GPA is very important when applying to college. However, in Afghanistan, high school GPA is irrelevant when applying to a public college. It all comes down to one exam (Kankor). What are your thoughts on this? Do you agree with this?

> **SN:** I personally believe in considering multiple factors when reviewing a student's college application to get a more comprehensive assessment of a student's abilities. I think having an exam as one of the measuring tools can be beneficial in the application process, but I wouldn't recommend it being the only factor considered. A student's ability to be creative, think critically, and lead is difficult to measure using an exam. A student's grade point average (GPA) gives an indication of how the student performed in the different courses throughout their high school years. Extracurricular activities like sports, clubs, and other programs can provide more insight into what a student is capable of.

Summary

This chapter focused on the importance of high school for opening up more opportunities in academics. The current high school system in Afghanistan needs reform. For example, the Kankor exam that is completed by high school students is not an equitable assessment for all students throughout Afghanistan. One exam should not determine a student's ability to go to a public university or not. The current high school system in Afghanistan is designed for the elite and does not help with ending the cycle of poverty that many Afghans have faced for generations. According to Conchas (2008), "Education creates a multigenerational cycle of prosperity powerful enough to push aside cycles of poverty." Students who are successful in high school should have more opportunities to attend college.

Chapter Two Discussion Questions

1) How will you use high school as a vehicle to continue with your education?

2) What should your number one priority be in high school?

3) Discuss your experiences in high school that you believe have shaped the person that you are today, and that should be highlighted in your application process for university admissions.

4) How will you ensure that a teacher writes you a positive letter of recommendation?

5) What are some ways to indicate to colleges that you are in fact a well-rounded applicant?

6) What are some ways that administrators and other education professionals can ensure students are getting the highest quality education?

3

UNDERGRADUATE EDUCATION

"Education is the most important weapon you can use to change the world."
— President Nelson Mandela

With high school and the infamous Kankor exam out of the way, students in Afghanistan are now ready for the challenges of college. Being able to balance home life and school life can become overwhelming without proper time management skills. In the case of Afghanistan, undergraduate education is very important because students acquire skills and training in a field that will prepare them for their next strategic step. In the US, many students are able to enroll in specific high school "Pathways" and learn more about a specific field that they are interested in through both theory and application. More specifically, instead of completing general education courses and random electives, students are able to substitute their electives with pathway courses from their chosen pathway that are taught by professionals in a specific field with the correct teaching credentials. For example, some high schools offer a business pathway, biomedical pathway, engineering pathway, and/or a computer science pathway. To complete the pathway, students need to complete at least one pathway course per year throughout their high school tenure. The final course is usually a capstone course. The earlier a student is exposed to a specific career or field, the more likely they will be able to determine whether or not the career or field is a good fit for them, which will help with taking the correct courses while in college, thereby not wasting time and money.

College life is very different from high school life because students are faced with a myriad of decisions. For example, the subject matter a student decides to study as an undergraduate will have an impact on his or her career, graduate education, and quality of life. Deciding what to major in is the most critical decision that a student will ever have to make because a student is committing to a long and strenuous journey that will open up other doors and adventures. In Afghanistan, your score on the Kankor exam not only determines whether or not you can go to a public university for free, but it also determines what you will be studying based upon the minimum score for each academic department. Thus, if your dream is to become a civil engineer but you only scored high enough on the Kankor exam to meet the requirement to study agriculture, then you will be admitted as a student in the Agricultural department.

Brief History of Higher Education in Afghanistan

Samady (2001) provides a valuable timeline on the progress made in higher education. Modern higher education in Afghanistan began with the establishment of the Faculty of Medicine in Kabul in 1932, followed by the Faculty of Law in 1938, the Faculty of Science in 1942 and the Faculty of Letters in 1944. In 1946, these were combined into the University of Kabul. The

Faculty of Theology and Islamic Studies was established in 1951. With the launching of the first five-year economic development plan in 1956, new facilities were constructed, including a central library, a building for university administration, and residential facilities. In 1957, the Faculty of Economics was added to the University of Kabul; in 1959, the Faculty of Pharmacy; in 1962, the Faculty of Education; and in 1967, the Polytechnic Institute. The University of Nangarhar's Faculty of Medicine was established in 1963. In the 1960s, the Ministry of Education established several other institutions of higher education, including teacher-training institutes and the Institute for Industrial Management, which opened in 1962. Universities were established in Balkh (1986), Herat (1988) and Kandahar (1991).

The Minister of Education retained authority over the University of Kabul, but its administration was entrusted to a university president, a dean for each faculty and an academic senate. According to the Constitution of Universities in Afghanistan, enacted in 1968, all policy matters related to development of each university were entrusted to the Board of Trustees (chaired by the Minister of Education) and the Academic Senate, chaired by the university president. In 1977, the government proposed to establish a Ministry of Higher Education.

The WEED (War, Economy, Education, Dependency) Curse

The Russian invasion of Afghanistan and the subsequent 10-year war (1979-1989) is one of the main reasons why Afghanistan has been struggling to recover for decades. The war created a diminishing economy, which caused a brain drain and severely impacted the education in the country, and ultimately, caused Afghanistan to regress and become dependent on foreigners and foreign aid. The WEED acronym not only describes Afghanistan's tragic situation (curse) but also what some other countries have been dealing with for many years (e.g., Liberia, Eritrea, and Burundi).

Lack of Educational Resources in Contemporary Afghanistan

Lack of educational resources is a fundamental issue for why Afghanistan is unable to improve the quality of education that students receive. Samady (2014) explains:

> One of the most important constraints in the development of education in Afghanistan is a lack of resources. The education system is largely funded through international contributions. It is hoped that with exploitation of natural resources including minerals and other economic activities, the country will be able to finance its development. The important challenges are not only lack of capacity in the education system, but also the quality and efficiency of education. These challenges include shortage and qualification of teachers and university faculty, lack of adequate physical and learning facilities such as laboratories and libraries, outdated curricula and lack of appropriate textbooks especially in vocational and higher education. The achievement of a basic education for all children, which according to the

Constitution should be compulsory up to middle school level, and also adult literacy will be a continuing challenge in education. Social and cultural constraints for the education of girls and women especially in the South and East of the country will affect the development of education. Peace and stability will be the most important factor for progress in education.

The following Tables from the *Ministry of Higher Education* (2009) illustrate the disparity between different provinces throughout Afghanistan. Furthermore, it should be mentioned that the data may have increased or possibly even decreased since 2009 due to ongoing war and instability, corruption, and a lack of oversight.

> **"Libraries store the energy that fuels the imagination. They open up windows to the world and inspire us to explore and achieve, and contribute to improving our quality of life."**
>
> **-Sidney Sheldon**

Based upon the data that is available, Kabul University may have approximately 7,000 books and 500 computers in their library while the Institute of Higher Education in Badakhshan may only have approximately 2,500 books and 2 computers in their library. Paktia University may have approximately 3,000 books in their library and 5 computers. Although this data is from 2009, the lack of resources in different Provinces should be noted.

Table 9: Disparities Between Afghan Provinces

Institutions, Number of Books and Computers and Collaborating Countries

#	Institutions	Number of books in Library	Number of computers	Countries of Collaborating Universities
1	Kabul University	7,000	500	Germany, USA
2	Kabul Medical University	2,500	30	Japan, France, USA
3	Kabul Education University	15,000	60	Japan, USA
4	The Polytechnic University of Kabul	72,000	165	–
5	Nangarhar University (Jalalabad)	4,000	70	–
6	Heart University	40,000	100	Germany
7	Balkh University (Mazar-e-Sharif)	25000	200	Pakistan, Germany, USA
8	Kandahar University	18000	10	–
9	Takhar University	5000	24	–
10	Alberoni University	2000	15	–
11	Bamyan University	6000	30	Switzerland
12	Khost University	3000	50	Germany
13	Paktia University	3000	5	–
14	IHE, Baghlan	700	0	–
15	IHE, Parwan	4000	27	France
16	IHE, Jowzjan	3000	17	–
17	IHE, Kunduz	4000	12	–
18	IHE, Faryab	3000	8	–
19	IHE, Badakhshan	2500	2	–

Note: (–) =No collaboration, IHE=Institute of Higher Education
Source: Ministry of Higher Education

When reviewing the data from the Ministry of Higher Education in Afghanistan (2009) regarding the education level of instructors throughout different provinces, it becomes apparent that there are some major obstacles. The first issue is the lack of female instructors. For example, Balkh University has 94 female instructors which represents 42% of the instructors but Kandahar University has 8 female instructors which represents 13% of the instructors. Furthermore, the education level of the instructors also provides valuable evidence regarding the disparities between the Provinces throughout Afghanistan.

Lack of Qualified Instructors in Afghanistan

According to the data that is available from the *Ministry of Higher Education* in Afghanistan (2009), approximately 9% of the faculty at Kabul University have a PhD degree, 30% of the faculty have a Master's degree, and 60% have a Bachelor's degree. At Herat University, less than 1% of the faculty have a PhD degree, 19% of the faculty have a Master's degree, and 80% of the faculty have a Bachelor's degree. The harsh reality is that these numbers may be significantly less due to the fact that thousands of educated Afghans fled the country after the Taliban took over in August 2021.

> **"A good teacher is like a candle—it consumes itself to light the way for others."**
>
> **– Mustafa Kemal Atatürk**

> **"It is the supreme art of the teacher to awaken joy in creative expression and knowledge."**
>
> **–Albert Einstein**

Table 10: Instructor Credentials

#	Institution	Number of Teachers and their Qualifications								Grand Total
		PhD		MA/MSc		BA/BSc		Total		
		M	F	M	F	M	F	M	F	
1.	Kabul University	47	1	134	13	214	81	395	90	485
2.	Kabul Medical University	4	0	131	15	52	7	187	22	209
3.	The Polytechnic University of Kabul	36	0	71	18	10	0	117	18	135
4.	Kabul Education University	6	1	47	11	59	27	112	39	151
5.	Paktia University	1	0	1	0	8	0	10	0	10
6.	Bamyan University	2	0	8	0	21	5	31	5	36
7.	Takhar University	1	0	3	0	20	0	24	0	24
8.	IHE, Jowzjan	0	0	15	0	21	13	36	13	49
9.	Balkh University	4	0	70	11	100	36	174	47	221
10.	IHE, Faryab	0	0	1	0	19	10	20	10	30
11.	IHE, Badakhshan	0	0	1	0	4	7	5	7	12
12.	Alberoni University	1	0	4	0	38	1	43	1	44
13.	Nangarhar University	8	0	100	6	147	2	255	8	263
14.	Baghlan University	0	0	0	0	20	2	20	2	22
15.	IHE, Kunduz	0	0	1	1	12	4	13	5	8
16.	Heart University	1	0	26	4	107	19	134	23	157
17.	Kandahar university	0	0	11	2	43	2	54	4	58
18.	Khost University	3	0	16	0	18	0	37	0	37
19.	IHE, Parwan	0	0	4	0	5	4	9	4	13

Note: M=Male. F=Female. IHE=Institute of Higher Education.

Since the supply of Afghan PhDs (the intelligentsia) is low and the demand is high, Afghan PhDs should be paid a premium to return to Afghanistan.

Supply and Demand

The principle of *supply and demand* is a construct from the field of economics but is relevant to everything. Those who understand the rules of supply and demand are able to make sound and logical decisions about the different choices people are exposed to on a daily basis. For example, if there are a number of students (high demand) who apply to a specific university with a limited amount of seats available (low supply); then the supply and demand rules would yield a competitive enrollment rate that minimizes the chances of a potential student being enrolled.

Excerpts From A 2014 Interview with Dr. Saif Samady (Former Deputy Minister of Education in Afghanistan)

Dr. Saif Samady completed his secondary education from Habibia High School in Kabul, earned his undergraduate degree in chemical engineering from the University of Illinois, and a doctoral degree in Chemistry from the University of Colorado. He has done research at the American Potash and Chemical Company and at the University of Durham in the United Kingdom. In terms of employment in Afghanistan, he was an associate professor (Faculty of Science) at Kabul University, and served as the President of the Department of Vocational Education and Teacher Training, and Deputy Minister of Education (1962-1967). Years later, he was an elected Chairman of the Independent High Commission of Education for Afghanistan.

Dr. Samady is a well-known educator in Afghanistan. In his capacity as President of the Department of Vocational Training and Teacher Training, he has been involved in the administration of technical schools. Dr. Samady is one of the most experienced and well-informed educators around the globe.

In addition to the posts noted above, internationally, he has served as UNESCO Regional Education Advisor (Bangkok, Thailand), Director of UNRWA/UNESCO Department of Education (Beirut, Lebanon), and Director of Division of Science, Technical and Environmental Education in UNESCO (Paris, France).

Dr. Samady has contributed in the preparation of many
international publications on education policy, science
education, environmental education and technical
education. He has also produced studies and documents
on the development of education in Afghanistan. Some
of Dr. Samady's publications are available on the
UNESCO website. The following are the author's
questions and Dr. Samady's responses.

Author: When did you begin teaching in Afghanistan,
and what was the situation at that time? Could you
mention one or two significant experiences?

> **Samady:** I began teaching inorganic and
> analytical chemistry to science and pre-medical
> students (PCB) at the Faculty of Science in 1959.
> It was an interesting period, as the Faculty of
> Science including the chemistry department was
> being developed. I was appointed assistant dean
> of the Faculty, and I was able to participate in this
> process. The University of Kabul had initiated
> significant reform and development projects. The
> Faculties of Engineering and Agriculture were
> being established in new facilities. A team of
> professors from the University of Illinois was
> invited in 1960 to advise the education authorities
> on the training programs and structure of Kabul
> University. An important development during
> 1960 was the introduction of coeducation for the
> first time in Kabul University. In 1963 the
> university administration was moved to new
> facilities in Ali Abad, and a modern central library
> was established. In the early 1960s several

Faculties were cooperating through an affiliation arrangement with universities in Europe and the USA.

A significant personal experience for me was the preparation of a short paper on applied research, at the request of the President of the University, Professor M. Asghar. He endorsed my proposal and with the assistance of the Asia Foundation (USA), the first research laboratory was set up at the Faculty of Science in 1960. Based on this initiative, the university set up a research center and a board for promotion of scientific research. In the 1970s different Faculties carried out some 20 research projects.

Author: You have been an educator for many years and have also been involved in the rebuilding process of education in Afghanistan over the past decade. How are things different now in the country?

Samady: It should be recognized that the development of modern education in Afghanistan was slow due to government policy, cultural constraints and limited resources. In the 1960s and 1970s some progress was made in the development of education according to government policy and strategies in the context of a democratic movement, peace and stability. The role of dedicated education leaders, Afghan experts and teachers was significant. The war and conflicts of the 1980s and 1990s devastated the social and economic infrastructure including the education system in the country. In 1980, there were 1.2 million students including 18% girls in all levels and types of education in Afghanistan. After 20 years at the end of the century the total enrollment in the education system was less than one million with only 7% girls. During this period the quality of education suffered and the system did not function effectively due to conflicts and instability. Since 2002, with the assistance of the international community, efforts have been made to develop the education system. There has been significant expansion of education. In 2012 the enrollment in general education was 8.6 million including 2.9 million girls (38%). The enrollment in higher education was 110,000 including 19,200 female students (19%). However, the quality and efficiency of education continue to be a major challenge. There has been no significant progress in adult literacy, which remains under 30%.

Author: The Afghan government established an Independent High Commission of Education in 2002. What was the role of the Commission?

Samady: The Commission was established, with the support of UNESCO, to propose policy, objectives and strategies for the revival and development of education in Afghanistan. It was composed of 23 Afghan educators and experts from within the country, Europe and the USA. The Commission completed its report in August 2003, which contained recommendations concerning modernization and development of the education system. The education of girls and women and promotion of education for peace and human rights were emphasized. The Commission also made specific proposals concerning future education policy and objectives, which were reflected in the new Constitution of Afghanistan. The report of the Commission under the title 'The Revival and Development of Education in Afghanistan' is available on the UNESCO website.

Author: What is the status of general education in Afghanistan now? In one of your recent publications, you wrote that since 2002 schools in Afghanistan increased from 6,040 to over 14,456 today. During the same time period, the number of teachers in Afghanistan have tripled to about 181,640 and 32% of these educators are women. Despite this growth, many young children and young teenagers are not able to get the education that they deserve as they cannot get into schools. Given the available resources, what can the Afghan government and the people of Afghanistan do to make the best of use of their available resources to educate more people?

Samady: The development of education requires resources. In Afghanistan the education system is financed through the government budget, contributions of the international community and public participation. Currently the development of education depends largely on external assistance and support. To make the best use of available resources, it is necessary to develop relevant strategies and ensure the efficiency of the system. This requires proper management, transparency and accountability. The support of communities and civil society, professional organizations such as teachers' associations and school councils will contribute to the improvement of quality and efficiency of education. The use of new technologies and innovative methods such as distance education can increase educational opportunities. There has already been significant development of private vocational and higher education in Afghanistan. This trend can be further encouraged and facilitated by the authorities. The enterprises can participate in the training of young people. According to the Education Law in Afghanistan, education in government schools and institutions is free. Ways and means should be explored to encourage voluntary participation and contribution of the people in education.

Author: There has been a great increase in the establishment of private education institutions in Afghanistan. These private educational institutions are operating as profit-making entities. What are your thoughts regarding the privatization of education as for-profit institutions in Afghanistan? Will this be a positive transition or should education be made available to people at a cheaper cost by the government?

Samady: According to the Constitution of Afghanistan the government has a responsibility to provide education. The Constitution and Education Law allow private education, and that is why a number of private institutions have been developed in the last few years especially in economics, business and management, computer science, engineering, medical technology, journalism, etc. Not all private education institutions are for-profit. For example the American University of Afghanistan is a non-profit private institution. I believe the number and capacity of private higher education institutions will rapidly increase. Hopefully the majority will be non- profit or minimum-profit to allow young Afghans to have higher education and contribute to the development of the country. Many private universities in Europe and the USA find additional funds from philanthropic foundations, charities and private contributions from individuals and enterprises in order to keep the cost to students at a minimum. The concept of making significant profit in universities is not generally appreciated by the public. In Afghanistan, the ideal situation will be for the government to increase the capacity of university education as much as feasible and for the private sector to offer higher education at a reasonable cost. The wealthy people and enterprises have a moral responsibility to contribute to the education of young people. The government should provide incentive for enterprises and private individuals through the tax system for their contribution to education. Ways and means should be explored to help qualified needy students with scholarships or low interest loans.

Author: Finally, have you visited Afghanistan recently and been involved in the promotion of any educational activities?

Samady: The last time I visited Kabul was in August 2010. I was invited to participate at the inaugural conference of the Association of Natural Science and Mathematics Educators. I spoke on the subject of science and society in Afghanistan. Another recent activity was a short paper that I prepared in early 2013 for setting up a national science museum in Kabul, which could be developed in cooperation with universities. The ministry of higher education and a senior American advisor seem favorable to the proposal. I believe non-formal programs of science education and information such as a science museum can be an effective means for inspiring children and young people in science and technology. I hope the Afghan scientists and engineers in the United States, especially the Society of Afghan Engineers (SAE), could support a science museum in Kabul.

Benefits of English Instruction

A major outcome of acquiring an education is being able to find employment and contributing to a profession that will help a society prosper. Unfortunately, Afghanistan has not been able to provide employment opportunities for the majority of its graduates. As such, new strategies must be considered in order to create employment opportunities.

Due to decades of war and being refugees in neighboring countries (e.g., Pakistan and India), the Afghan youth have learned the basics of the English language. Furthermore, technological advancements such as the internet, YouTube, and social media have allowed

Afghans to further develop their understanding of the English language.

While English may not be the native language of many people across the world, it is universally accepted as the *lingua franca* for international commerce. Businesses must communicate efficiently, and English provides a common platform for global communication that allows for seamless operations. Afghanistan is in a strategic position to leverage this opportunity because the English-speaking world comprises over 80 countries where English is either the official, administrative, or cultural language.

If the model proposed in this book is implemented, where Afghan students study English as a foreign language in primary school, then at the secondary level at least 25% of the curriculum is taught in the English language, and at least 50% of the curriculum is taught in the English language at the university level, then students will be fluent in English. In return, this will provide them with a skill that can be transferred to employment opportunities because companies all over the world outsource some of their services to countries who have a workforce fluent in the English language. This can be a win-win situation for all parties involved.

As a case in point, the Philippines assists many companies around the world with providing English-speaking staff for working at their call centers. Several international companies, including Microsoft, IBM, and Wells Fargo, outsource to the Philippines. India has the second largest English-speaking population in the world and is able to provide software development services to assist English-speaking customers and clients. As a final example, Malaysia also has a large population of English-speaking citizens. Their high proficiency enables

Malaysian talent to perform any English-speaking outsourcing services efficiently. This includes customer services, content development, and technical support with an English-speaking target audience. Samady (2014) explains:

> There is currently no mechanism for communication and effective cooperation between universities and business enterprises. The employment system for recruitment of new graduates is also inadequate. Companies with foreign participation find it convenient to hire experienced professionals from neighboring countries. The English language ability and experience could also be in favor of foreign professionals.

With job opportunities, the Afghan population will instantly be motivated to complete their educational aspirations and as a result, the Afghan economy will start to flourish.

The other major benefit of providing instruction in the English language is that teachers and professors will have access to more educational resources such as textbooks, articles, and research studies. Furthermore, there are a number of open education resources (OER) available but the majority of the resources are in English. Instruction in the English language will also prepare students for graduate programs outside of Afghanistan and other scholarships such as the prestigious Fulbright Scholarship or Chevening Scholarship.

The last benefit that should be mentioned is that there are highly qualified Afghans living in the United States, Canada, England, Australia, and other English speaking countries who are able to provide services to their fellow Afghans in the English language. An Afghan American engineer can easily use Zoom to help explain a solution to a civil engineering problem in Afghanistan. Using technology to reverse the brain-drain in Afghanistan is a viable option. As a different example, there are many Afghan psychologists, therapists, and counselors who were born and raised outside of Afghanistan who are able to assist their fellow Afghans via WhatsApp as long as they are able to communicate in English with their clients.

Community Colleges

In 1901 the first junior college in America was founded. Since then, junior colleges (also known as community colleges) are becoming more prevalent throughout the country. Many students use the community college option as a way to save money, stay closer to home, and buy time for deciding on a major. The reality is that a student who goes to a community college or straight to a university must first take their general education courses which give students the opportunity to explore different subjects in different departments: humanities, music, foreign language, anthropology, geography, and many other subjects. For many students, general education courses help filter out majors and subjects that are of no interest, while for others it helps with narrowing down a major to study.

In the US, there are some significant differences between community colleges and universities. Generally speaking, community colleges provide two years of general education while universities provide two years of general education plus two additional years of specific subject matter education; the majority of instructors at community colleges have master's degrees, and at universities, the majority have doctorates. At universities, the professors are required to teach and conduct scholarly research whereas in community colleges, the focus is mainly on teaching.

The community college atmosphere is calmer and less competitive. At community colleges and universities, class sizes are about the same and instructors usually do not take roll. Students range in age, and many adults are coming back to further or continue their education because, "By the fast-approaching turn of the century, over half of all available jobs will require a college education and over half of those studying for undergraduate degrees will be twenty-five or older" (Kegan, 1994, p. 271).

Similar to the US, community colleges in Afghanistan can be very helpful for students who need more time to figure out what major they are interested in, students who are unable to take the Kankor exam or who did not perform well on the Kankor exam, and/or students who may simply need to live closer to home. Samady (2014) explains:

> The number of secondary school graduates will substantially increase in the years to come. It is necessary that greater efforts should be made to expand post-secondary and higher education. The ministry of higher education intends to develop community colleges.

In the US, community colleges have implemented transfer agreement contracts for students who are interested in transferring to specific four-year universities that are usually very competitive to get into. In California, the actual contract is called a *Transfer Agreement Guarantee* (TAG). There are specific guidelines that must be met in order for a student to transfer to a specific university. For example, a student must complete all prerequisites and have an acceptable GPA in order to be guaranteed admission into specific universities. Each campus and department has different requirements and it is highly recommended to schedule an appointment with a college counselor for further information. Signing the TAG contract also ensures that a student will be taking classes that will count toward their major as opposed to taking classes that are not transferable.

Afghan universities can also create TAG contracts between community colleges and public universities. Some students can attend a community college first for two years and then can transfer to a university to complete his or her education. This will help with the situation of students being admitted into majors that they are not interested in or passionate about. The majority of university professors in Afghanistan currently hold a master's degree. Thus, it makes sense to have community colleges where most of these professors can teach and thrive. Ideally, each province should have at least one community college and a university.

The need for significantly more PhDs in Afghanistan is mandatory and will be discussed in the next chapter.

A conversation with Dr. Marina Aminy - The Importance of Community Colleges

Dr. Marina Aminy has over 20 years of experience in education and is currently the Associate Vice Chancellor at Foothill-De Anza Community College District, and Executive Director of the California Virtual Campus. She holds a BA, MA, and Ph.D. from UC Berkeley. Her doctoral degree is in Education. The entire interview can be found in Appendix A.

Authors: From your vast experiences, can you please explain the main benefits of community colleges for students in the US?

MA: The main benefits are:

- Ease of admissions: students don't need to apply 6-9 months in advance and wait anxiously for replies of acceptance. Most community colleges have a quick turnaround time of days if not hours to inform students of their acceptance and most have an open-access policy where no one is turned away.

- Affordability: The costs of community colleges are often a fraction of the cost of four-year institutions, and oftentimes that is subsidized through financial aid for qualified students. Some states make the first two years free for everyone, regardless of financial status. For example, California passed Assembly Bill 19, which pays for the first two years of community college for qualified students, regardless of their income status.

- Support: The levels of access to faculty, smaller classes and support is typically stellar at community colleges. There are specific programs developed to support various student groups such as veterans, disabled students, former foster youth, formerly and currently incarcerated students, parents, and other at-risk populations.

Authors: Why do you think most developing countries have not looked into having community colleges similar to the US model?

> **MA**: The answer may not always be something Americans want to acknowledge: it could be that they have been involved in intensive socio-political and economic turmoil in some instances, and interference from foreign governments in other cases. In many developing countries there is a lack of basic K-12 schooling and funding, so the attention to post-secondary or college levels is just not there. In other countries, famine, war, occupation, economic hardship and lack of medical care keep the priorities away from education and toward basic survival. In wealthier countries, such as some post-colonial European countries for example, the differences may be more around workforce development or terminology. For example, in Germany students are tracked early on, as young as 10 years of age into vocational or more academic paths, and their bachelors programs are typically only three years long.

Authors: What other big changes are community colleges considering and/or implementing?

> **MA**: CCs are known as a hub of innovation and experimentation. Some exciting shifts that have already come to the CCs include:
>
> - Strong career/workforce partnerships and development
>
> - Growth of Zero Textbook Cost and Open Educational Resources in courses and programs
>
> - Strong professional development for online education
> - Increased focus on technology and consistency of the student experience (for example, all of the community colleges in California now use the same LMS - Canvas)
>
> - Guided pathways to help students decide their career/major tracks early on with lots of support
>
> - A strong consideration of and focus on equity in all matters and programs
>
> - Unique partnerships that serve underrepresented students (such as previously or currently incarcerated students and foster youth).

Accreditation

Many students have also learned that a program's accreditation is significantly important and should be researched ahead of time. Some private universities claim to be accredited but in reality are nothing more than a scam. Accrediting agencies hold universities and programs accountable for following rules and regulations, emphasizing the importance of transparency to all of its stakeholders (e.g., gainful employment numbers), and focusing on continuous improvement efforts. Programmatic accreditation is different from institutional accreditation. Some students believe that if a college or university is accredited, then all of the programs within the college or university are also accredited by the appropriate and most prestigious accrediting agencies, which is absolutely false. In the case of Afghanistan, a university can be accredited by the Ministry of Higher Education but the programs within the university should be accredited by reputable global accreditors. As an example, Computer Science programs should be accredited by ABET (Accreditation Board for Engineering and Technology). According to the ABET website,

> ABET accreditation assures confidence that a collegiate program has met standards essential to prepare graduates to enter critical STEM fields in the global workforce. Graduates from an ABET-accredited program have a solid educational foundation and are capable of leading the way in innovation, emerging technologies, and in anticipating the welfare and safety needs of the public. To date, over 4,500 programs at over 850

colleges and universities in 40 countries have received ABET accreditation.

Business programs should also be accredited. A student explained how she received a doctoral level degree in Business Administration and was unaware of the different accrediting institutions for business programs. She explained,

> I received a doctoral level degree in Business Administration from a well known university that was very expensive. When I was seeking employment, I found out that the majority of universities prefer a doctoral degree in Business Administration that is from an AACSB accredited program and my doctoral degree is from an ACBSP accredited program. I was flabbergasted and felt cheated. No one ever explained to me the different accrediting institutions for business majors. As a result, I am limited to where I can teach.

This student, like many others, realized after the fact that her four-year doctoral program was not accredited by the highest business school accrediting institution which is the Association to Advance Collegiate Schools of Business (AACSB) and as a result is unable to teach in *some* of the top-tiered business programs that require that AACSB stamp of approval. The following job posting illustrates the importance of accreditation:

> Qualifications for the position include: (1) an earned doctorate in Business Administration from an AACSB accredited institution, with an emphasis in Management; (2) evidence of

effective teaching; (3) evidence of a strong research agenda. Preference will be given to candidates with refereed publications in the field and presentations at national and international conferences. The College of Business Administration is fully accredited by AACSB.

The Association to Advance Collegiate Schools of Business (AACSB), International Assembly for Collegiate Business Education (IACBE), and Association of Collegiate Business Schools and Programs (ACBSP) are three examples of accrediting agencies for business schools and programs. Many believe that the "gold standard" is the AACSB accreditation for business schools. One university stated the following on their website:

> Undergraduate and graduate programs at the College of Business are accredited by AACSB. Less than 5% of business programs worldwide have earned this distinguished hallmark of excellence in business education. AACSB standards relate to curriculum, faculty resources, admissions, degree requirements, computer facilities, financial resources and intellectual climate.

The same is true for students interested in law school. The top law schools around the nation are ABA (American Bar Association) accredited. Those who have graduated from an ABA accredited law program will have more employment opportunities. Medical schools are accredited by the Association of American Medical Colleges (AAMC). This does not necessarily mean that someone who graduates from a non-ABA accredited law program or a non-AACSB accredited business program will be less successful. The point here is that students should be aware of the different accrediting institutions that relate to their subject matter and should make informed decisions. A student can easily check the status of each school by simply doing a quick search online or calling the school.

By having different programmatic accreditations, a university is forced to hold high standards for students, faculty, and administrators. This equates to stringent policies and procedures which lead to continuous improvements, accountability, transparency, and standardization. For example, being accredited prevents a university from being hyper-focused on rote learning (short-term memorization). A major goal for Afghanistan should be to provide the same quality of education at all schools, colleges, and universities throughout Afghanistan. The Ministry of Education and the Ministry of Higher Education must work collectively to create strategic collaborations to promote high quality education throughout Afghanistan. According to Samady (2014):

> I believe the training of faculty for higher education in Afghanistan is of utmost importance, which could be organized by developing graduate studies and sending qualified candidates abroad for higher degrees. The ministry of higher education has undertaken such programs, largely through scholarships to the USA, Europe and other countries. Currently 175 faculty members study abroad for the master's and doctoral degrees. There are also 16 master's programs in several faculties of the universities in

Kabul and another 7 programs have been approved in 2013. I understand the ministry of higher education intends to expand these programs as soon as the conditions permit. It is important to ensure the quality and standards of graduate studies. It is also necessary to make the employment conditions (salary, opportunity for research and professional growth) of the higher education faculty more attractive and interesting to encourage trained Afghans to return home. Peace and security is also a factor. In general Afghans love their country, and in the 1960s and 1970s the majority of Afghans who were trained abroad came back to Afghanistan.

Summary

This chapter focused on undergraduate education in Afghanistan. Community Colleges can fill an important gap by providing opportunities for students who do not perform well on the Kankor exam. An important interview is conducted with the Associate Vice Chancellor of a Communications College in the US. International accreditation is also emphasized for all programs being offered in Afghanistan. A recommendation is made for 50% of the curriculum to be taught in English at the undergraduate level so students have more global opportunities upon graduation.

Chapter Three Discussion Questions

1) Based upon the information and data presented in this chapter, what is the most alarming and why?

2) What did you learn from Dr. Saif Samady's interview?

3) What did you learn from Dr. Marina Aminy's interview?

4) Why is it important for all programs to be accredited on an international level?

5) What global opportunities will students have if they are also fluent in English?

6) What are some benefits of countries implementing a community college system?

4

GRADUATE EDUCATION

"Education is our passport to the future, for tomorrow belongs only to the people who prepare for it today."

—Malcolm X

*I*n the past, those who were interested in graduate education were either overachievers or interested in higher level positions. However, today many believe that a prerequisite to living comfortably in the 21st century is having a graduate level degree. There is definitely a correlation between higher levels of education and higher living standards. With the competitive global economy, graduate education is becoming more prevalent and many individuals have multiple graduate degrees. Although graduate school consists of programs after the bachelor's level, this chapter will focus mainly on doctoral programs because Afghanistan desperately needs more specialized "academic doctors" in all fields.

Afghanistan has not been successful with offering graduate degrees. More specifically, Afghanistan has very limited experience with offering rigorous, respectable, and research-based Ph.D. degrees at any of its public or private universities throughout its history. Most students interested in earning a Ph.D. degree have been forced to find a program outside of Afghanistan. As an interesting anecdote, decades ago the famous Afghan singer known as "*Nashenas*" supposedly earned his Ph.D. in Pashto Literature from Russia due to the lack of academic opportunities in Afghanistan. Currently, there are only a couple of Ph.D. programs that focus on Farsi Literature and Pashto Literature that are offered at Kabul University. However, the quality, impact, and effectiveness of the two Ph.D. programs cannot be verified. For benchmarking purposes, the US has over 400 doctoral-granting institutions with each of these institutions offering a myriad of Ph.D. disciplines (Survey of Earned Doctorates, 2022).

Having highly skilled individuals with graduate degrees in all fields is crucial for a society to prosper. Countries like the United Arab Emirates are actively recruiting and attracting Ph.D. holders by offering a "Golden Visa" which includes a 10-year residency permit for the Ph.D. holder and their family. In most countries around the world, less than three percent of the population have earned a Ph.D. degree. Afghanistan started producing minimal Ph.D. recipients in the last decade or so. In comparison, the US produced over 57,000 Ph.D. recipients in 2022 according to the latest data provided by the Survey of Earned Doctorates (SED). The 2023 data by SED will be available in October 2024. Due to its significance, the SED has been collecting data in the US since 1957 and is sponsored by the National Center for Science and Engineering Statistics (NCSES) within the National Science Foundation (NSF) and by three other federal agencies: the National Institutes of Health, Department of Education, and National Endowment for the Humanities. The SED collects information to assess characteristics of the doctoral population and trends in doctoral education and degrees.

The Ph.D. is the highest degree that is offered by academic institutions around the world, and many of the recipients of a Ph.D. degree enter the field of academia to teach, influence, and train future generations. Ph.D. holders publish textbooks and manuscripts for students and practitioners to learn from. Moreover, faculty members with a Ph.D. are required to conduct impactful research studies to help provide solutions to some of the problems that their society is facing. Furthermore, Ph.D. holders can use their research to influence policy, and ultimately promote changes that positively impact society at various levels. The contributions of Ph.D. recipients to not only improve their own society but also the global society is worth highlighting- the following are some examples of this:

- Woodrow Wilson, the 28th President of the US from 1913-1921, had the most extensive academic career of any United States President. He is the only United States President who has earned a Ph.D. degree. Wilson was able to transform American foreign policy from isolation to internationalism. President Woodrow Wilson won the Nobel Peace Prize in 1919 as the leading architect behind the League of Nations.
- In 1936, while studying for his Ph.D. at Princeton University, the English mathematician Alan Turing published a paper, "*On Computable Numbers, with an application to the Entscheidungsproblem*," which became the foundation of computer science.
- Albert Einstein completed his Ph.D. in 1906 from the University of Zurich. He received the 1921 Nobel Prize in Physics for his services to

theoretical physics, and especially for his discovery of the law of the photoelectric effect, a pivotal step in the development of quantum theory.

- Amartya Sen completed his Ph.D. from the University of Cambridge, UK. He received the 1998 Nobel Prize in Economics for his work on poverty and famine in developing countries.
- Valerie Thomas earned her Ph.D. and is an American scientist and inventor who, while working at the National Aeronautics and Space Administration (NASA), invented a way to transmit three-dimensional images, or holograms, that appear to be real. In addition, she helped to develop processing software to convert scientific data captured by satellites into information that scientists could use.

As with every graduate program, there are specific requirements that must be met in order to graduate. In the academic world, the most common graduate level project is a thesis or dissertation, which consists of producing original research in a specific field.

Afghanistan must be transformed into a merit-based society. Afghans holding high positions in the Afghan government must have a graduate degree. The days of merely having a bachelor's degree and leading a Ministry because of who you know must never be repeated.

Graduate Level Entry Exams

When applying for graduate school, most programs require students to take an exam that is related to their field of study. For example, if a student in the

United States is interested in law school, he or she is required to take the LSAT (Law School Admission Test) or different assessment (e.g., GRE), and if a student is interested in medical school, the requirement is to take the MCAT (Medical College Admission Test). A graduate level entry exam is used by universities as an indicator of how successful a student will be in a specific program when compared to his or her peers. Also, the results of graduate level entry exams are used for accreditation and re-accreditation purposes. The mean, mode, and median scores for each program can usually be found on a university's website and can be used as a benchmark. Graduate level entry exams play a significant role when admissions personnel make recommendations on who will be admitted; the assumption is that a graduate level entry exam is objective. Each university has their own method of evaluating student applicant files and have their own minimum requirements that are at times kept a secret from the general public.

Each graduate level exam is unique and has different sections. There are many resources that offer useful information about each exam. The following table represents the most common graduate level exams; however, it should be mentioned that many universities in the US are experimenting with different types of equitable enrollment requirements. For example, some law schools will now accept either a student's LSAT or GRE scores.

Table 11: Graduate Level Exams in the US

Program	Exam	Full Name of Exam
Business	*GMAT*	Graduate Management Admission Test
Sciences	*GRE*	Graduate Record Exam
Education	*MAT/GRE*	Millers Analogy Test
Pharmacy	*PCAT*	Pharmacy College Admission Test
Law	*LSAT*	Law School Admission Test
Medical	*MCAT*	Medical College Admission Test
Social Sciences	*GRE*	Graduate Record Exam
Dental	*DAT*	Dental Admission Test

Preparing for a graduate level exam requires time, motivation, and a competitive drive because the final outcome will determine where a student will end up going to school.

Master's Programs

According to the Kabul University website (2024), the university started offering master's programs in 2005. Once a student has been admitted into a master's program, he or she will soon realize that there will be assignments, projects, and group presentations on a regular basis. Students become overwhelmed with their careers, ongoing homework assignments, and projects. Graduate students are pushed to their limits, and those who survive master the art of efficiency, improvisation, and efficacy. Most programs consist of approximately ten to fifteen courses, which can take about two years to complete. Also, classes are usually held in the evenings. Those who benefit the most from a master's program are the individuals who have practical work experience and can make connections from theory to practice (*praxis*). Some universities require their students enrolled in a Master's program to complete a Thesis while other universities allow students to complete a challenging capstone course. If a student is planning on continuing their education to the doctoral level, then they may want to enroll in a university that requires the completion of a Master's Thesis.

Students should understand that graduate school is a serious commitment that will last several years but will open more opportunities. Being able to balance graduate school and life at the same time has been described by many as "the ultimate test" with many unforeseeable obstacles.

The 10,000 Hour Rule

Many people do not know about the "ten thousand hour rule" and its relevance to becoming successful. The ten thousand hour rule is a concept that has been proven to be accurate time after time. The rule emphasizes the amount of time that is needed in a specific field to acquire a set of skills that can be recognized on an international level. In the early 1990s, a psychologist by the name of Dr. K. Anders Ericsson conducted a study and concluded that ten thousand hours of practice are required to achieve the level of mastery associated with being a world-class expert in anything. Thus, ten thousand hours is the magic number of greatness.

Many researchers have interviewed successful basketball players, soccer players, ice skaters, and chess players and have determined in all cases that the same amount of time has been invested to reach such high levels. A case in point is Dr. Bill Joy, the computer programmer who "co-founded the Silicon Valley firm Sun Microsystems, which was one of the most critical players in the computer revolution. There he rewrote another computer language—Java—and his legend grew still further" (Gladwell, 2008, p. 37). The reality is that Dr. Bill Joy had access to computers at an early age and spent countless hours working on these machines. By the time real opportunities presented themselves, Dr. Bill Joy had acquired 10,000 hours of experience and was able to apply his skills to great advantage.

Doctoral Programs

Being admitted into a doctoral program is an accomplishment and finishing the requirements of a doctoral program is an even bigger accomplishment. Doctoral programs are meant for people who are interested in conducting research and teaching students at the undergraduate and graduate level.

In the US, there are many different doctoral level programs and degrees. For example, a person can get the traditional Doctor of Philosophy (Ph.D.) degree, a Doctor of Business Administration (D.B.A.) degree, a Doctor of Education (Ed.D.) degree, a Doctor of Judicial Science (S.J.D.) degree, a Doctor of Engineering (D.Eng.) degree, a Doctor of Psychology (Psy.D.) degree, a Doctor of Pharmacy (Pharm.D.) degree, Medical Doctor (M.D.) degree, a Doctor of Osteopathic (D.O.) Medicine degree, a Doctor of Optometry (O.D.) degree, a Doctor of Nursing Practice (D.N.P.) degree, and more. The "D" in each title signifies an expert who is considered a doctor in that specific field. All programs require dedication, motivation, and inspiration to be completed. An interested student can apply to a Ph.D. program in Business Administration or a D.B.A. program which is very similar because they are both doctoral level degrees in the field of Business Administration and are considered academically equivalent. A Ph.D. in Business Administration focuses more on developing new theories while a D.B.A. focuses more on the application of theory. As a matter of fact, many business departments have an even distribution of D.B.A.s and Ph.D.s who teach and conduct research.

Advanced degrees are becoming more prevalent as specialized programs are becoming more popular. For example, a student can earn a doctorate in Public Administration (D.P.A.) if he or she is interested in managing a government affiliated organization. In the US, doctoral programs are expensive and usually take about four to six years to complete.

Students in doctoral programs should be actively publishing in their fields. This point cannot be stressed enough because many students neglect the importance of publishing because they are so busy with their doctoral dissertation. As a result, students graduate with a doctoral degree but are unable to find teaching positions because of their lack of scholarly work. Many job postings state, *"Candidates must demonstrate an active research agenda, and have excellent teaching and communication skills"* or *"Evidence of teaching effectiveness is desired as is evidence of the potential to produce peer reviewed published research."* As many have realized, publishing in peer-reviewed academic journals takes time, patience, and determination. Students become discouraged when their work is not published in academic journals, but the key is to find the right journal to complement the article. As mentioned above, students should subscribe to academic journals to learn more about publishing requirements, new trends in their field, and the etiquette of publishing in journals.

Those who are in a doctoral program should also consider teaching at the college level to gain experience. Instructors at the college level are expected to have at least a master's degree. Teaching experience and research publications will help significantly when applying for a teaching position at a larger university.

A crucial requirement for all doctoral programs is the notorious doctoral dissertation. The doctoral dissertation is similar to the master's thesis but is more comprehensive, detailed, strenuous, and meaningful. This project can take anywhere from two to five years to complete because the data gathering process can be difficult depending on the study methodology. The doctoral dissertation topic should be chosen ahead of time and should be chosen strategically. Some conduct a quantitative research study while others conduct a qualitative research study. Regardless of a student's research methodology, a doctoral dissertation is highly research-oriented and will help others understand more about a specific topic.

A Conversation with Dr. Bahaudin Mujtaba on the Importance of Ph.D. Programs

Bahaudin G. Mujtaba is a Professor of International Management and Human Resources. He earned his doctoral degree in Business Administration from Nova Southeastern University, has 16 years of corporate and management experience, and 25 years of education experience locally in Florida, nationally in the United States, and globally in over ten different countries such as Afghanistan, Pakistan, China, Vietnam, Thailand, Morocco, and several others. The entire interview can be found in Appendix A.

Authors: From your perspective, why is it important for a country such as Afghanistan to offer Ph.D. programs?

> **BM:** Having a rigorous and quality doctorate program in Afghanistan will enable research possibilities based on science and facts, and it will empower talented Afghans to become regionally and globally competitive with any workforce in developed economies.

Authors: In Afghanistan, which 3 departments should start with offering Ph.D. programs and why?

> **BM:** Afghanistan needs Ph.D. scholars in all subject matters. I would recommend starting with faculty areas such as education, information technology, and business administration as these departments can be initiated with the least resources. And, the best option might be to partner with accredited foreign universities so Afghan students can have access to the latest available research.

Authors: Why is it important to have faculty members with doctoral degrees?

> **BM:** Doctorally-qualified professors will provide students the guidance and rigor needed for research so Afghan leaders can become the drivers of major decisions through science and evidence.

Authors: Where would you like to see Afghanistan in 10 years in regard to education?

> **BM:** Through a focus on quality and equitable education of young men and women in Afghanistan, the country can become not just a competitive regional economy in South Asia, but it can also compete with other nations around the globe. I would like to see Afghanistan as a thriving economy, following the example of Singapore, South Korea, and other such successful nations.

Authors: Why is international accreditation so important for different programs being offered at Afghan universities?

> **BM:** International accreditation in Afghanistan is a necessary starting point so Afghan graduates can research with and find jobs in any university across the globe. However, after accreditation, universities must find their narrow niche and differentiate themselves from others in Asia, Europe, and North American through excellence.

Post-Doctoral Research Programs

Postdoctoral research programs are on the rise because of the growing competition in academia. A postdoctoral program offers specialized training in a specific subject matter, endless research opportunities to publish with scholars in the field, and experience teaching courses at the undergraduate and graduate level. For many, postdoctoral programs are unnecessary while for others, it's a priceless experience.

With baby boomers (born between 1946-1964) retiring from the workforce, the younger generations are ready to take over those positions. Those who have completed postdoctoral programs will be more competitive and will have an upper hand when applying for positions. Each year, a limited number of students are admitted into postdoctoral programs. A student by the name of Jessica explained her postdoctoral program:

> It was a demanding program that developed me into an expert in my field. A postdoctoral program is similar to a medical doctor's residency where a doctor receives specialized training in a

specific field. I was also able to do a lot of networking as a postdoc student.

A postdoctoral program appointment can be anywhere from one to three years long. One job posting stated,

> The Graduate School of Business anticipates appointing one Postdoctoral Fellow for a period of two years. The Postdoctoral Fellow will collaborate in research projects of mutual interest with the faculty. In addition, the Postdoctoral Fellow will teach two sections per year of MBA level courses.

Each university and department will have their own expectations of what a postdoctoral researcher will be required to do. As a result, some programs provide a stipend, while others provide intrinsic rewards.

With education being so important, many spend countless amounts of time and energy learning and mastering their fields. A person who is committed to success will sacrifice many years to education in return for a more promising future. Earning an undergraduate degree takes about four years, a master's degree takes about two years, a doctoral level degree takes about four years, and a postdoctoral degree can take another two years. With global competition, the elite student can anticipate going to school for 12 years and earning multiple undergraduate and graduate level degrees.

Global Competition and Human Capital

With globalization, countries are interconnected implying that additional competition is on the rise. As developing nations attempt to become more modernized and industrialized, they also create a high demand for educated professionals. There is a large wage gap between those with a high school education compared to those with a college degree. With technological advancements, there is a wage premium for highly educated workers which encourages people to acquire more education. Education is a luxury throughout the world.

Human capital is the set of skills a worker has as a result of education, training, and experience that can be used in production which is why recruiters ask for resumes that highlight such knowledge and abilities. It is important to have a significant amount of education, training, and experience in this competitive society in order to stand out from the rest of the competition because demand (the number of jobs) is currently low and supply (the number of applicants) is currently very high. The importance of doing research, being proactive, and figuring out what skills are in demand must be emphasized because of this highly volatile global society. An example is how companies are outsourcing customer service call centers overseas to developing countries due to technological advancements, which means that the demand for customer service agents in the US has decreased. Furthermore, the "dot-com bubble" during the late 90's was a time when there was a high demand for many professionals who were computer savvy. During that period, employment levels sky-rocketed and many college students decided to major in Computer Science (CS) or Computer Information Systems (CIS) because of the high demand and the low supply of qualified workers. In fact, at some universities the CS and CIS programs became "impacted" and students were waitlisted. Many of the students who graduated with a CS or CIS degree after 2002 were disappointed to find out that the "dot-com bubble" burst and more importantly, no one was hiring. The moral of this story is to spend time researching economic trends because there are jobs out there that are in high demand and that will stay in demand because of continuous technological advancements, globalization, and the demand for highly-skilled professionals who are willing to work abroad. The economy continuously fluctuates, which requires each individual to improvise, continuously learn, and be creative.

Summary

Afghanistan must offer additional Ph.D. programs domestically to help create a more stable educational system. Ph.D. programs should be highly competitive and should have the following components: (1) coursework in the subject, (2) some coursework in educational pedagogy because many professors know their subject matter very well but struggle with teaching, (3) oral and written qualifying exams, and (4) a final dissertation or thesis that is defended. Ph.D. students and recipients should be treated with the utmost respect by the government and society and teaching should become the highest paid profession in Afghanistan.

Chapter Four Discussion Questions

1) Based upon the information presented in this chapter, what is the most alarming and why?

2) Why is it important for a nation to offer Ph.D. programs?

3) From your perspective, what Ph.D. programs do you think Afghanistan can immediately benefit from?

4) What criteria should be used for Ph.D. admissions in Afghanistan?

5) What incentives can be provided to Ph.D. students in Afghanistan who are interested in working in academia?

5

VOCATIONAL EDUCATION

"Tell me and I forget, teach me and I may remember, involve me and I learn."
– Benjamin Franklin

Vocational education, also known as career and technical education (CTE), is becoming more prevalent for students throughout the world because of the shortage of qualified workers in specific fields. Students who prefer to learn and master a vocation go to a vocational or career-oriented school where they are trained to start a career upon graduation. The difference between a vocational school and a traditional university or college is that a vocational college is career-oriented and teaches a student a specific skill. Some believe there is a stigma behind going to a vocational school but in reality, vocational schools produce high-quality and skilled workers who contribute significantly to the workforce.

Many vocational schools offer fast-paced programs that last anywhere from three months to two years. Many vocational schools require students to complete an internship or externship before graduating which helps students put the theory they have learned into practice. Also, the experience gained through an externship or internship helps students acquire the confidence that is needed to be successful in their new careers. The reality is that many students go to a four-year traditional university and then are unable to find work in their field because there are no job openings in their field, which is the case in Afghanistan and many other countries.

At a vocational school, many of the students who complete their internship or externship are usually hired by the site where they interned because they have already built rapport and have proven to be extraordinary workers. Most vocational colleges and programs are accredited and go through extensive programmatic reviews by their accrediting bodies on a regular basis. Vocational education may not be for everyone; however, it has the potential to be a great option for those who need a quicker path to start a career.

Vocational Education Programs

Vocational schools offer many different programs to accommodate students with different interests. Most vocational programs require students to have a high school diploma. In recent years, many programs have become "impacted" (meaning they have more students wanting to declare that major than can be accommodated), which has forced students to be waitlisted. This suggests that many see the benefits of going to a vocational college and learning a specific skill in a field, obtaining hands-on training, and in some cases, earning an associate's degree.

There are a myriad of vocational programs available to students. For example, students have the choice of studying pharmacy technology, construction, plumbing, medical assisting, dental assisting, nursing, massage therapy, graphic design, radiology technology, respiratory therapy, sonography, computers, criminal justice, veterinary technology, and many other interesting fields. Many vocational schools also offer career placement upon graduation.

With the job market becoming more specialized, government agencies and businesses are investing more in the future of vocational programs to help balance the supply and demand. Many vocational schools are focusing on providing high-end programs related to the health field such as nursing, nuclear medicine, radiation therapy, and electro neuro-diagnostic technology. Students who graduate from such high-end programs are in high demand and do not have to worry about acquiring multiple graduate level degrees, lacking job security and stability, or spending more than a decade in school.

Students are starting to realize that traditional colleges and universities are unable to provide job placement for their students and as a result, many students are left with a college degree, student loans, and unemployment. This phenomenon has become more apparent during the current economic crisis. At the end of the day, it is important for a student to do his or her research ahead of time by figuring out what fields are in high-demand.

Vocational Education in Afghanistan

Based upon the limited data that is available, Afghanistan appears to have been actively enhancing its vocational training system to foster national growth through skilled labor. From 2001 to 2012, there was significant growth in Afghanistan's vocational training sector. For example, in 2001 there were only 26 high schools and 12 institutes and a total of 1,152 students taught by 470 teachers. By 2012, the sector expanded to 130 high schools and 80 institutes, catering to 70,094 students with 2,622 teachers.

This remarkable increase underscores Afghanistan's dedication to vocational and technical education as a cornerstone for providing the necessary skills for employment and contributing to the country's development. Table 12 was retrieved from a report that was published in 2012 by the *Deputy Department of Technical and Vocational Education in Afghanistan.*

Table 12: Technical and Vocational Education in Afghanistan from 2001-2012

The School Year	Location	Number of Technical and Vocational Schools and Institutes		The Number of Teachers	The Number of Students
		High Schools	Institutes		
2001	Capital	11	6	310	472
	Provincial	15	6	160	680
	Total	26	12	470	1152

Year					
2002	Capital	11	6	321	617
	Provincial	18	6	160	737
	Total	**29**	**12**	**481**	**1354**
2003	Capital	11	8	330	1522
	Provincial	19	6	168	930
	Total	**30**	**14**	**498**	**2452**
2004	Capital	11	8	394	3104
	Provincial	20	8	193	1110
	Total	**31**	**16**	**587**	**4214**
2005	Capital	11	8	340	5272
	Provincial	20	8	220	3682
	Total	**31**	**16**	**560**	**8954**
	Capital	11	8	381	6183

Year					
2006	Provincial	20	8	280	4712
	Total	**31**	**16**	**661**	**10895**
2007	Capital	11	8	643	6995
	Provincial	21	11	352	3096
	Total	**32**	**19**	**995**	**10091**
2008	Capital	6	13	490	9839
	Provincial	28	12	412	4426
	Total	**34**	**25**	**902**	**14265**
2009	Capital	7	13	581	12504
	Provincial	32	13	566	8462
	Total	**39**	**26**	**1147**	**20966**
2010	Capital	6	15	622	12832
	Provincial	59	22	640	13145
	Total	**65**	**37**	**1262**	**25977**

2011	Capital	6	18	699	16885
	Provincial	88	30	752	23747
	Total	**94**	**48**	**1451**	**40632**
2012	Capital	5	22	943	21071
	Provincial	125	58	1679	44523
	Total	**130**	**80**	**2622**	**70094**

Strategic plans from earlier regimes aimed to expand to 300 learning venues within 3 -10 years (based upon the amount of international aid received and the budget provided by the government) to accommodate 150,000 students and 3,000 teachers. The vision extended further to establishing 500 training centers, including 100 institutes and 400 high schools, aiming to educate 400,000 students with the help of 8,000 teachers. This expansion plan also focused on diversifying the curriculum and initiating a research center, with the government seeking external funding to achieve these significant educational advancements. However, at this time, it is not clear how the Taliban regime will move forward with the educational strategic plans of the past.

Fortunately, there are many opportunities (e.g., mining and coding) in Afghanistan that can be taken advantage of.

Mining Education and Jobs in Afghanistan

Afghanistan can enhance its infrastructure and economy by tapping into the mineral deposits that geologists have uncovered. The capital can also be used to create educational opportunities that have been discussed throughout this book. According to Horowitz (2021), "Afghanistan is one of the poorest nations in the world. But in 2010, US military officials and geologists revealed that the country, which lies at the crossroads of Central and South Asia, was sitting on mineral deposits worth nearly $1 trillion." Afghanistan should strategically leverage this opportunity so that the country, and more specifically the youth of the country, are the main beneficiaries. However, it is important for Afghanistan to avoid the "resource curse" by hiring educated and just administrators to manage all projects. Unfortunately, Nigeria can be seen as a prime example of the "resource curse", a phenomenon where natural resource wealth leads to poor economic growth and development and an increased likelihood for civil conflict.

According to O'Donnell (2022), "Afghanistan's mineral wealth has been well documented for decades. The Soviets did surveys in the 1970s and 1980s, and the United States did plenty of its own during its 20-year adventure. Some big contracts were signed, notably a 30-year, $3 billion deal in 2007 with a Chinese consortium to develop a copper deposit near Kabul called Mes Aynak, though that sputtered to a halt. Little else was done to turn reserves into riches."

Vocational schools and programs can take advantage of this opportunity by creating programs that are focused on specific mining jobs that are needed for mining efficiently and safely. Some examples of mining jobs are: Field Assistants, Driller Offsiders, Mining Electricians, and Concreters. There are a myriad of other jobs in this field ranging in skills and responsibilities that need to be filled to help create a robust workforce- this will in turn improve the economy and open up other doors for creating other forms of revenue (e.g., tourism and ski resorts).

Pro bono partnerships can be created with universities in the west for collaborating on mining projects with the understanding that the partnerships are merely for advising and teaching purposes. For example, Pennsylvania State University boasts one of the largest and most recognized mining engineering programs in the United States. The program is one of the degree programs offered by Penn State's College of Earth and Mineral Sciences, which has achieved a long and distinguished history dating back to 1896 when it was founded as a School of Mines. Faculty from Penn State's College of Earth and Mineral Sciences can volunteer to provide expert advice to Afghan nationals on advanced technologies to obtain reports and data on past and present mines, mine prospects, and processing plants. Furthermore, best practices can be shared by different countries to help Afghanistan profit from this opportunity. India has learned a lot over the years about the dangers of mining and exploiting natural resources from underground. As a case in point, mica mines in India are now heavily regulated to prevent underage children from being hired as miners in harsh and dangerous conditions.

Code to Inspire

An outstanding example of a vocational program or career and technical education program that has provided immediate skills and employment opportunities to students is Code to Inspire (CTI). Code to Inspire was started by a visionary leader, Fereshteh Forough (Founder and Executive Director), a commendable individual who was born as an Afghan refugee in Iran. Over the years, she overcame countless barriers, including the denial of educational opportunities.

In 2015, driven by an unyielding sense of purpose, Fereshteh felt compelled to establish Code to Inspire, the first-ever advanced computer coding school in Afghanistan. The organization aims to educate young women and girls, empowering them to pursue a seemingly distant dream: the opportunity to study and evolve into the fullest versions of themselves.

CTI's vision is to narrow the gender gap in educational participation and empower Afghan women to become active contributors to their communities. Through their free educational programs, they create a safe environment where their students can thrive and develop their talents. By providing their students with the necessary skills to excel in the technology sector, CTI not only opens doors to economic opportunities but also cultivates a sense of confidence and independence.

Knowledge holds immense power, and technology serves as the key to empowerment. CTI firmly believes that education and technology have the power to transform lives and break down barriers. By addressing the unique challenges faced by Afghan women, CTI aims to create a more inclusive society, where women can play a pivotal role in shaping the future of Afghanistan. According to the CTI website, the impact of this important initiative has been educating 500 students, with 350 students graduating from their program, and 60% of their graduates becoming employed.

A Conversation with Fereshteh Forough of Code to Inspire (Founder and Executive Director)

Code to Inspire (CTI) is the brainchild of Fereshteh Forough, an extraordinary individual who, born as an Afghan refugee in Iran, overcame countless barriers, including the denial of educational opportunities. In 2015, driven by an unyielding sense of purpose, Fereshteh felt compelled to establish Code to Inspire, the first-ever advanced computer coding school in Afghanistan. The entire interview can be found in Appendix A.

Authors: Navigating the dynamic landscape of education and technology can be intricate. Could you delve into specific instances where Code to Inspire encountered challenges and elaborate on the innovative solutions or strategies you implemented to overcome them?

> **FF:** CTI has shown exceptional adaptability in the face of challenging circumstances. The Taliban's ban on education for girls above the 6th grade presented a significant obstacle to CTI's mission. Nonetheless, our immediate decision to shift from a physical location to an online platform reflects our commitment to providing education, irrespective of external challenges. This experience showcases CTI's ability to overcome adversity no matter the difficulty.

For our online education, we are using Google Classroom to demonstrate CTI's capacity to leverage digital tools for teaching and learning. This includes further curriculum development, video content creation, and interactive exercises tailored to the needs of our students. The students' limited access to laptops and the internet necessitated innovative solutions, such as conducting surveys and distributing essential hardware and connectivity packages.

Authors: Reflecting on the organization's journey, how has the operational landscape of Code to Inspire evolved amidst external factors, such as changes in the political climate pre and post-Taliban? Can you shed light on any notable adjustments or adaptations made during these transitions?

FF: In the wake of the Taliban's takeover of Afghanistan in August 2021, which included the prohibition of education of women and girls beyond the 6th grade up to university level, Code to Inspire was compelled to modify its facilities. This decision was made to ensure the safety of our staff and students, given the circumstances surrounding the ban on the education of women and girls. However, our commitment to our mission remained unwavering, and we swiftly adapted by transitioning our operations to an online platform while awaiting the opportunity to reopen our physical school. To facilitate this transition, we opted for Google Classroom as the medium through which we could provide educational content to our students, encompassing a wide array of resources such as videos, presentations, and interactive exercises. However, this digital shift was not without its challenges. The limited availability of laptops and reliable internet connectivity among many of our students' households caused significant problems in our ability to educate. Recognizing the pressing issue, we conducted a comprehensive survey to help meet the needs of our students. Subsequently, we embarked on a distribution initiative that provided laptops and monthly internet packages to each student's home, thus mitigating the digital divide. Thanks to this concerted effort, we successfully managed to reintegrate approximately 80 percent of our students into our online learning environment, thereby ensuring their continued access to education.

Authors: Your commitment to education is commendable. Could you elaborate on the societal impact you believe Code to Inspire has had, and how does this align with your personal philosophy? Do you identify as a social entrepreneur, and if so, how does this perspective influence your approach?

FF: CTI is dedicated to transforming Afghan women's lives through technology education, fostering inclusivity and breaking down barriers. Our primary goal is to bridge the education gap for women in Afghanistan, offering free, high-quality coding and graphic design education. By empowering women with these skills, we enable their participation in the digital economy, addressing educational disparities and promoting social empowerment.

Driven by a commitment to narrowing the gender gap in education, CTI creates a supportive environment for female students to thrive economically. Our free programs provide unique opportunities for Afghan women to excel in the technology sector, fostering confidence and independence. Beyond individual empowerment, CTI's impact extends to the overall economic growth of Afghanistan, aiming for a multiplier effect where our students' success contributes to broader economic advancement and sustainability in local communities.

Authors: Expanding access to quality education is a pressing concern. Have you explored integrating online education platforms to extend the reach of Code to Inspire? How do you envision leveraging technology to bridge gaps and provide coding skills to a broader audience?

FF: Code to Inspire is integrating online education platforms like Google Classroom to overcome geographical constraints and provide quality coding education to students from diverse regions. In addition, the organization is developing its own online learning platform, offering a variety of tech skills in Farsi and Pashto. This initiative promotes self-paced learning, aligns with industry standards, and

fosters a sense of community through virtual
forums and collaborative elements.

Authors: Recognizing global shifts in education, do you
envision a parallel benefit for Afghan students if coding
were integrated into primary school curricula? How
might this influence both individual skill development
and contribute to the broader economic landscape?

> **FF:** Introducing coding at the primary level
> fosters computational thinking, problem-solving,
> and critical creativity, providing foundational tech
> literacy applicable in various aspects of life. This
> early exposure enhances problem-solving skills,
> contributing to a versatile skill set applicable
> across disciplines. Moreover, it breaks gender
> stereotypes by promoting inclusivity, ensuring
> that all students, including girls, are prepared for
> the evolving tech landscape and fostering a
> diverse workforce.

Authors: Celebrating the success of your graduates is
crucial. Could you share specific success stories and
highlight industries or sectors where your alumni have
found meaningful employment after completing the
program? How does this align with Code to Inspire's
mission?

> **FF:** We have provided education to over 550 girls
> in our coding and graphic design classes. Over
> the past years, our alumni and students have
> successfully completed 50 remote projects in
> coding, graphic design, and animation, totaling
> $60,000 in value. These projects were delivered to

clients located in the United States, Europe, and
Afghanistan.

Based on the data gathered from the alumni
survey conducted in July of 2023:

- 80% of our alumni work in Afghanistan
  helping to improve the overall economy of
  the region.

- 88.5% of students/alumni believe that
  CTI has had an impact on their personal
  well-being.

- 94.4% of students/alumni believe that the
  skills and knowledge they received from
  CTI's program contribute to their personal
  growth and development.

- 86.6% of students/alumni believe that
  CTI helped improve their employment
  opportunities.

Students and alumni of CTI report that they
spend a large amount of their income on their
healthcare, savings, education,
personal/professional development, and the
reinvestment of themselves.

Momtaz, one of our graphic design graduates,
says: "CTI has completely transformed my life.
Through their comprehensive program, I not
only became a skilled graphic designer but also
had the opportunity to work on several paid

graphic design projects, earning income for the first time. These experiences not only improved my skills but also instilled a sense of financial independence. With an enhanced portfolio and gained experience, CTI opened doors for me that I never imagined possible. Through CTI, I secured an internship at Binance, one of the largest cryptocurrency exchanges in the world, where I worked on their social media promotional materials. This opportunity has been truly life-changing, providing me with invaluable experiences and opening new horizons for my career. I am immensely grateful to Code to Inspire for paving the way to financial independence and empowering me to pursue my passion. CTI has not only equipped me with the necessary skills but has also provided a supportive community that believes in the potential of Afghan women. I cannot thank CTI enough for the life-changing opportunities and the platform they have provided me to thrive as a graphic designer."

Wajiha, one of our Front-end coding graduates, says: "Code to Inspire (CTI) has been the pivotal point in my life, where curiosity met opportunity. This transformative coding school for Afghan girls provided me with a nurturing environment that encouraged me to explore the vast world of technology. CTI became my guiding light, equipping me with the knowledge, skills, and unwavering support to pursue my dreams and thrive as a full-stack developer. The comprehensive curriculum and dedicated mentors at CTI struck the perfect balance between theoretical knowledge and practical experience, enabling me to sharpen my coding skills and embark on a rewarding career path. Armed with the invaluable education and experience gained at CTI, I confidently embraced the role of a full-stack developer. This career not only fulfilled my professional aspirations but also became a means of supporting my extended family. Each milestone I reached allowed me to contribute to their financial stability and well-being, uplifting them towards a brighter future. I am grateful to Code to Inspire for unlocking my potential, shaping my career, and providing opportunities that transcend geographical boundaries. With their support, I am embracing a future filled with possibilities, making a positive impact on the tech industry and creating a better life for my loved ones."

Authors: Diving into the heart of education, could you provide insights into the creation of Code to Inspire's curriculum? Were there specific philosophies or industry needs that guided its creation? Additionally, how does the curriculum ensure graduates are well-equipped for entry-level coding roles?

FF: Code to Inspire's curriculum, rooted in student-centered and project-based learning, emphasizes hands-on experience and practical coding application. It's designed to be engaging, interactive, and tailored to diverse student needs. Updated regularly to align with industry trends, the curriculum collaborates with experts to enhance graduates' employability. Recognizing diversity, it's inclusive, accommodating varied learning styles and backgrounds. The iterative curriculum development process, fueled by feedback from students and industry partners, ensures constant improvement and relevance to evolving industry needs.

Authors: Bridging the gap between traditional education and the demands of the tech industry is a unique challenge. How does Code to Inspire tackle the shift from memorization-focused education to fostering critical and logical thinking? Have there been notable challenges or successes in this regard?

FF: Code to Inspire places a strong emphasis on project-based learning. Instead of memorization, our educational model revolves around hands-on projects that require students to apply coding concepts in real-world scenarios. This approach not only enhances their technical skills but also fosters critical thinking as they problem-solve and create tangible outcomes. We believe in the power of collaboration. Our learning environment encourages students to work together on projects, share ideas, and learn from each other. This collaborative approach helps develop not only technical skills but also interpersonal and communication skills, crucial for success in the tech industry.

Authors: Looking ahead, what strategic visions or expansions do you envision for Code to Inspire in the next decade? Could you elaborate on any plans to empower graduates to contribute to the establishment of vocational schools across different provinces, creating a ripple effect of positive social and economic impact?

FF: In the next decade, Code to Inspire envisions an expansive approach to empower women economically. This includes the extension of educational and job placement programs throughout Afghanistan, ensuring that women in various provinces have access to coding and tech education. The organization also plans to launch a comprehensive online educational platform, providing a flexible learning environment for women who may face geographical or logistical challenges.

Additionally, recognizing the displacement of Afghan refugees, particularly women, Code to Inspire aims to expand its operations into neighboring countries with significant Afghan refugee populations. By reaching out to these communities, the organization seeks to provide educational opportunities and support the economic empowerment of Afghan women who may be rebuilding their lives in new environments.

Furthermore, the establishment of a mentorship hub is integral to this vision. The mentorship program will connect experienced professionals with aspiring women in the tech industry, fostering a supportive network that goes beyond formal education. This mentorship initiative aims to guide women in making informed career choices, navigating challenges, and building successful pathways in the tech sector.

Authors: Many educational initiatives face resource challenges. How has Code to Inspire overcome resource constraints and ensured sustainability, especially in the context of financial or infrastructural limitations as Afghanistan continues to face political challenges and crises?

FF: Code to Inspire actively fundraises, reaching out to donors and partnering with organizations committed to empowering women through tech education. Recognizing the importance of tech access, the organization distributes laptops and provides internet support for students facing financial constraints. Collaborations with tech companies secure additional resources, including in-kind donations and financial support. Building community engagement is crucial for sustainability, fostering collective responsibility and grassroots support for educational programs.

Authors: Technology is always changing - considering the growing influence of artificial intelligence in various industries, how does Code to Inspire incorporate AI and other emerging technologies into its curriculum? Are there specific initiatives or strategies to prepare students for the evolving landscape of technology?

FF: Code to Inspire's curriculum integrates the latest technology advancements, focusing on AI, machine learning, and emerging technologies. Students gain a foundational understanding and

practical skills through hands-on projects,
implementing AI algorithms and analyzing data.
This approach enhances problem-solving skills
and prepares them for AI applications in various
industries. The curriculum also emphasizes ethical
considerations, educating students on responsible
AI practices, promoting fairness, transparency,
and accountability for well-rounded and
responsible technologists.

Vocational Education Curriculum

The curriculum at vocational colleges and schools
is robust and vigorous. Students are expected to learn
and retain a significant amount of information in a small
period of time. The focus should not be on rote learning.
At a traditional college or university, students are either
on a semester or quarter system. A semester system is
approximately eighteen weeks long and a quarter system
is approximately ten weeks long. Most vocational
colleges and schools use a modular term system that
runs approximately six weeks. It is important to mention
that it is not the length of the semester, quarter, or term
that is important but rather the hours that are spent in a
classroom.

For example, if a student is going to a traditional
college or university that is on a semester system (18
weeks) and is taking two courses and is expected to be in
each course once a week for three hours, the student will
receive a total of 108 hours of class time instruction for
the two courses. If a different student is enrolled at a
vocational college that is on the modular term system (6
weeks) and is expected to be in class four times a week
for a total of four and a half hours each day, the student

will receive 108 hours of class time instruction per term. Thus, those who are on the modular term system are on the fast-track and cannot fall behind.

The truth is that students need to be constantly challenged in order to learn and retain information. If a class only meets once a week, there are six days in between each class where the student can easily forget valuable information because with memory, if a person does not use it, he or she can lose it. Vocational programs are investing in their curriculum by following the strict rules and regulations of their elite accrediting bodies. For example, vocational programs have enhanced their learning objectives for each course, implemented learning outcomes for each course, and have standardized the entire curriculum for each program.

Many do not fully understand the difference between course objectives and outcomes. A simple definition for course objectives can be the course goals that are usually listed on the course syllabus. A simple definition for a course learning outcome is what a student will be able to do at the completion of the course. Learning outcomes are the current popular trend in education because they allow an educational environment to continuously improve in all aspects of learning and teaching. Many vocational colleges have implemented pre-tests and post-tests that measure how much a student has learned after taking a class with a specific instructor. This not only puts pressure on the instructor but also on the student. Instructors no longer have as much academic freedom because they are now focused on the assessment that each student takes at the end of a class to determine what was learned. On the other hand, students must do well because a significant

percentage of their grade is on the line with the end of
term assessment. By default, instructors and students
must put in more effort into the class. Critics of learning
outcomes have pointed out that learning outcomes are
neither fair nor accurate because certain matters (student
retention and student motivation) are not taken into
consideration.

Instructors take on a big responsibility when they
are in the classroom because they are constantly being
evaluated and must be able to please all constituencies.
Not only do students and supervisors rate instructors
but now learning outcomes rate an instructor's
performance as well.

Vocational Education Instructors

Instructors at vocational schools and colleges are
highly trained professionals who have a passion for their
profession. The majority of the instructors have a
significant amount of work experience (10 or more
years) but do not necessarily have high levels of
education. For example, a criminal justice instructor
could have 20 years of experience as a police officer but
may only have an associate's degree. To teach at a
vocational college or school, experience is important
because it is the responsibility of the instructor to be able
to teach a student a specific skill. To be a successful
vocational instructor, an individual needs to have the
sound technical, human, and conceptual skills that assist
an instructor with teaching complex information in a
short period of time. Many vocational colleges and
schools have implemented educational incentive
programs where instructors are reimbursed for
continuing with their education. As a result, each year

more and more instructors are enrolling into graduate level programs.

Vocational colleges are also encouraging their instructors to obtain higher levels of education because accrediting bodies are also requesting that instructors have both the experience (professionally qualified) and the education (academically qualified). According to Samady (2014),

> Technical education is very important for economic development in Afghanistan. Engineers and technicians need to be trained for all sectors of development. In 2012 a total of 18,112 students including 893 female students were enrolled in the Faculties of Engineering, computer science, geology and mining, and agriculture. There were also 350,000 trainees in about 600 public and private technical and vocational centers. A survey of 420 centers found that 58% of trainees are in computers, mechanics, electronics, and construction, and 17% received training in business. The quality of teachers and facilities are not always at desired standards. The government departments, agencies and the private sector have developed separate strategies, and there is a need for coordination and a comprehensive national strategy for the training of engineers and technicians. The application of technologies in the management of education has been very limited and used primarily for data collection and statistics, communication, libraries, etc. The application of new technologies initially in higher education and teacher training in Afghanistan will improve the quality of education.

The gradual provision of appropriate facilities including hardware and software and necessary training programs will be required.

Dependency Theory and Afghanistan

Vocational schools and colleges can help provide specialized training to Afghan students so that the country does not feel obligated to request assistance and eventually become dependent on neighboring countries with hidden social, political, and economical agendas. For example, the former Soviet Union (Russia) helped build tunnels, bridges, roads, apartment complexes, and other infrastructure throughout Afghanistan. "The Macroyan Kohna apartment district, built by the Soviets a half-century ago, still flourishes despite many eras of trauma" (Zucchino, 2020). According to Putz (2015), "A marvel of Soviet engineering when it was first opened in 1964, the Salang Pass tunnel remains the major artery in Afghanistan's sparse transportation network."

> **"We will never allow you [Soviet Union] to dictate to us how to run our country and whom to employ in Afghanistan. How and where we employ the foreign experts will remain the exclusive prerogative of the Afghan state. Afghanistan shall remain poor, if necessary, but free in its acts and decisions."**
>
> **— President Daoud Khan (1973-1978)**

In 1979, the former Soviet Union used some of the infrastructure that they built in Afghanistan to invade Afghanistan and ultimately kill over 1 million Afghans. "By the time the last Soviet troops pulled out in early 1989, rumbling back across the ironically named *Friendship Bridge*, the conflict had cost the lives of an estimated 1 million civilians" (McGee, 2023). Thus, the people of Afghanistan cannot depend on foreigners to build or rebuild their country.

The dependency theory concludes that "poverty in the developing nations is the result of their dependence on high-income nations" (Tregarthen & Rittenburg, 2000, p. 675). Influence is exerted over Afghanistan by many other nations. According to Tregarthen and Rittenburg (2000), "Dependency theory holds that the industrialized nations control the destiny of the developing nations, particularly in terms of being the ultimate markets for their exports, serving as the source of capital required for development, and controlling the relative process and exchange rates at which market transactions occur" (p. 675).

Despite much foreign aid, Afghanistan still lacks in many professional and technological fields (Mujtaba, 2005). This is perhaps normal as well since "the benefits of trade between a rich country and a poor country will go almost entirely to the rich country" (Tregarthen & Rittenburg, 2000, p. 675). Even though the majority of the benefits are going to the richest countries, poor countries do not have many options if they want to live peacefully with the international community. In this case, the future does look brighter if the citizens of the developing country educate themselves and become self-reliant. Ultimately, the people of a country must take initiative and help themselves if they want to prosper.

However, it has been suggested that the people of each country must realize that "Capital and technology from the West do not lead to development but can only deepen underdevelopment" (Munck, 1999, p. 58).

Poor countries are often stuck in the cycle of oppression until they are able to put an end to this cycle through entrepreneurship, development, and education.

Such countries must develop a comparative advantage for themselves to trade with their neighbors, both regionally and globally. Gradually, they must strive to escape the dependency trap since dependency is said to be a theory of underdevelopment: "Poor countries exiled to the periphery of the world economy could not develop as long as they remained enslaved by the rich nations of the center" (Velasco, 2002, p. 44). Long-term dependence cannot be sustained. Dos Santos (1970) explains that, "By dependence we mean a situation in which the economy of certain countries is conditioned by the development and expansion of another economy to which the former is subjected" (p. 231). Dependency can be best converted into sustainable development through equal and speedy education of all citizens of a country. Equal and public access to a speedy education can help avoid the disparity between the upper and lower classes. As stated by researchers, "dependency theory holds that economic development widens the gap between the rich and the poor because most new jobs are for educated middle-class and skilled blue-collar workers rather than for unskilled workers" (Tensey & Hyman, 1994, p. 31). Independence is part of the journey toward the ultimate goal of living interdependently with the global community. This, however, is not a long-term solution in today's interconnected global community. Today's economic productivity and work environment are dependent on an "open system" where people can receive resources from anywhere worldwide and sell them globally, rather than functioning in a "closed system" which requires independence on all fronts.

Overall, dependence is especially harmful when the nation is forced to rely upon less-developed countries. "Dependence" must be converted to "independence" and then to "interdependent relationships" globally; in this way, Afghanistan can benefit from certain comparative advantages which are afforded to it through its natural resources. As a result of long-term dependence, the majority of Afghans have neglected education and innovation which has resulted in a society that has mainly embraced culture. While culture provides the foundation of a society, education provides the means to a civil society (Kaifi, 2010).

Summary

Vocational education is flourishing and the benefits are becoming more noticeable to the general public. Many students do not have the time to spend four to ten years in a traditional school without a guaranteed position waiting for them upon graduation. Students who have graduated from vocational colleges and schools learn a specific skill in a short period of time that will help them start a career which will help the economy in many ways. Initiatives in Afghanistan, such as Code to Inspire, can help jump-start the process of vocational training for underrepresented groups, and having instructors with proper training and experience will only help in the long run. Ultimately, vocational education can transform a dependent country into an independent member of the global community.

Chapter Five Discussion Questions

1) Why is vocational education becoming more popular both nationally and
 internationally?

2) What are the drawbacks to vocational education?

3) Should vocational education curriculum be standardized?

4) What are your observations on the new vocational training centers like Code to Inspire? Will they be beneficial in the long term for a country?

5) Do you believe that by promoting a culture of improvement in education, and specifically in vocational education, Afghanistan could overcome dependency in the future? If so, what are the arguments supporting this belief?

6) How does the increase in vocational training affect job creation and the rise in employment opportunities in the market?

6

ONLINE EDUCATION

"If we teach today as we taught yesterday, we rob our children of tomorrow."
– John Dewey

Online education is becoming more prevalent throughout the world as students have the luxury of completing programs without physically being in a classroom. Furthermore, research is showing that online education provides more equity in the classroom. Online education has been around for nearly three decades, and Nova Southeastern University (NSU) was one of the first higher education institutions to offer graduate programs in an online format (Mujtaba, 2007). Interestingly enough, Nova Southeastern University has been offering online programs since 1983. Schools and universities that embraced and invested in online education had no issues navigating through the COVID pandemic. Afghanistan has observed practical advancements in online education following the COVID-19 pandemic, making it an important topic of discussion. Most of the universities which had sound financial resources used technology (e.g., Zoom) to continue their teachings during the pandemic. Online education has allowed millions of students to complete their education in a non-traditional format that has led to many debates. Some believe that online education is unfair and unjust because students do not learn the course objectives. Others have mentioned how online educators are disconnected from their students. The reality is that online education has proven to be successful, convenient, and beneficial based upon years of research by educators and administrators which is precisely why it is becoming more prevalent. As a case in point, Saudi Arabia started Saudi Electronic University (SEU) to help provide additional opportunities for its citizens.

Saudi Electronic University (SEU) is located in the capital Riyadh and has expanded by opening branches in other regions according to the university's approved plan. SEU aims to obtain national and international academic accreditation to elevate the quality of its programs. SEU also provides higher education based on optimal learning models, applying applications and technologies of electronic and blended learning, which combines direct attendance and attendance via technology. In addition, SEU supports the mission and concept of lifelong learning for all society members. Furthermore, the United Nations continues to promote the importance of blended education in many formats. More specifically, the United Nations Educational, Scientific and Cultural Organization (UNESCO) is a specialized agency of the United Nations with the aim of promoting world peace and security through international cooperation in education, arts, sciences and culture. UNESCO emphasizes that blended learning is a valuable approach to help promote learning and achieve the fourth sustainable development goal known as Education 2030: ensuring quality and equitable education and lifelong learning opportunities in all forms of formal

and non-formal education. The adoption of blended
education is increasingly seen in higher education
institutions, and researchers expect that blended learning
will become the new "traditional model" (Ross & Gage,
2006) or the "new norm" in the introduction of higher
education courses (Norberg, 2011). According to
Samady (2014):

> Virtual education or e-learning has developed
> extensively in the United States, Europe and
> many developing countries. The first successful
> distance teaching university was the Open
> University, which was established in 1970 in
> London. There are many advantages in virtual
> education, as it provides flexible distance
> education for working people, who may not have
> access to standard universities. It is assumed that
> the cost of online education will be less than the
> cost of standard education. Virtual education
> depends largely on computers and
> telecommunication. There is a need to plan and
> manage effectively this new mode of teaching and
> learning. While hundreds of thousands of
> students receive education through distance and
> virtual modes around the world, questions remain
> about accreditation and the quality of assessment.
> In Afghanistan, distance education was used for
> teacher training as early as the 1960s. In recent
> years some higher education institutions have
> made limited use of e-learning. At present the
> technical capacity (computers and internet
> facility) and managerial experience for virtual
> education in Afghanistan is very limited. But it is
> important that higher education institutions and

teacher training colleges consider the development of distance education modalities in their system.

According to the World Bank (2024) website, Broadband (or high-speed) internet access is not a luxury, but a basic necessity for economic and human development in both developed and developing countries. The challenge is to expand broadband access to all—only about 35 percent of the population in developing countries has access to the Internet, versus about 80 percent in advanced economies. Broadband has also become a foundation for smart infrastructure (e.g. Intelligent Transport Systems and Smart Electric Grids) that is facilitated by new wireless technologies. It can help create jobs in information and communication technology (ICT), engineering and other sectors, as well as help catalyze job skills development, an important avenue toward poverty reduction and shared prosperity.

Implementing online education throughout Afghanistan can be challenging because the majority of the people in Afghanistan do not have stable electricity, internet, and/or bandwidth. However, the following conversation with a subject matter expert, Mr. Mansoor Haidari, provides plausible solutions to bridge this connectivity gap.

A Conversation with Mr. Mansoor Haidari: Expanding Online Connectivity to Pave the Way for Digital Transformation in Afghanistan

Mansoor Haidari has 15 years of experience and expertise as an Intelligence Analyst, a Cybersecurity Analyst, and in Network Security. Mansoor completed his Bachelor's degree in Computer Science (Network and Security) from the University of the Pacific and is planning on starting a Master's degree in Information and Cyber Security at UC Berkeley. He is an employee at the Lawrence Livermore National Laboratory (LLNL) in the US. The entire interview can be found in Appendix A.

Authors: How can all of Afghanistan have access to the internet—even in the most remote and rural areas? Based upon my research, the generally accepted method is to invest a lot of capital in getting a developing nation onto a major fiber optic backbone, either terrestrial or undersea (e.g., most African coastal nations are on a backbone that rings the continent). However, planning and deploying an undersea cable can take a decade or more, and the cost is enormous. The lifespan of a cable is typically around 25 years. Terrestrial cable is less costly but might be challenging due to Afghanistan's terrain. It may also be possible to bring it in wirelessly from a neighboring country, as Haiti has done from the Dominican Republic (and even that is an alternate path to an existing fiber optic route), however that is severely limited in capacity.

> **MH:** Providing internet access to remote and rural areas in Afghanistan comes with a lot of challenges that need to be assessed and considered. For example, network infrastructure limitations, landmark or geographical barriers, and social and economic factors all need to be examined. From the network perspective at this stage Afghanistan has two options which are wireless mesh networks or TV White Space

(TVWS) Technology. I will explain each option but there are some other options that we will discuss.

Option # 1 is Wireless Mesh Networks which consist of interconnected nodes that communicate with each other to extend network coverage. Each node in the network serves as a router, relaying data to other nodes until it reaches a gateway that connects to the internet. Nodes can be strategically placed to create a network that covers vast regions, even in rugged terrain. The use of solar-powered nodes can enhance sustainability in areas with unreliable power sources. This approach can be very beneficial and is cost-effective, scalable, and adaptable to the geographical challenges of Afghanistan since Afghanistan is a mountaineer country. It can be quickly deployed and expanded, making it suitable for remote locations.

Option # 2 is TV White Space (TVWS) Technology which is the inactive or unused space found between channels actively used in the UHF and VHF spectrum. TVWS frequency spans from 470 MHz - 790 MHz. Currently, TVWS radios are being deployed in rural communities by ISPs (Internal Service Provider) to provide broadband. Spectrum in the VHF and UHF bands was originally reserved for analog television broadcasts. This spectrum can be repurposed for wireless communication without interfering with existing television signals. It is very easy to deploy, and the technology is using frequencies that are not in use for TV broadcasting. TVWS signals can cover longer distances and penetrate obstacles better than higher-frequency signals, making them suitable for remote and rural areas. Access points using TVWS technology can be strategically placed to create a network. TVWS technology is effective for reaching remote areas with limited existing infrastructure. It requires fewer base stations compared to traditional wireless technologies, making it a cost-effective solution. It is the best method that can provide connectivity over challenging terrains.

Creating or establishing internet connectivity in a remote and rural area of Afghanistan requires a collaborative and systematic approach from the international community, local population, and the Ministry of Afghan Telecommunications. The lack of enthusiasm of Afghanistan's neighboring countries to support certain projects stems from concerns over Afghanistan's rapid advancements in telecommunication infrastructure and a robust internet network. The fear among neighboring nations is that Afghanistan's technological progress may pose an economic threat to their own economies. The worry is that Afghanistan's enhanced capabilities could lead to increased competition, potentially impacting market dynamics and economic interests in the region. This apprehension has contributed to a lack of support for certain initiatives, highlighting the complex interplay of economic interests and geopolitical considerations among neighboring countries in the region.

Authors: I recently learned that "Afghanistan and China will be connected to a fiber optic network via Wakhan port. Apparently the Ministry of Communications and Information Technology is working on the implementation of the Wakhan corridor project and is also undertaking programs to be connected to the fiber optic networks in Tajikistan and Kyrgyzstan through the Silk Route fiber optic network." What are your thoughts on this, and what are the pros and cons?

MH: The Wakhan Corridor is a narrow strip of territory in northeastern Afghanistan that extends to China's Xinjiang region. The area and its people were abandoned by both countries for years with no support and humanitarian assistance. In recent years, there have been discussions and plans to enhance network connectivity and other infrastructure projects in this region, including the possibility of a fiber optic network. The Silk Route fiber optic network is part of broader regional connectivity initiatives, and various countries in Central and South Asia have been exploring ways to improve communication and trade links between Afghanistan, China, Pakistan, Kyrgyzstan, and Tajikistan.

When it comes to infrastructure projects that are funded by other countries, there are always potential pros and cons associated with projects like the connectivity initiatives between Afghanistan, China, Pakistan, Tajikistan, and Kyrgyzstan through the Wakhan corridor. Keep in mind that the success or challenges of such projects can depend on various factors, and perspectives may differ based on individual and geopolitical considerations.

Authors: Is Starlink the solution? Based upon my research, Starlink has the potential to revolutionize connectivity in developing countries. By leveraging its satellite network, Starlink can bring high-speed internet to remote areas, bypassing the need for costly ground infrastructure.

MH: In the recent year, Starlink, a satellite internet collection project developed by SpaceX, has shown potential improvement to address connectivity challenges in remote, warzone, and developing areas. Starlink's objective is to provide high-speed, low-latency internet access through a constellation of small satellites in low Earth orbit.

Starlink benefits:

Worldwide Coverage: Starlink has the potential to offer internet services globally, reaching remote and underserved areas where traditional infrastructure is challenging to deploy.

Low Latency: The low Earth orbit configuration of Starlink satellites is designed to reduce latency, making it suitable for activities such as online gaming and video conferencing.

Quick Deployment: By relying on satellite technology, Starlink can potentially be deployed more quickly than traditional terrestrial infrastructure, which involves laying cables and building ground-based infrastructure.

The satellite constellation can be expanded to accommodate increasing demand, allowing for scalability in providing internet services. However, it's important to note that as with any technology, there are challenges and considerations:

Cost: While Starlink may bypass the need for extensive ground infrastructure, the cost of satellite technology and user terminals could be a limiting factor for some individuals or communities.

Starlink Environmental Concerns: The large number of satellites in low Earth orbit has raised concerns about light pollution and space debris. SpaceX is working to address these concerns through measures like darkening satellites and implementing collision avoidance systems.

Regulatory Challenges: Different countries have various regulatory requirements for satellite internet services. Navigating these regulations can be a challenge for widespread global deployment.

Competition: Starlink faces competition from other satellite internet providers and emerging technologies, which may influence its market penetration and success, but one thing about Starlink that stands out compared to other providers is risk. Starlink's CEO is willing to take risks to support countries in need during times of war.

Starlink has the potential to provide reliable and high-speed internet access, and could play a role in supporting education initiatives, including those aimed at empowering Afghan women.

While Starlink and similar initiatives can contribute to addressing connectivity challenges, a comprehensive approach involving collaboration between government agencies, non-governmental organizations, and the private sector is often necessary to address the broader challenges in promoting education, especially for women, in regions like Afghanistan.

Authors: From my understanding, Nigeria became the first African country to access the Starlink satellite broadband service. Do you have any information or stats on this? Has it been successful?

> **MH:** Currently there isn't much information on how the network is doing but there was an article published in the Business Insider titled "SpaceX's Starlink is active in Africa for the first time" on January 31, 2023. SpaceX's Starlink satellite internet service has become operational in Nigeria, marking the first African country to receive the service. The announcement was made on Twitter (now known as X) by the company. Nigeria's Minister of Communications and Digital Economy, Isa Ali Pantami, expressed gratitude to SpaceX for the deployment. Elon Musk, CEO of SpaceX, had previously announced Starlink's

expansion into Africa in the preceding year. Despite operating in numerous countries with over a million users, Musk acknowledged that Starlink was not profitable to SpaceX.

An article authored by Francis Hook on November 3, 2023 explores the entry of SpaceX's Starlink satellite internet service into Africa. Initially met with enthusiasm, the service has encountered challenges related to pricing and regulatory considerations in markets such as Nigeria, Rwanda, Malawi, Kenya, Mozambique, and Zambia. The article highlights the disparity in pricing across countries, emphasizing higher terminal costs and variable monthly access fees.

The pricing strategy in Africa appears to target lower monthly costs compared to developed markets, aligning with the region's economic landscape. However, the relatively high equipment costs pose a barrier to widespread adoption. The article suggests that, with the current pricing structure, Starlink may only serve a niche market comprising remote businesses and high-income individuals, particularly in uncovered rural areas and specific urban segments.

Regulatory hurdles, including adherence to local ownership laws and licensing requirements, are discussed as additional challenges. Starlink's phased entry into key markets like Kenya and Nigeria involves navigating diverse regulatory landscapes and addressing issues such as taxation, employment, and payment channels. The article underscores the importance of regulatory bodies ensuring a level playing field for existing operators while considering access gaps in rural areas.

Looking ahead to 2024, the article anticipates a refining of Starlink's pricing strategy and a clearer go-to-market approach as it enters more African markets. It suggests that greater pricing harmony and simplified distribution partnerships could emerge, potentially leading to increased accessibility for consumers and businesses. The article speculates that, as Starlink accumulates more customers, prices may decrease, allowing the service to disrupt the market further.

According to an article by Harlem Solicitor, the impact of Starlink on Nigerian education has been notably positive, creating numerous opportunities for the delivery of online educational content to students in remote and underserved areas. Prior to Starlink, a significant portion of students lacked access to educational materials, but with the introduction of Starlink, they are now able to avail themselves of these resources. The improved connectivity has facilitated greater accessibility to educational content, thereby enhancing the learning experience for students in previously disadvantaged regions.

Authors: Do you agree with the following statement? "Satellite internet service has become increasingly popular in recent years, offering a viable alternative to traditional broadband connections. However, despite its advantages, there is one major problem that plagues satellite internet service: limited bandwidth and data caps. However much they've evolved, satellite internet doesn't compare to the speed of cable or fiber optics internet. Download speeds for cable range from 10 to 500 Mbps." What are your thoughts on this regarding Afghanistan's dire situation where fiber optics may not be a plausible solution?

> **MH:** In my opinion, the statement accurately highlights the challenges associated with satellite internet service, particularly limited bandwidth and data caps. Satellite internet has indeed become more popular in areas where traditional broadband connections like cable or fiber optics are not readily available, making it a viable alternative in certain situations.
>
> In the context of Afghanistan's situation, where deploying fiber optics infrastructure might be challenging due to various reasons such as geographical terrain, security concerns, or economic constraints, satellite internet can offer a practical solution. While it may not match the speed of cable or fiber optics, it can still provide internet access in areas where other options are not feasible.
>
> However, it's essential to recognize that deploying satellite internet, or any technology for that matter, might be more straightforward in a peaceful country with robust security measures in place. The current situation in Afghanistan presents numerous obstacles, including ongoing

conflicts and security challenges, making the implementation of any infrastructure a complex endeavor.

In regions with difficult terrain or areas affected by conflicts, satellite internet can be a crucial tool to bridge the digital divide and connect people to the online world. Despite its limitations, the reliability and accessibility of satellite internet make it a valuable option in such challenging circumstances.

While acknowledging the limitations of satellite internet compared to cable or fiber optics, it is important to consider the practicality and feasibility of deploying alternative technologies in regions facing unique challenges, such as Afghanistan. Satellite internet can play a crucial role in providing connectivity where other options may not be readily achievable, even though the current situation in Afghanistan adds an additional layer of complexity.

Authors: Satellite broadband holds exciting possibilities, providing improved access to digital opportunities for those previously left behind and offering reliable communication channels during critical times. As technology continues to evolve, the future of internet connectivity will likely involve a hybrid approach, with satellite broadband complementing traditional terrestrial networks to create a more connected and inclusive world. What should we be prepared for in the future in the US?

MH: Honestly, there is no precise answer – Safeguarding Active Transmission protection and mitigating risks during critical times with Satellite Broadband is not going to be possible with a lot of bad actors around. From Cyberspace and Cybersecurity perspectives we need to understand that technology is transforming and bad actors are developing new theories to exploit vulnerabilities to attack users.

Although we understand that reliable communication during critical times is a fundamental necessity, the integration of satellite broadband offers promising solutions. However, as we embrace this technology, it is crucial to recognize and address hypothetical risks that can compromise communication reliability during critical moments.

Satellite broadband is undoubtedly a crucial communication lifeline, but its singular dependence may expose vulnerabilities that adversaries could exploit. Unforeseen issues such as satellite malfunctions, space debris, or solar interference could disrupt connectivity precisely when it is most critical.

Weather conditions pose a significant threat to satellite signals during crucial moments. Storms, heavy rainfall, or atmospheric disturbances may affect signal strength and reliability, necessitating robust solutions to mitigate these weather-related risks.

Critical events often trigger a surge in communication demand, potentially leading to congestion in satellite broadband networks. Heightened usage may result in delays or interruptions, emphasizing the need for proactive network capacity planning and management.

Satellite signals are susceptible to intentional or unintentional electromagnetic interference. Deliberate jamming or unintentional interference from nearby electronic devices could compromise reliability, requiring countermeasures to maintain connectivity during critical periods.

Regardless of expanding satellite constellations, there may still be areas with limited coverage. In remote or challenging regions, the risk of communication blackouts during critical times remains, necessitating strategic planning for comprehensive coverage.

Satellite communication often introduces higher latency compared to terrestrial networks. While efforts are underway to reduce latency, critical applications such as real-time decision-making or emergency response may still be impacted, prompting the need for optimization strategies.

Continuously expanding and strategically planning satellite constellations to ensure comprehensive coverage, especially in critical regions, minimizes the risk of communication blackouts.

As we leverage satellite broadband for reliable communication during critical times, a proactive approach to identifying and mitigating risks is vital. Addressing issues related to infrastructure dependence, weather resilience, network congestion, interference, coverage limitations, and latency concerns fortifies our communication networks, ensuring they remain robust and dependable in the face of unforeseen challenges.

Authors: Based upon my research, companies are using LEO (Low Earth Orbit) Satellites in Afghanistan. However, affordability remains a barrier for widespread adoption. Is this accurate? If so, what can be done to make this affordable for all people throughout Afghanistan?

MH: To enhance accessibility to satellite services for the entire population of Afghanistan, a viable approach involves the allocation of funds by the Afghan government or international organizations specifically dedicated to satellite infrastructure development. This endeavor may encompass financial mechanisms such as subsidies, grants, or collaborations with private entities, aimed at mitigating the overall cost of satellite services.

An effective strategy entails fostering collaboration between the Afghan government and private companies through Public-Private Partnerships (PPPs) for the development and deployment of satellite infrastructure. Such partnerships distribute the financial responsibilities, establishing a sustainable framework for satellite services. To incentivize private sector involvement, the Afghan government could consider offering tax cuts or other relevant incentives.

Financial support from non-governmental organizations (NGOs), international entities, and donor countries can significantly contribute to the deployment of satellite infrastructure in Afghanistan. These contributions play a crucial role in alleviating financial constraints and facilitating the successful implementation of satellite technology.

Engaging the local population within communities is pivotal for generating demand and garnering support for satellite services. Educational initiatives about the advantages of satellite technology can stimulate interest and foster increased utilization. A surge in demand may result in economies of scale, potentially leading to a reduction in overall costs.

Collaborative efforts between countries, international organizations, and private enterprises are essential for leveraging resources, sharing expertise, and collectively addressing challenges associated with satellite deployment, especially in challenging environments such as Afghanistan. Tailoring strategies to the specific context and challenges of Afghanistan, including security considerations and existing infrastructure limitations, is imperative for the successful adoption of affordable satellite technology.

Drawing inspiration from successful models, such as Japan's advanced internet infrastructure, the Afghan government can adopt relevant telecommunications policies to achieve its goals. Japan's consistent investments in broadband access, promotion of high-speed internet services, and encouragement of technological innovation serve as valuable benchmarks for Afghanistan's own aspirations in this domain.

Online Platforms

There exist many online platforms (a.k.a. Learning Management Systems, or LMS) that are being used in education, such as: Canvas, D2L, Blackboard, Google Classroom, Web CT, and Ning. Each platform is unique and enables an instructor or facilitator to plan, organize, lead, and control the learning outcomes and objectives of the course. In 2009, California State University, East Bay implemented an AACSB accredited online undergraduate program in Business Administration. The university website states that it is "the only AACSB-accredited Online Business Administration degree completion program offered by a California university that offers adults the knowledge and skills necessary to understand the changing global business environment and prepare them for success in their professional careers." California State University, East Bay was using Blackboard as their learning management system and recently transitioned to using Canvas. The American University of Afghanistan also uses Canvas. Additionally, there are some free online learning platforms that are available to schools and universities.

Using Google Classroom For Free

Due to the fact that online education is becoming more prevalent around the world, there are more resources being created to help facilitate student learning. For example, Google created Google Classroom which is a free learning management system that can be used by educational institutes. The Teacher's College of San Joaquin in California uses Google Classroom as their learning management system. Google Classroom helps educators create engaging learning experiences they can personalize, manage, and measure. It is part of Google Workspace for Education, which empowers an institution with simple, safer, and collaborative tools. According to the Google Classroom website, Google Classroom was designed with feedback from the educational community, always building new features and functionality that lets educators focus on teaching and students focus on learning. Afghanistan can easily develop and implement online courses using Google Classroom as their learning management system. This will allow more students to study and the cost savings for each student and university will be significant.

Online Students

Deciding to be an online student is a serious commitment. Those who have discipline are able to handle the demands of an online course while reaping the many benefits. For example, most organizations depend upon computer-savvy individuals who are able to utilize specific software programs for completing tasks in an efficient manner. Furthermore, organizations depend on individuals who can constantly adapt to new technologies to help reduce errors. Thus, it makes logical sense for students to be highly knowledgeable with computers and capable of producing high quality work without much guidance. A college instructor explained,

> I have two graduate level degrees. I received my first graduate degree from a traditional university and my second graduate degree from a non-traditional university where I completed my program online. I can honestly tell you that I worked twice as hard for my second graduate level degree that was completed online. In both programs, I graduated with honors. Being an online student is strenuous but rewarding. As a result, I prefer hybrid programs.

Hybrid programs can be extremely beneficial for most courses and programs. For example, many local colleges offer a hybrid speech course where students complete the majority of their coursework online and are required to come in once a week to deliver a speech to their peers. Many other colleges that offer hybrid courses require their students to come in on exam days. An online student by the name of Robert stated,

> Being an online student has allowed me to keep my job while going to school. I do not have the comfort of going to a traditional university where I sit in the classroom and learn. I take my classes online and have trained myself to learn new

theories based upon the information that is provided to me. Of course, when I have questions, I can easily send my instructors an email.

Many believe that online education can be extremely beneficial for adult learners (*andragogy*) as opposed to child learners (*pedagogy*) because adult learners can draw upon their knowledge and experiences from different fields. Adult learners are encouraged to make connections and use their prior knowledge to grasp new concepts. Over the years, many students have completed their undergraduate, graduate, and even doctoral degrees online and have spent over $120,000 on tuition fees. This phenomenon is becoming more prevalent and may become the status quo of the future.

Online education can be expensive and unfortunately, some universities overcharge their students. There are currently many "online diploma mills" where students can purchase a degree online. Students should pay close attention to the institution's accreditation when deciding on a specific program to study at a university. This is precisely why institutional accreditation and programmatic accreditation are so important.

Online Faculty

Online faculty members are usually instructors who are looking for additional experience, extra income, or may be full time faculty who specialize in online education. They are responsible for teaching or facilitating a course or two every term. Generally speaking, instructors spend about 15-25 hours per week teaching online courses. Depending on the college or university, online faculty members usually have limited interactions with their students.

Online instructors are usually required to take an orientation course prior to teaching an online course. The orientation course introduces the instructor to the different mediums of communication, how to check for plagiarism, how to grade papers using rubrics, and ultimately, how to facilitate the course efficiently and effectively. Many retired professors have come back to academia to teach online. Some professors teach at a number of colleges or universities. In the case of Afghanistan, if there is a subject matter expert in one province, then the expert or professor can easily reach a wider audience by teaching online. This strategy can be extremely beneficial for a country such as Afghanistan that does not have an abundance of PhDs. Afghans with PhDs living outside of Afghanistan can assist with teaching specific online courses.

The student evaluations at the end of each term are what measure the success of online instructors. This means that if an instructor is teaching a number of courses for different colleges and universities, he or she cannot neglect any student in any way because at the end of each term, students are usually required to take an online survey where they evaluate the quality of education, the attentiveness of the instructor, and whether or not they would recommend the instructor. Successful online instructors will have the required educational background to teach a course, practical experience in the field in which he or she is teaching, research publications in their field, and will have above average computer and technological skills.

Education Technology (EdTech)

Many online programs have invested in resources to help create a more interconnected virtual classroom. For example, several universities have implemented VoIP (Voice over Internet Protocol) in each course so instructors can lecture "live" and students can ask questions. Of course, this requires both the instructor and the students to be on the course website simultaneously. Other colleges and universities have used *YouTube* as a medium for communicating and explaining concepts. A new and growing wave of instructional resources is offered online by using simulations and adaptive Artificial Intelligence (AI). Generative AI has the ability to create content, simulate scenarios, and provide personalized feedback. It's a tool that can democratize access to education, adapt to diverse learning styles, and prepare students for a world where AI is ubiquitous. Instructors can use the following AI tools to help with creating and developing curriculum:

- ***Brisk*** is a free AI-powered Chrome extension that simplifies teaching by integrating seamlessly with tools like Google Classroom, Docs, Slides, YouTube, and articles. Brisk enhances productivity by overlaying your existing tools without the need for a separate app, offering an all-in-one solution that saves time and reduces hassle for educators.

- ***Sherpa*** is a tool designed to help teachers scale oral evaluations in the classroom.

- ***Eduaide.Ai*** is an AI-driven platform that helps educators create lesson plans, teaching resources, and assessments.

Unfortunately, some students are becoming dependent on AI and as a result, submit assignments and exams that have been completed using AI technology. With this type of plagiarism becoming more rampant, instructors can consider using the following plagiarism detection tool:

- ***ZeroGPT*** is a reliable Chat GPT, GPT4, and AI content detector.

The reality is that technology is constantly evolving and both students and instructors need to receive proper training on how to use AI in an ethical and professional manner.

Flipped Classroom

Hybrid education can help teachers and professors be more efficient in the classroom. The "flipped classroom" concept helps with allowing a student to encounter information before class, freeing class time for activities that involve critical thinking, creativity, and communication. There are many Open Education Resources (OER) that can easily be posted online before class for a student to read so that they are better prepared for a lecture in class. Digital books, presentations, and articles are becoming more common and are typically free to use for educational purposes. As an example, students can prepare online to participate in class activities before school. During school, students can practice applying key concepts with feedback from the teacher or professor. After school, students can check and recheck their understanding online to extend their learning.

The Legitimacy of Online Education

With online education becoming more prevalent, many question whether or not degrees that are earned from online colleges and universities are weighted equally to degrees earned from traditional universities. A professor of sociology stated the following:

> If one has earned all of one's degrees online, then that individual will most likely be qualified to teach in online programs as opposed to traditional on-ground programs. At this time, I would recommend a student to obtain all of his or her degrees the traditional way and to have an additional online degree. This way the individual will have all of the bases covered and will be more employable.

Being able to advance in the corporate world with an online degree is highly possible. For example, there are many first-line managers who have undergraduate degrees and want to be promoted to middle-management positions without having to physically go to a classroom several times a week. Many end up enrolling in a graduate online program. A marketing director explained:

> I was very fortunate to be able to complete my MBA program online because it contributed to my promotion at work. There was no way I could

have completed my program the traditional way because of my different obligations. My next goal is to earn a doctoral degree online and strategically position myself for a VP position.

Earning a degree online will definitely help those who are working in the corporate world but can limit those who are interested in working in academia. Online education may be a plausible solution for the people of Afghanistan and more specifically, the Afghan girls and women who have been banned from acquiring an education.

Online Education in Afghanistan

Since seizing power in 2021, the Taliban have banned girls above the sixth grade from going to school and women from attending university, which has provoked international condemnation. As an unintended but fortunate consequence, thousands of Afghan women and girls have been able to join online study programs despite the Taliban government's ban on female education (Jack & Parkin, 2024). The online education providers say they have seen strong demand from Afghanistan for courses on subjects including English language, science, and business. Consequently, universities and institutions around the world have attempted to assist Afghan girls and women. For example, University of the People, a US-accredited nonprofit higher education institution, said that more than 21,000 Afghan women applied in the past year for its degree courses, with more than 3,100 currently enrolled to study subjects including business, computer science, health, and education. As a different example,

Canadian Women for Women in Afghanistan (CW4WAfghan) has implemented a fully online secondary school serving Afghan girls and women since 2022 as a response to the closure of girls' schools.

A conversation with Dr. Marina Aminy - Online Education

Dr. Aminy has over 20 years of experience in education and is currently the Associate Vice Chancellor at Foothill-De Anza Community College District, and Executive Director of the California Virtual Campus. She holds a BA, MA, and PhD from UC Berkeley. Her doctoral degree is in Education. The entire interview can be found in Appendix A.

Authors: Is online education trusted? Are courses online interactive and engaging?

> **MA:** This question alone would need its own book. Of course, the answer is that it strongly depends on the faculty member, the services and the policies of the institutions. The preparation and professional development of the faculty member is paramount, as is the course design (to ensure quality and accessibility). The policies of the institution around regular substantive interaction (RSI) are critical as well to ensure interactivity in that online classroom. Furthermore, the institution's ability to provide wraparound services for online students will also impact success, such as the availability of online tutoring, counseling, and other services.

Authors: What impact will Artificial Intelligence (AI), ChatGPT, and other similar apps have on online education? Will plagiarism become a larger issue in the future? Will the use of these types of apps prevent students from learning and being successful in the workplace?

> **MA:** This is a question a lot of our colleges are currently grappling with. Generative AI is certainly a major disrupter in the classroom (online or not), and students, faculty and institutions are in the midst of some very critical conversations around how to respond. In general, policies and clear guidance are needed for faculty and students on the ethical and appropriate use of AI in the classroom. I would also add we need policies for use of AI in faculty publications toward tenure and retention, scholarly work, classroom materials, and curriculum. There needs to be a conversation around equity as well, since students can have access to "better" AI if they pay a fee, versus the free versions available to the public. Do these varying levels of access in turn impact the resources and quality of work that students can produce? I truly believe that AI can be a powerful tool for education rather than a scary unknown; however, to fully realize its potential, we must pull together and respond thoughtfully and in student-centered ways. For example, using plagiarism or AI detectors as a "response" to AI can be very harmful due to the prevalence of false flags, and rather futile as AI improves and deterrents like those become less effective. I would like to see, instead, that we use

more authentic assessments and project-based learning in the classroom, which are much harder to replicate with AI. Let the AI question serve as a challenge to all faculty and administrators to fundamentally rethink their approaches to learning, assessments, and supporting students in the classroom.

Authors: How does online education break barriers?

MA: Online education provides access as a key element. This means it helps the student who is disabled and cannot come to a physical campus, the student who has two young children and cannot afford childcare, the student who cannot afford the parking fees or gas needed to drive to campus, and the student who may be caring for a sick parent or family member. These are the students who have traditionally been locked out of education because they cannot easily come to a physical campus. Online education provides an avenue for these students to learn and have a seat at the table. One of my favorite online content creators on LinkedIn is Jessica Lopez, a student at a local community college. She was born with no hands and feet, so it's clearly difficult for her to travel and physically navigate a college campus. She speaks at length about the transformative value of online education in her life, and how access to a computer and online courses have allowed her to get a degree, have a job, and live a fulfilling life where she contributes to society in meaningful ways.

Authors: What will the future of online education look like?

MA: The future of online education will certainly incorporate AI, but we don't know for sure just how this will look. It will be flexible, student-centered, and driven by student needs rather than institutional needs. Moreover, boundaries will increasingly blur for students' experiences. The Bachelor degrees being offered by community colleges is just a first step. I oversee the California Virtual Campus, or CVC, which allows for cross-enrollment across California's 115 colleges. Whereas before a student at a small community college had no choice but to wait for an online course to be offered by their home institution, today that student has access to the online inventory of dozens of other colleges. The CVC Exchange basically removes the walls between colleges and allows students to enroll in courses at any of the state's 115 colleges. This happens in a matter of minutes, and our platform takes care of all the details like admissions, records, transcripts and other business processes. We ask: why should the student have to keep filling out applications each time they need a class outside of their college? Basically, we cut a lot of the red tape for students to be able to enjoy a seamless experience. That's the future – a marketplace of education and learning experiences at the students' fingertips.

Summary

This chapter provided information on online education and opportunities. As online education expands, elements such as online platforms, students, faculty, and costs continue to develop. While its legitimacy was once questionable, online programs having proper accreditation and other accolades are quickly making virtual education a promising option for underserved communities. Online education is definitely becoming more prevalent throughout the world and can be used strategically throughout Afghanistan to promote education for all students. As a result, more students will be able to complete their educational objectives. Providing online education is possible even in the most remote areas of Afghanistan. Furthermore, there are free platforms available for creating courses. Online education can break barriers in Afghanistan by providing opportunities to students and ultimately, transforming their lives.

Chapter Six Discussion Questions

1) Why is online education becoming more popular both in Afghanistan and internationally?

2) What are the drawbacks to online education?

3) Should online education curriculum become standardized?

4) What impact will AI have on online education?

5) From your own perspective, what will be the next innovative educational evolution after online education?

6) Considering the pros and cons of in-person and online education, which one do you prefer and why?

7) In what ways do you think online education has evolved since the onset of the COVID-19 pandemic?

8) When the first handheld programmable pocket calculator (Model Name: HP - 65) was introduced during the 1970s, professors and teachers were upset that the calculators would eliminate math education and critical thinking. From your perspective, how was math education impacted by the invention of handheld programmable pocket calculators?

9) Today, ChatGPT is nothing more than a more advanced and sophisticated rebirth of the first handheld programmable pocket calculator. Similar to how the calculator allowed students to quickly calculate numbers, ChatGPT empowers students to get a quick snapshot of information. What are your thoughts on ChatGPT and do you believe that student learning will be positively or negatively impacted by the use of ChatGPT?

7

AFGHAN STUDENT FOCUS GROUP

"Education is for improving the lives of others and for leaving your community and world better than you found it."
—Marian Wright Edelman

*I*n order to figure out how to structure the book and to identify the actual educational gaps and needs in Afghanistan, a focus group consisting of 20 Afghan students provided their perspectives, attitudes, and opinions on the education system in Afghanistan. Their responses helped shape the content of each section of the book. For example, when students mentioned that the Kankor exam is ineffective and unfair, the authors of this book conducted additional research and conversations in order to provide plausible recommendations for enhancing the Kankor exam to make it more effective and fair. Without the help of the focus group, the information in this text would not be as meaningful and practical. The purpose of a focus group was to gain insight into the experiences and perspectives of a group of people with similar backgrounds. According to Nyumba et al. (2018), the focus group discussion is frequently used as a qualitative approach to gain an in-depth understanding of social issues. The focus group method aims to obtain data from a purposely selected group of individuals rather than from a statistically representative sample of a broader population. The following selected responses from Afghan students provide useful information that will give the reader an idea of how complex the political, economical, and social landscape in Afghanistan really is and more importantly, the need for immediate educational reform. Some descriptive questions were asked to paint a picture of the focus group. The names of the participants are not included for security purposes. Furthermore, the focus group also answered questions about their experiences with the Taliban.

Demographic Information

Age

Highest Level of Education Completed

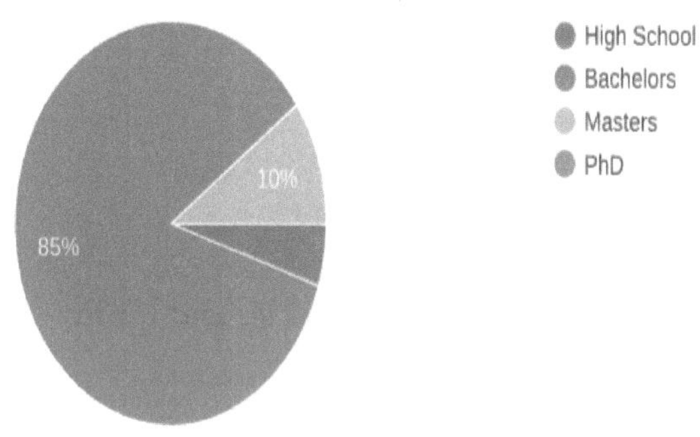

Gender

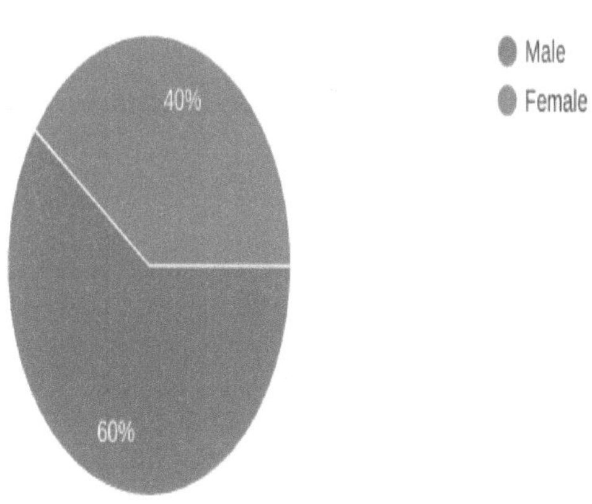

Languages Spoken

Farsi and English
Farsi and English
Farsi, Pashto, Urdu, Arabic and English
Farsi, Pashto, and English
Pashto, Farsi, and English
Farsi and English
English, Pashto, Farsi, and Urdu
Farsi and English
Pashto, Farsi, English, Turkish, and Urdu
Farsi and English
Farsi and English
Farsi, Pashto, English, and Hindi
Pashto and English
Farsi, Pashto, and English
English, Farsi, Pashto
English, Farsi, Pashto, Urdu, and Hindi
Pashto, Farsi, and English
Pashto, Farsi, English, and Urdu
Pashto, Farsi, and English
Farsi, Pashto, and English

Marital Status

20 responses

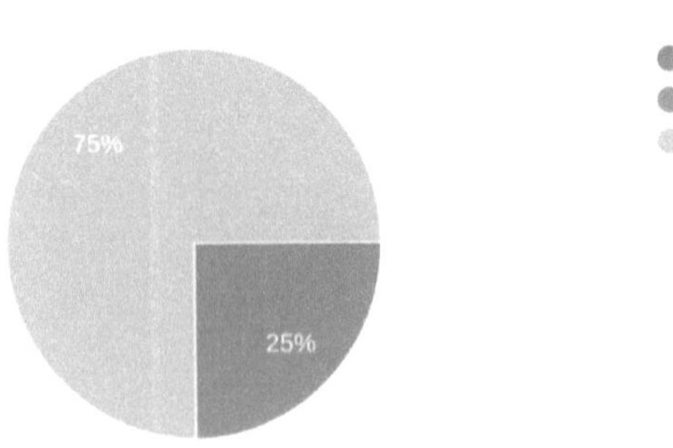

Employment Status

20 responses

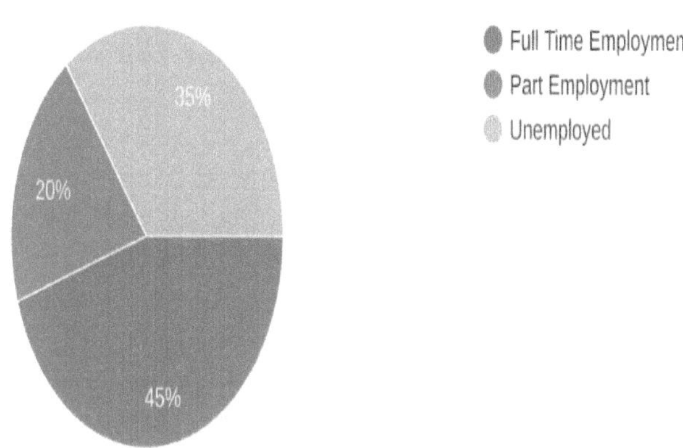

Interview Questions and Responses

From your perspective, should Afghan women be required to wear a headscarf or should it be a personal choice?

- They need to wear it as per Islamic principles
- It must be a personal choice; they know best for themselves.
- Should wear one.
- As we are Muslim it is a must to wear it.
- It should be a personal choice.
- The decision to wear a headscarf should ultimately be a personal choice, respecting an individual's autonomy and freedom of expression. Mandating or coercing women to wear headscarves infringes upon personal

liberties. Instead of emphasizing to women about hijab we should avert our eyes.

- I believe it should be a personal choice. Women should have the right to choose whether to cover their hair. At the end of the day, it is the woman who is affected by the decision. Her wearing or not wearing the headscarf does not affect anybody.
- It is a personal issue.
- It should be a personal choice because everyone has their own rights to choose what to wear.
- Considering that we are Muslims and Islam has ordered the hijab, yes, we must wear a headscarf.
- It should be a personal choice. In our society the problem is other people dictating behavior on others. I believe that women should have the choice to either wear or not wear a scarf. Having the ability and freedom to choose is important.
- I think it should be a personal choice because clothing is a personal choice for everyone.
- It should be a personal choice because we live in an Islamic country and everyone is aware of the fundamental principles of Islam in the headscarf and the hijab.
- Yes. I suggest that Afghan women wear a headscarf in public for two main reasons: 1) this is recommended in Islamic literature, and 2) wearing Hijab and a headscarf in public is part of Afghan culture. Therefore, wearing a headscarf in public, particularly in Afghanistan's type of culture, helps them with social protection and also respect for women.
- Based on our religion which is Islam women are recommended to wear it. So, I believe that it's a choice, and everyone has their own justification for their choices whether they accept or deny.
- Because we are from a Muslim country and the majority of our people are Muslims, we should follow whatever the true direction of our religion is. Hence,

females should be required to wear a headscarf as directed in our religion.

- Yes, women should wear a headscarf.
- I think that Afghan women should wear a headscarf because of two reasons. First, covering the head and hair of women is part of our Afghan culture. As a culturally independent nation, we should protect and continue with our culture. Second, the majority of Afghans are Muslims, and it is an Islamic rule for women to wear a headscarf. Also, we Afghans identify ourselves as the best Muslims in the world. Hence, we should stick to our interpretation of Islamic Sharia.
- Based on my own perspective and the religion I follow, women should wear a headscarf. They should not consider it unnecessary because it is considered as compulsory in Islam. I believe that when women wear a headscarf, they are greatly respected by everyone.
- From my perspective, wearing a headscarf should be a personal choice.

Would you support a highly qualified, responsible, respectable, and righteous female to lead Afghanistan?

- No, as the context of Afghanistan is not suitable for such a scenario and it will create problems in governance.
- Yes, if she is a highly qualified, responsible, respectable, and righteous female among all the candidates.
- Yes, because women are the makers of family and community.
- Yes, everyone has this right if they are qualified enough to lead a country.
- Yes, because I believe in equal human rights and values, I support a highly qualified, responsible,

respectable, and righteous woman to lead our country towards development and prosperity. Moreover, in the history of Afghanistan, we haven't seen a female leader, so from that aspect, it would be better to give a chance to a female to test how well she could govern Afghanistan.

- Without any doubt, my mother is my heroine. She is the reason why I believe that a woman can lead. She is the best leader I know. Moreover, for the Afghan society to fully accept and support a female leader, it would require a shift in traditional beliefs and an emphasis on meritocracy. A female leader, embodying integrity and capability, could potentially inspire positive change, promote gender equality, and represent the diverse needs of Afghan citizens. Unfortunately, we don't have such a leader, but men should accept that women are half of their society and women should accept that they have the power to bring change even in a cultural society like Afghanistan.

- No. I believe that women do not have the emotional courage and logical ability to lead a country of such a magnitude. This statement of mine does not mean that women are inferior logically compared to men. However, leading a country needs strength in both qualities to exist within that person. One must ask about the countries currently led by women and the developed state they have acquired. Yet, it must also be considered that these countries were already in a state of peace and development when the women rose to power. For a country like Afghanistan, with such a complex social structure, it is impossible for a woman to successfully lead the country due to emotional weakness and logical inadequacy. Furthermore, a society where men dominate almost every aspect of life is unlikely to accept a woman leader.

- I would support a leader with the mentioned characteristics regardless of gender.
- Yes, if a leader is qualified, responsible, respectable and accepted by people of Afghanistan then gender should not be prioritized.
- Yes, of course, because women are half of the society and Afghan women should have this right like women in other countries.
- I would definitely support a highly qualified, responsible, respectable, and righteous female to lead Afghanistan. I am pro merit and if a leader has the ability to lead, being a male or a female does not matter.
- Afghan women need support from their females and educated women; by having these kinds of women we can have greater achievements.
- With confidence, I will support such women because I care more about skill, responsibility, and righteousness that benefit our nation than I do about gender.
- Yes. For me, gender does not matter and I strongly support highly qualified people who have the capability to thoroughly lead the country. In the past, females have contributed to the peace and development of the country significantly. We had lots of Afghan women who brought the most pride to Afghan people through their achievements in different arenas.
- Absolutely yes, I look for quality, so if a female has the appropriate qualities why wouldn't I support her?
- Yes, for sure. I don't see gender as a condition for leadership. We have women and men with outstanding leadership skills, some better than others. A good leader would not be determined or known by their gender. There is no issue with a woman leading our country.
- Yes, not an issue at all.

- Yes. Afghan males and females are both capable of leading Afghanistan because there is no difference between them in terms of their natural capabilities of leadership.
- I would definitely support the appointment of a highly qualified, responsible, respectable, and righteous female to lead Afghanistan. Gender should not be a barrier to leadership, and it is important to recognize that women possess the same capabilities, skills, and dedication as men in effectively leading a nation. Having a female leader in Afghanistan could bring numerous benefits and opportunities. First and foremost, it would be a powerful symbol of gender equality and women's empowerment, inspiring and motivating women across the country to pursue their aspirations and contribute to the nation's progress. Furthermore, a female leader may excel in building diplomatic relations and fostering international cooperation. Women leaders have often demonstrated exceptional skills in diplomacy, negotiation, and building relationships, which could contribute to stronger ties with donors, neighboring countries, and the international community. This could potentially lead to increased support, investment, and collaboration, benefiting Afghanistan's development and stability. It is important to recognize that leadership qualities and capabilities are not determined by gender but by an individual's competence, integrity, and dedication. By embracing gender equality and providing equal opportunities for women in leadership roles, Afghanistan can tap into the immense potential and talents of its entire population, paving the way for a brighter and more inclusive future.
- Support for a leader, regardless of gender, should be based on their qualifications, capabilities, commitment to justice, and ability to address the

needs of the people they serve. In the context of
Afghanistan or any other country, promoting gender
equality and empowering women in leadership
positions is a positive step towards building more
inclusive and diverse societies.

What was a typical day like for you in primary (elementary) school?

- Elementary school wasn't a good experience for me at
  all. The teachers' behavior wasn't good. However, the
  education system was somehow fair but the teachers
  weren't able to implement it perfectly. Most of the
  teachers were not qualified enough. The teachers were
  focusing more on religious subjects rather than any
  other scientific subjects. The teachers beating
  students was a normal thing.
- I strongly opposed the education system in
  Afghanistan. The classes were not selective, and the
  subjects were limited. It was monotonous, requiring
  sitting for six straight hours and learning something
  you didn't necessarily need or have an interest in. We
  were in school six out of seven days a week.
- Although it is hard to remember all the details, I
  remember those days to be quite fun. I was in a
  public school where you had classmates of all
  backgrounds. It was interesting to be classmates with
  them; I still remember them up to this day. I would
  wake up early for school, which was the most
  challenging part; the primary school classes used to
  start at 7 and end at 12, right at noon. I learned what
  was necessary for me, which at the time was to learn
  how to read and write. Not to forget, learning
  mathematics was the most fun part for me. I don't
  recall having well-qualified teachers. Most teachers
  were just recent high school graduates. Since the

materials were easy, schools did not find it necessary to hire well-qualified teachers. Usually, students would go to school 5 hours a day, 6 days a week.

- A typical day is listening to the lecture by the teacher and discussing a topic with my classmates. I would feel like I learned something. Our teachers had specialties in the fields they taught. We had to stay 4 hours in primary school.
- Compared to other countries' school systems, the school system for me was not a perfect one, yet I remember it helped a lot to enter the stage of life where as a little girl I learned responsibility, communication with people my age, and learned from my instructors. I used to go 6 days a week at school and was there 5 hours per day.
- First of all, students go to school 6 days of the week and they're free on Friday; in school they study different subjects for a maximum of 5 hours. Lots of teachers were qualified but some of them were teaching subjects that they didn't have any ideas about. Sometimes we felt so bored because we learned lots of subjects in 4 hours without a break.
- Each day I looked forward to going to school. Everyone could teach these kids because it was a primary school with an elementary-level curriculum, and I learned a lot. Parents made an effort to encourage their children to attend school, and as a result, students consistently showed up for the six days of instruction each week. Every day, we were there for around 2.5 hours total.
- I completed my primary school at a public/government school in a rural area (Logar province) of Afghanistan. Therefore, my typical day in primary school was a mix of challenges and determination. While the structured schedule involved attending classes, the overall learning experience was often hindered by several factors which varied from

lack of proper classrooms and the school building itself, the high number of students in one class, and unqualified teachers, lack of teaching materials including the textbook which was always changing, and lack of regulation and discipline in the school... I can list many others. Thus, the education quality was not optimal, leading me and many of my classmates to seek additional private courses. In most cases, we ended up studying a subject in private accelerated courses from the same teacher who taught these subjects in the school. Obviously, it was much better in the private courses as we paid the teachers and they had to make sure that we understood the subjects. Unfortunately, the lack of qualified teachers was a significant hurdle. Many educators struggled to impart knowledge effectively due to their own limitations in subject expertise. Most of our teachers had never attended teaching training courses or if they had attended, were not teaching the same subject that they had studied. This circumstance made self-driven learning and private lessons crucial for my academic development. In terms of the school week, we attended primary school for six days, typically adhering to a standard six-day school week from Saturday to Thursday with Friday off. Usually, the school was a half day, starting from 8 am-12:00 pm. We had to study 4 to 5 subjects in a day and each subject's teaching duration was 35 minutes. There were 15-30 minute breaks in the middle between the three classes. The effectiveness of these days varied, considering how many subjects teachers were present. On the luckiest days, we studied 2 or 3 subjects, and for the rest of them either the teachers were absent or there was another issue that prevented teachers from coming to teach and lead the classes. Since the number of students was high in each class, usually between 50-70 students, it was very crowded and conflict between the students in some cases led to physical injuries of the students. Therefore, the secondary school classes were not very effective and usually, most of the students dropped out of the school at this stage. In rural areas, usually, the student needs to commute a long way to attend school. Personally, I needed to walk around 2.5 hours every day to and from school. Therefore, personally I don't feel that I had learned effectively during secondary school because I was always exhausted.

- I was studying in a private school in Kabul. Our daily routines and studies were quite a learning experience. Our teachers usually had bachelor's degrees or were people that were about to finish their bachelors. We were only excused on Fridays, and we studied the remaining six days of the week. We had eight studying hours for eight subjects each day. Each of the study hours was 45 minutes.

- When I started school, I remember the first days when I was very excited that I started school and also I was going to Masjed to recite the Qur'an. Our primary school was 6 days a week and 4 hours a day. I learned a lot of lessons such as reading books, writing, and memorizing words. Although while I was going to school I could read the billboards and station names easily. It helped me a lot to start school from the primary class and continue.

- My primary school experience was more traumatic than a real and well-rounded education. The issue was language teaching and learning. Some of my classmates mimicked me in the class while our teacher was present. The only subject in which they could not laugh at me, and I could challenge them was math, but my math language was also Pashto. When I was starting the calculation, I was trying to keep my voice low and only to myself, so nobody else could hear it. Now, thinking back about those days, I feel that all I learned at primary school was not considering others' opinions about me. All the school curriculum subjects I have been taught at home by my older siblings. Although our teacher had a bachelor's degree, her teaching method was really bad. It was boring and dictatorial. Punishment was the only solution to our childish kind of disobeying acts in the class. I went to school six days a week. Every day was about four hours.

- A typical day for a primary school student varies depending on the school, location, and educational system. In Afghanistan, primary school students attend classes six days a week, typically from Saturday to Thursday. The number of hours per day was often around 4 to 5 hours. Our schedule included a combination of subjects such as mathematics, language arts, science, social studies, and physical education. There was usually a break for recess, providing students with time for physical activity and social interaction. Also, the quality of education and the qualifications of teachers can vary widely. In general, my primary school teachers had completed relevant education and training programs. Their effectiveness also depended on their teaching methods, ability to engage students, and the resources available to them.

What was a typical day in high school like in Afghanistan?

- Typically the school day starts from 7am to 11am for elementary and for high school students it is from 7am to 1pm, but in some schools as there is a lack of classrooms they use three different timings (7-10:30am, 10:30 to 1:30pm and 1:30pm to 5pm). The high school teachers were good but not qualified enough. Students spent 6 days a week for 6 academic hours per day which are from 45 to 60 minutes.

- I had to go to the class at 7:30. We had 6 classes per day, and the classes were finished by 12:00. I learned a lot from my teachers during my high school. Our teachers were well qualified for the subjects they were teaching us. We attended school 6 days a week, 5 to 6 hours a day.
- Good and full of scary stuff because of the Kankor Exam. I graduated from high school in Peshawar, Pakistan, though that was an Afghan high school but still the student enthusiasm and the education system was very good. The participation was also perfect. The teachers were very qualified. We had a small laboratory for experimentation purposes and I still remember the memories and the practical lessons I learned in that laboratory. However, some teachers were very aggressive and they were beating students with big sticks.
- High schools have become more frustrating as we're compelled to study additional subjects that hold no interest for us. Spending eight consecutive hours in classes, six to seven days a week, feels overwhelming. While some teachers are excellent, others seem to merely pass time to collect their monthly salary. I graduated from Dunya Private High School, equipped with nearly every facility a student could imagine. However, the education system in Afghanistan lacks many essentials. Upon high school graduation, another stressor gets added to our education journey: the Kankor exam.
- I attended a prestigious high school where you must pass three exams to enroll. Afghan Turk high school reminds me of the best days of my life. This was one of the few schools across Afghanistan with breaks between lessons. This would help us take the time off and prepare for the next. Thus, we got to learn a lot.

The teachers were well-qualified, and the majority were of foreign origin. A typical day would have us studying, playing football, and having fun. We would go to school 8 hours per day, 5 days per week. Thursdays and Fridays were off days. On Thursdays, we had lesson recitation sessions.

- I do not believe that I have learned a lot from high school in Afghanistan. Even though I was studying in a private school, the teachers were not qualified enough to transfer knowledge and share it with the students. In school, we had classes from 7:00 in the morning until noon. We used to have 4 classes, then a break of 15 minutes, and then 3 more classes till noon. The tables were packed, and sometimes the classes were either too hot or too cold for the students. Additionally, controlling the students in Afghanistan was also not easy because I saw many of the students starting to use drugs in schools.

- In high school we learned lots of subjects in 5 hours and most of the teachers were unqualified.

- Similar to primary school, we attended high school six days a week for about four and a half hours. In fact, our school lacked qualified teachers in certain subjects, particularly science and English. I remember that in our physics, English, and chemistry classes in grade 12, these subjects were significant and required further analysis. We didn't have qualified teachers; we just read from the book, and I didn't learn anything new.

- I completed my high school at a public/government school in a rural area (Logar province) of Afghanistan. We were transferred to another school as the previous school did not teach classes beyond grade nine. My typical day in high school was a mix of challenges and determination. While the structured schedule involved attending classes, the overall learning experience was usually hindered by several factors which varied from lack of proper class setup to lack of qualified teachers and other challenges. Thus, the education quality was not optimal, leading me and many of my classmates to seek additional private courses, particularly for difficult subjects including math, geometry, chemistry, and physics. Obviously it was much better in the private courses as we paid them and they had to make sure that we understood the subjects. In high school, we got used to this and we understood that even good marks in school in some subjects depended on if you had attended the private courses by the subject teachers in the school. Thus, we were considering this as a usual practice to learn a subject and receive good marks. Unfortunately, the lack of qualified teachers remained a significant hurdle in high school. Many educators struggled to impart knowledge effectively due to their own limitations in subject expertise. I remember that our math teacher got mad at me when I asked him difficult questions in algebra that he was not able to answer. Unluckily that question caused me to receive a very low mark in that class and I regretted asking that. Therefore, after that, I always tried not to ask any difficult questions from the teachers in the class and tried to ask them personally at the end of the class if it was possible or in the private courses. The same as the primary, in the high school most of our teachers had not attended specialized teaching training courses or if they had attended were not teaching the same subject that they had studied. The school duration remained the same as the primary at secondary school with the difference that we needed to take additional courses. We still needed to attend high school for six days, from Saturday to Thursday with Friday off. Usually, the school was a half day, starting from 8 am to 12:30 pm or 1:00 pm to 4:30 pm which was very hot during the summer days.

Usually, schools are off for around three months during the winter in that area. We had to study 6 subjects/classes in a day and each subject's teaching duration was 45 minutes. There were 15-30 minute breaks in the middle between the three classes. The same as the primary and secondary school, the effectiveness of these days varied, considering how many subject teachers were present. On the luckiest days, we studied 3-4 subjects and the rest of them remained untouched. The number of students in each class was still high between 40-60 students. To sum up, high school classes were not very effective for me, but still better than primary school as I was able to read and write and was able to study in a group with my other classmates, sharing teaching materials. I was also able to self-study easy subjects such as biology, history or Islamic studies. The same as in primary school, most of my classmates were commuting a long way to school passing through agricultural lands, gardens and muddy ways. I was among the luckiest people who were cycling to school. Since our school was located a bit far, I still needed to cycle around one and a half hours each way from school to home. Unfortunately, with transferring to the high school, the conflict started in our areas which caused serious challenges for us. Most of our classes or school altogether were canceled due to the active conflict between Taliban and foreign forces and movement soldiers at that time. This added another excuse for canceling our high school classes. Sadly, I lost three of my classmates in a blast and firing on our school at that time.

- My High school era was 4 hours per day and 6 days per week. Honestly this era was not too productive but to recover I was studying with my father at home most of the time.

- I graduated from the same private school I started in Kabul. Same duration of 8 periods each of 45 minutes. For our high school classes our teachers were better. Some were graduates, some were even masters. The learning environment was way better than governmental schools. We used to study during all the 8 periods of the day.

- I studied in Lycée Istiqlal (Istiqlal High School) in Kabul. It was an elite school in Afghanistan. Our classes began in the early morning and continued until 1:00 pm. The school uniform and regulations were closely followed and respected by the students, teachers, and administrative staff. There were several security checkups at the school gate. Students had half an hour to walk around the school building area and read or play football before the beginning of the classes. The teaching and learning language was Dari, the lingua franca of Afghanistan. Each class was taught by a teacher who was proficient in his or her fields. Our teachers had bachelor's, master, and doctoral degrees in their respective fields. I learned a lot in this school and gained new experience. Like other high schools in Kabul City, we were required to attend the classes six days a week.

- In Afghanistan, the education system in secondary school can be quite challenging for students. A typical week at school was often filled with a heavy workload as we had to study nearly 20 subjects. However, the reality was that the quality of education varied greatly. I remember my first day at school being exciting, but unfortunately, some of our teachers would frequently arrive late or not show up at all. This resulted in a less structured learning environment. As a result, attending school sometimes became more about socializing and having fun rather than focusing on academics. Throughout my time in secondary school, I had mixed experiences with teachers. Some were dedicated and innovative, making the learning process engaging and effective. However, there were also instances where teachers lacked qualifications or expertise in the subjects they were teaching. It was not uncommon for a teacher to be assigned multiple subjects even if they were only skilled in one area. For instance, I remember one particular teacher who taught us physics, biology, and English in grade 9. He was like an all-in-one package just because he had a good understanding of English. In terms of the school schedule, we attended school six days a week. The school day typically lasted around 6 to 7 hours, allowing for a substantial amount of time dedicated to learning. However, it's important to note that the specific hours and days may vary depending on the school and region.

- In Afghanistan, the education system may vary, and experiences in high school can be influenced by factors such as the location, school infrastructure, and available resources. High school education typically involves a more specialized and in-depth curriculum compared to primary school. As a high school student in Afghanistan, I often attended classes six days a week, with the same length of the school day. The number of hours per day ranged from 5 to 6 hours, including a break for recess. The curriculum in Afghan high schools typically included subjects like mathematics, sciences, language arts, social studies, and sometimes vocational or technical courses. The goal was to provide students with a well-rounded education that prepares them for higher education or the workforce. Moreover, the quality of education and the qualifications of teachers can vary, and it depends on factors such as government policies, school resources, and the overall education system. In my school, qualified teachers should have had relevant education and training to effectively impart knowledge to students. Finally, as for whether students feel like they learned a lot, it can depend on individual experiences, the effectiveness of teaching methods, and the resources available. I am among those students who feel like they learned a lot.

If you earned a Bachelor's degree in Afghanistan - What was a typical day in university like in Afghanistan?

- There are two times for bachelors in public universities (morning or afternoon); the morning's timing is from 7:30am - 12pm, and the afternoon is from 1pm to 4:30pm). Some of the private and public universities offer late day programs which go from 5pm - 8pm. I feel I learned enough considering the lack of equipment and technology. The professors at the university during my bachelor's program were qualified, but there were professors who were not willing to teach, although this was not an overall issue.
- I did a bachelor's degree at Kabul University. The university opened at 08:00 am. Everyday was different. It depended on the amount of credits we took each semester. The professors were excellent in their field of study. I went 6 days a week and 2 to 5 hours a day.
- I completed my university in Nangarhar in one of the private universities named Khurasan and studied English literature. The teachers were very qualified and well mannered.
- I learned but not as much as I wanted. Professors were good but there were some people with less knowledge and experience in teaching. I went 5 days a week and studied 4 hours a day.
- Overall, the education system in Afghanistan is a bit similar at every level. You face the same type of

teachers and lecturers all over the education centers. The university lecturers were mostly engaged in political discussions. Despite being qualified lecturers, they still had issues about how to inject and carry out their knowledge to the students. Students' participation was at first good and then gradually decreased significantly. I believe I've learned more things in university, compared to high school.

- I chose this university because of its liberal arts education system. Here, I had the choice to select what I wanted to study. At the university, I discovered numerous new things that were culturally limited in other universities. I met many new people who influenced my student life in various ways. From every professor, I learned something new. Meeting every professor was something special. Typically, we attended university four out of seven days a week.
- A typical day on campus would normally be only a few hours long for other students. However, since the university community was close-knit and offered many extracurricular opportunities, a typical day on campus would begin in the morning, and I would be on campus until the evening. Only a small part of my time was dedicated to in-class learning; the rest was devoted to learning outside the class. This process would be repeated almost every day, and based on my experience, it was typically 4 days per week.
- Online education was the education system that I was seeking. It made me prepared for the real world and showed me the path to the international system of education. My major was Computer Science and my instructors were qualified enough. I had classes 4 days a week, and it was mostly 3-5 hours per day .
- Yes, I believe that university helped me learn and get a different view of the world. The classes were more flexible, and you had more freedom within the walls of the university. The environment was academic and

interesting. The days and classes depended on each student's timetable and degree plan. However, most of my classes were four days a week.

- Typical days for university were the same as school. Students went to university 6 days a week and we had qualified teachers. Some of them were absent but at the end of semester they would appear and teach to students.
- I completed two years of study at a government institution and two more years of study at a private university to obtain my bachelor's degree. I studied three or four days a week at my private institution, and I believe Afghanistan has a true shortage of highly trained university lecturers. For example, it is not appropriate for a bachelor to come and teach a bachelor's degree but one of our teachers had a master's degree and the other had a bachelor's.
- Yes, I completed my first bachelor's degree at Kabul University and successfully passed the Kankor examination on my first attempt, graduating from the Faculty of Agriculture in 2014. A typical day at Kabul University started with preparing for classes. As a student from another province, living in the hostel or private rented accommodation near the university, I often shared a room with 2-8 other students. We would have breakfast together with our roommates or alone before heading to the faculty. Depending on the distance, students commuted by walking, cycling, or using private transport. The attendance system was stringent, and punctuality was essential. Students arriving late were not allowed into the class. Each class consisted of a 90-minute lecture. Instructors used presentations or whiteboards, and sometimes they delivered lectures without any visual aids. It was the student's responsibility to note down the essential points. Lecture notes were typically available as chapters for purchase from a nearby private

photocopy shop. Unfortunately, these notes were often in use for years, making them illegible after copying from the original. Lecturers were not very supportive in sharing teaching materials, causing difficulties in finding lecture notes or other study materials. We usually had one final exam for each subject at the end of the semester. Some instructors assigned homework or group assignments with minimal marks. The exam system was challenging, with paper-based exams and no standardized question formats. The number and type of questions depended solely on the lecturer, creating stress among students. Tough and complex exams were seen as a source of power for professors. The university operated six days a week (from Saturday to Thursday), with up to four classes (each lasting 90 minutes) per day, depending on the timetable. Personally, I don't feel that I learned much despite putting in significant effort in each subject. Memorizing Latin names/terms or botanical names of plants, often asked during exams, proved to be futile as they were easily forgotten afterward. When I graduated, I realized I never applied what I studied in my job, rendering my degree seemingly useless. Consequently, I decided to pursue another diploma in business management at a private institute and obtained a second bachelor's degree in pharmacy from a private university in Kabul. While most professors at the Faculty of Agriculture were well-qualified, possessing PhDs from other countries, they were not very collaborative in their teaching methods. Issues with university curriculum and teaching systems persisted, with professors clinging to traditional teaching methods that often resembled a dictatorship. Many professors were not friendly, leveraging the complexity of subjects and the difficulty of exams to command respect from students. In conclusion, I regret the four years I spent studying at the Faculty of Agriculture, as the knowledge gained was limited, and what I did learn proved to be of little use in my professional life.

- The university and faculty I attend have USA universities' curriculum. I attend the full day engineering faculty 5 days per week. All of my professors earned their masters or PhD from USA, Japan, India, and European universities.
- I started my bachelor's in 2018. I studied on campus for three years. We could take a maximum of 5 classes equivalent to 15 credits and we could take a minimum of 3 classes equivalent to 9 credits. Our professors were all PHDs and we barely had any professor with a Master's degree. We learned a lot; everything was new and we are taking in a lot of information each day.
- I started my bachelor's degree in Business Administration. The university was full of students, both male and female students. Our university management encouraged everyone to learn and finish their bachelor's with high marks. We had foreign professors in university beside our Afghan professors. Both were good enough and qualified to teach at that international level. I learned lots of things, especially business and economics while studying, although I was working as well as studying. Our class was for 3 hours 5 days a week.

Based upon your experiences, what are the differences between the education you received in Afghanistan compared to your current university?

- The only difference is that my current university uses a different assessment approach. At my current university, the assessments are distributed each week, while in Kabul University all the assessments were completed at the finals. Moreover, at my current university there are many other events and activities in addition to our regular classes.

- At my current university, you learn a lot. The first thing emphasized is critical thinking and recognizing the value of your opinions. They truly appreciate your thoughts, ideas, and words, which is a rarity in other universities.
- The language of the instruction was different, and the teachers didn't require us to memorize the textbooks but to learn from them.
- My current university has an international based education system where it was more than just books.
- The unique aspects of my current university include its diverse approach, highly qualified professors, and high quality of education. In Afghanistan, a student will read one book during the course of the semester. We use various books in a single subject at my current university consistent with assignments with various group projects.
- In the preceding question, I provided a brief overview of my experience at Kabul University, considered one of the top public universities in Afghanistan. Upon transitioning to my current university, I observed a stark contrast. My current university stands out with its updated curricula, aligning with international standards. Access to teaching materials is readily available, and the examination system is standardized and well-defined. Professors at my current university are notably friendly and supportive, marking a departure from the authoritarian system prevalent at Kabul University. My current university professors encourage questioning and are open to challenges to their teaching methods, appreciating creativity and hard work. The grading system is diversified, incorporating various activities and assignments throughout the semester to keep students engaged. While there are some administrative issues, they are

generally acceptable for a university based in
Afghanistan. Personally, what I have learned at my
current university as part of my degree has been
directly applicable in my professional life. The
practical relevance of the knowledge gained is evident
in its real-world usage. To be candid, I don't believe it
would be fair to compare the standards of the
Agriculture faculty at Kabul University with my
current university's Business School. The two
institutions operate on different scales, and the
superior standards at my current university
underscore its commitment to excellence in
education.

- First, my current university education is well rounded
  and has components of various disciplines such as
  science, mathematics, and computer science. The
  main aim of such education is not to prepare students
  for a specific vocation but to become educated,
  engaged citizens, and life-long learners. However, the
  main focus of traditional universities in Afghanistan
  education is to train students through rote learning
  for a specific profession, mainly future bureaucrats.
  Secondly, in traditional Afghan universities,
  mathematics and physical science related subjects are
  thought to be better than social sciences subjects.
  Students who are better at math than history or
  geography are perceived to be smarter than those
  who are interested in history or any other social
  science subject.

- There are significant differences in various aspects,
  and some of the notable ones that I recall are as
  follows: 1- There is a great respect for instructors at
  my current university, which can rarely be found in
  schools in Afghanistan. 2- The grading approach in
  the Afghanistan education system is highly
  competitive, with students striving to be in the top
  three positions rather than focusing on learning.

However, at my current university, there is no race among students for positions, as the Credit and GPA system is implemented. 3- The education system in Afghanistan lacked an environment that fostered student motivation. However, my current university strives to promote student engagement and motivation through its welcoming environment.

Did you take the Kankor exam in Afghanistan? If so, what are your thoughts on the Kankor exam?

- Yes I took it. The Kankor exam was good but not an accurate assessment. The way that each student selects the major and how they introduce you is very unfortunate. Most of the students fail and 50 percent of those who pass are not happy with what they are given to study.
- Yes I took it. It was fair, credible and accurate under the Control of Islamic Republic of Afghanistan, but some small numbers of students just had some issues while taking the exams, which resulted in their dissatisfaction. It could be solved by applying some new rules after the results announcement. Now, at the Islamic Emirates of Afghanistan, I have no idea.
- Yes, I took it once. I passed it for German literature but due to family problems I was not able to study.
- Yes I did. This Kankor is useless and it's not fair for students who want to become a lawyer and have to study all of the subjects in order to get a good score on the Kankor.
- Yes, I've taken part in Kankor and successfully made it to the university from this exam. For me it was fair unless there was another better option. I can't say it is credible as it can be intervened by humans and we've witnessed many wealthy people who paid (a bribe) for a specific faculty of their choice.

- No, I didn't take it because I hate it. I believe that evaluating all your hard work from 12 years of education through a single exam is unfair. What if, on that day, you lack the energy or the right mood? What if stress causes you to forget everything? What if you lose someone dear to you on that day?
- Yes, I took the exam. This exam only tested people's abilities in memorization and calculation. However, a significant portion of the exam was only based on how well you memorized, as the questions would ask for factual and historical details. Hence, it is not a fair representation of students' knowledge. For instance, even if a student was interested in Arts, for which you would only need a relatively low score, they had to study all subjects even if they were unrelated.
- I did not take the Kankor exam because I was dissatisfied with the education that Afghan secondary schools were providing. The teachers were not qualified and could not teach students well.
- I took the Kankor exam, which is unfair because the results vary every year. For instance, I received a score of 256, but I was successful in my institution, which was two years of studying, called 14th grade. However, currently, students with that score can choose from the best faculty at any university, and Kankor offers more opportunities for provinces than for Kabul.
- Yes, I took the Kankor exam in 2010, which led to my admission to Kabul University's Agriculture Faculty. As a national-level examination, Kankor remains the sole method for assessing students' abilities and determining admissions to public universities offering free education up to the bachelor's level. Several countries in the region, including Iran, Tajikistan, and India, have adopted similar nationwide examinations. Given the substantial number of students participating in the

Kankor exam and the limited available seats at public higher education institutions, it requires fundamental reform. While there have been recent changes in the exam, they fall short, and the fairness of the exam nationwide remains a concern. For instance, in rural areas where the quality of education in schools is subpar, students face challenges passing the Kankor exams. Additionally, the difficulty of exam questions varies across provinces, as does the control over examinees during the Kankor exams. Regrettably, in the past, the influence of warlords and political figures has been evident, and at times, I have witnessed corruption in the examination process. Exam results from certain years reveal a disproportionate number of students from specific provinces receiving high marks and gaining admission to prestigious universities, raising questions about the fairness of the exam. Fundamental reforms are necessary to address these issues and ensure a more equitable and transparent higher education admissions process nationwide.

- Yes I did. Until 2014, the Kankor exam was not accurate but they made some changes and so far it has been accurate since then.
- Yes, I did. I think that it is not a fair exam as a university entrance exam since it is based on rote learning and testing memory. After taking the test, students forget the facts they memorized during the years' test preparation. It is the same all across Afghanistan.
- After graduating from Grade 12, I took the Kankor exam without any intention of studying at any Afghan university. I felt that I wouldn't be able to pursue my favorite field because of the perceived weaknesses in the education system. From my perspective, I find the Kankor exam to be unfair, particularly because certain top universities require high grades. For instance, if I

have an interest in engineering but struggle with subjects like Math, Algebra, and Calculus initially after graduating from school, it may prevent me from obtaining the passing grades required for the engineering field. However, this doesn't necessarily mean that I am incapable of studying engineering. I believe that once I start studying engineering, I would be able to comprehend the lessons and further develop myself. The Kankor exam's limitations lie in its inability to accurately assess an individual's future field and career based on a specific number of multiple-choice questions. Ultimately, I believe that the Kankor exam restricts individuals from achieving their dreams, especially those who struggled in school, leading them to choose labor work or pursue opportunities in foreign countries.

What do you think about the student ranking system (Number 1 and Number 2 and Number 3 ..... etc.) in Afghanistan?

- Nowadays this ranking system is over, as it was not helpful. When it was used before, the number 1 students were the best among all, and sometimes they were responsible for taking attendance and helping the teacher during teaching hours.
- I don't know either how this ranking works if universities do not use this info.
- The student ranking system does not work in Afghanistan. It only counts for self-glorification and bragging. Although it didn't have a tangible impact on student learning, it was problematic sometimes. For instance, those who were aiming for top ranks, were used to bribing their teachers to earn points. I fear in rural areas, it could cause abuse from some opportunists' teachers.

- It was more of an issue. Not everyone is perfect or interested in every subject. People have preferences for specific subjects—liking some and disliking others. Additionally, individuals excel in certain areas while facing challenges in others. I think it was more of a discouraging thing for most of the students.
- In Afghanistan, they had a student ranking system to pick the best students based on their grades. This made students feel pressure to compete. Overall, the competition was helpful. However, this would also create pressure on students who rank lower. They would underestimate their cognitive and intellectual abilities, being ranked low. Even though the scores rewarded some students, the universities didn't really use this information. Being the top student usually meant setting an excellent example for others, making the class a nice place to learn, and sometimes helping classmates.
- The ranking system has changed. Now, we rank students in terms of A, B, C, and D grades.
- I think it was not helpful. They were actually the only top students in the class. A student may be top in science courses but not in social studies. The number 1 student may have been a good student in 3 subjects but there were other students as well who had the same capabilities.
- In Afghanistan, it was a tool for your relatives to compare who was smarter. However, for me, it was not important because my mother had told me that as long as you were within the range of 1 to 10, you were good.
- It is a bad idea at school. It decreased the confidence of students, and also the number one student's responsibility was to manage students and their classmates.
- I disagree with this ranking system. As I have already stated, provinces are preferred above Kabul;

therefore, when they achieve the top rank and travel to Kabul, they are unable to complete their education. Ranking systems, in my opinion, are useless and don't change anything in education. When a student achieves top rank on the Kankor and is referred to as an elite member of the class, they ought to assist other students in the class.

- This traditional approach to student ranking has been in use for decades in Afghanistan. However, the intended objective is to foster a competitive environment among students, encouraging them to study harder and achieve top positions in the class. In practice, though, I find it to be neither very useful nor effective. Personally, I don't perceive it as beneficial. Based on my experience, holding the number 1 position in the class doesn't necessarily indicate the highest level of intelligence. The examination system, as described earlier, allows someone to perform exceptionally well, securing high marks and claiming the top position in the class. I have been the number 1 student in a few classes, witnessing other classmates achieving the same status. However, from an understanding of the subject and overall knowledge perspective, they may not truly be in the highest position. Furthermore, I've observed other factors influencing class rankings. For instance, the sons of a school principal consistently received good marks and secured the number 1 position in two classes, even though there were other more intelligent students in our classes. Similarly, at the university, the number 1 student in our class was the son of a professor at Kabul University, benefiting from his father's influence. The significance of being number 1 at Kabul University even led this student to become an instructor at the Agriculture Faculty. Personally, I don't support this system, as I believe it lacks fairness and is not merit-based. The number 1 student in the class carries both responsibilities and benefits. They are tasked with keeping attendance records and acting as a liaison between the class, professors, and administration. This visibility makes them well-known to professors and administration, potentially influencing leniency in grading and exams, which helps them maintain their top position.

- Number one students have the responsibility of all the affairs related to student and class management and class organization. Most of the time this ranking was not accurate. I think ranking students based upon overall grades is more effective.
- In my opinion it was a good system for promoting healthy competition among the students. However, my view may be biased, because I was the first position holder for 12 years straight. In my opinion, that ranking should only be for the top students, like the top 5 students of the class, as a reward and recognition. The rest of the students should not be shamed by the ranking of students to the lowest score. The rest of the class beside the top 5 should get categorized grades of A, B or C.
- Based on my personal experience, it promotes healthy competition and motivates students to excel. However, it also fosters stress and negatively impacts students' mental health.

Before taking online classes, what were your thoughts on online education?

- I thought it was useless and could not benefit students.
- It was okay for me since I previously was watching online videos to understand my subjects better.
- Well, for online education we need resources for Afghan women to continue their higher education.

- Online education is as useful as in-person learning but there are big obstacles that prevent Afghans from learning online education. The first obstacle is poor economy, followed by unstable electricity, lack of internet (particularly fast internet which is required for online streaming), high prices of internet packages, lack of internet connectivity in rural areas, rural students' lack of familiarity with modern technology, English language, and many more.
- I never even thought of taking online classes in my life; it was more of a surprise.
- Before I started doing classes online, I wasn't sure what to expect. I thought it might be a bit challenging because I wasn't used to learning that way. I was curious but also a bit worried that I'd miss out on things compared to traditional classes.
- Before the Covid-19 pandemic when I wasn't involved much with online classes, my thoughts about online classes were entirely different. I believed that online classes were less effective and not worth attending, especially as part of an academic degree.
- I felt like online education is unreal and is not effective.
- To be honest, I had no idea about online classes. I thought they would not be as effective as synchronous classes because there is no one to monitor students and check if they are on the right path or not.
- Before taking online classes, I had concerns and reservations about online education. I believed it would be a waste of time, as I doubted its effectiveness in providing a quality learning experience compared to traditional in-person education. I was worried that I would have difficulty hearing and understanding the learning due to potential issues with internet access. Additionally, I anticipated a lack of student engagement and

interaction, which I believed would hinder my ability to learn effectively. These concerns led me to believe that online education would not be as beneficial or meaningful as learning in a physical classroom setting.

Now that you have taken online classes, what are your thoughts on online education?

- After taking online classes I understand it as an evolution for the educational system and very effective.
- It is really great and we have more sources that we can learn from. We are limitless now. Previously we just were restricted to our books. After online classes, we became skilled in using different resources.
- It's great because some can't join classes in person so it has its advantages.
- It was boring with some professors and enjoyable with others. The lack of physical presence in class made it feel at times less like a classroom environment, as there was limited interaction with both students and professors.
- Online classes turned out to be pretty cool! I found them flexible and convenient. It was nice being able to learn from home and create my own schedule. But sometimes, it was a bit tricky not having face-to-face interaction with teachers and classmates. Overall, it worked well, but I do miss some aspects of being in a physical classroom.
- Online classes have several benefits such as receiving good knowledge through our mobile phones simply in our houses and it helps us to speak in English fluently. Besides that we now know how to work in English settings confidently.
- It is an incredibly easy method to achieve our degree from a great university, even while having a job and

continuing our studies at night. The lessons are sometimes too severe, even compared to the verbal or physical classes.

- During the Covid-19 outbreak, I became accustomed to attending online classes and other events, which became the only way to connect and communicate with others. This experience has changed my perception of online classes, as I now believe that taking them is highly beneficial, saving time and energy, and proving to be cost-effective. Through online education, I can connect with people from around the globe, learn the most up-to-date topics, and receive a quality education.
- Online education is a good approach to save resources and time. It's more applicable when there are too many restrictions on education, but we need electricity and internet with devices to attend the class.
- As explained in the previous question, things have become better. The students that want to learn something have started self-study and research which has led us to a better understanding of the course material. Previously we solely relied on our instructors.
- Online education is interesting as you can ask questions easily because instructors allow students to talk about topics and activities openly.
- I think it is one of the best ways for learning and teaching. Students and teachers can join from any part of the world; knowledge can be shared easily. In this system, students understand that there is no need for teachers to monitor their actions during exams or doing homework. Students should take control of their studies just as they should do in real life. In short, online classes prepare students for life better than offline classes.

- After taking online classes, my perspective on online education changed significantly. Contrary to my initial concerns, I found that I was able to understand the course material effectively. The flexibility of online classes allowed me to work part-time while pursuing my education, providing a better balance between my studies and other responsibilities. I also appreciated the diverse and unique approaches of the instructors, as they brought different perspectives and teaching styles to the virtual classroom.
- From my experience, online education offers flexibility and accessibility but poses challenges like the need for strong self-discipline. Benefits include improved digital literacy and diverse learning tools. Challenges involve reduced face-to-face interaction. Success depends on the quality of platforms, course design, and engagement levels.

With better infrastructure such as cheap, fast, and more stable electricity and internet throughout Afghanistan, can online education help all people in Afghanistan access better education?

- Yes, it will make the flow of knowledge fast and everyone can get access to knowledge, avoiding some obstacles they face, such as cultural barriers.
- Yes, the only limit they face now is having unstable electricity and slow internet.
- Yes, as females, we have only this option.
- I think it'll help if the above-mentioned obstacles are cleared.
- Absolutely. It truly depends on individuals whether they want to learn something or not. The internet offers numerous learning skills and lessons online, but many choose not to engage with them. Most of our young generation have access to these facilities, yet

they are unfortunately preoccupied with things that don't significantly impact their lives. A prime example is TikTok, especially the Afghan TikTok community.

- Absolutely! Improved infrastructure like reliable electricity and fast internet across Afghanistan would be a game-changer for education. It could make online learning accessible to many more people, especially in remote areas where traditional schools might be scarce. Online education could bridge gaps, giving students access to quality resources and teachers they might not have had before. It could empower learners of all ages to access better education regardless of location, potentially opening doors to new opportunities and knowledge.

- I would say a part of education can be online classes because now everything is found on the internet and online.

- I believe it can help them with education, but the people of Afghanistan do not just lack education, but also a platform to implement and learn many different social and academic skills to use within their careers.

- The important thing for every person in Afghanistan is to have access to a quality education and professional teachers. Most people, especially women, are frustrated with not being allowed to go to school. With better infrastructure, girls and women will be able to take online education classes which can help them so much. It would be a great opportunity for all women.

- Indeed, access to affordable, high-speed internet and reliable energy will facilitate education for the people of Afghanistan. For the younger generation who choose to use their time for studying or who are busy, online education is preferable. However, it can be challenging for young students to study over the phone and understand the lesson's objectives.

- In Afghanistan, improving infrastructure, particularly in terms of cheap, fast, and stable electricity and internet access, can indeed significantly enhance the potential for online education to reach and benefit people throughout the country. This improvement can contribute to better education in different ways including but not limited to: 1) Enhance accessibility, which will extend educational opportunities to individuals who may not have had access to attend educational institutions in person. 2) Flexible learning opportunity: as online education is more flexible in terms of scheduling and pacing. Therefore, better infrastructure will enable individuals to access educational content at times that suit their personal or professional commitments, enabling more people to engage in learning. 3) Less cost and save energy: Online education can be a cost-effective solution for both learners and educational providers. Reduced need for physical infrastructure, such as classrooms, can result in lower costs for educational institutions, making education more affordable for students. 4) Quality and updated learning materials: with a stable internet connection students will have access to updated and a diverse range of learning materials, including videos, interactive simulations, and real-time collaborations. This enhances the overall quality and effectiveness of education. 5) Access to learning opportunities globally and out of Afghanistan: Improved connectivity allows Afghan students to connect with educators and peers globally. This exposure to a broader educational community can enrich the learning experience and expose individuals to diverse perspectives and knowledge.
- For sure. If we can somehow provide internet and electricity to Afghans, we can expand online learning in Afghanistan and help all Afghans. The system is already checked and experienced. As a student I can

vow that those who want to learn will learn a lot from an online system. Besides, online education is way better than no education.

- At this moment it helps a lot, because the education system is failing, but it requires a strong internet connection as well as stable electricity in order to attend the class. But it's not cheap as the internet network providers which people are using are expensive, especially if students keep watching online videos.

- I think that online education is the best possible way for Afghans to have access to education in the current situation. Taking different factors like the Taliban de facto totalitarian regime, fragile infrastructure like buildings, and heating and cooling systems in rural Afghanistan, and Deobandi religious obstacles into consideration helps us to realize how important online education is in Afghanistan.

- No, online education alone may not be sufficient to ensure that all people in Afghanistan have access to better education, even with improved infrastructure such as cheap, fast, and stable electricity and internet. One of the challenges lies in the home environment, which may not always be conducive to effective learning. In many households, there may be overcrowding with 10-20 individuals living together, making it difficult for students to concentrate and create a suitable learning environment. Additionally, online education requires students to have self-discipline and motivation to actively engage in their studies, which may be hindered by various factors in the home environment. Therefore, while improved infrastructure is a crucial step, additional measures and resources, such as supportive learning spaces and community engagement, are necessary to ensure that all individuals in Afghanistan can access and benefit from a quality education.

- Improved infrastructure, including affordable, fast, and stable electricity and internet, has the potential to significantly enhance access to online education in Afghanistan, especially for the Afghan girls who are deprived from going to schools and universities. This could bridge educational gaps between urban and rural areas, offering flexibility, diverse learning resources, and valuable digital literacy skills. Global connectivity could broaden perspectives and foster international collaboration. However, challenges related to affordability, digital literacy, and appropriate educational content must be addressed to ensure the effectiveness of online education in complementing the existing educational infrastructure.

Do you think it would be helpful to have more vocational schools and vocational colleges throughout Afghanistan so that Afghans could quickly learn specific skills that will help them in their respective careers immediately instead of taking extra general educational courses?

- Yes, this is a necessity for Afghanistan, as it needs more vocational training than any other country in the world
- It depends on their own plans in life. Some people are interested in learning some helpful general knowledge and some people want to focus on a specific skill.
- Yes, that would be great.
- I think having more vocational schools and vocational institutions will help in having a self-reliant generation which can take care of their poor economic situation by themselves. The vocational schools and vocational institutions should help Afghan students to be able to work outside of Afghanistan and count as a big workforce for the country. There should be more

focus on vocational schools and vocational institutions, curriculum, and qualified teachers.

- Expanding vocational schools and colleges across Afghanistan would offer immediate, career-focused training, equipping individuals with practical skills tailored to industry needs. This approach could bridge the skills gap, providing quicker entry into the workforce and enhancing employment opportunities. While emphasizing vocational education, it's important to maintain a balance with general education to ensure a well-rounded learning experience catering to diverse career paths and fostering critical thinking.
- Yes, having more vocational schools and colleges in Afghanistan could be incredibly beneficial. These institutions focus on practical skills needed for specific careers, offering a quicker path to employment. They provide hands-on training that directly applies to real-world jobs, which is incredibly valuable in quickly preparing individuals for work opportunities. This approach can be especially useful in catering to the immediate needs of various industries and sectors, potentially reducing unemployment by supplying a skilled workforce. It offers an alternative educational pathway that emphasizes practical skills over generalized education, aligning more directly with job market demands.
- Yes, some students are not interested in learning theoretical subjects. They are eager to learn practical things.
- It would be really helpful for people within Afghanistan, especially in the current context where there is a lack of skills.
- I think if people, especially students, have an opportunity to choose what they want to learn and pursue as a career, they could achieve much more by having such vocational courses available. By creating

vocational courses, students would be able to choose among more professional careers, leading them to become more productive as students and workers.

- It is beneficial to have vocational colleges and schools in Afghanistan since the country is poor and people cannot afford to study further. Instead, they can acquire a vocational skill and immediately enter the labor market.
- Yes, I believe the establishment of more vocational schools and vocational colleges around Afghanistan could be highly beneficial for the reasons below among many others: 1) with more vocational training centers, individuals can quickly acquire specific skills relevant to their chosen careers and the market demands. This enables them to enter the workforce sooner and contribute to their families as well as the country's economy. 2) more centers teaching vocational skills would diversify career options and provide a broader range of occupational choices for individuals who may not be inclined toward traditional academic paths. 3) More vocational centers will create more entrepreneurship opportunities, and 4) training labor forces through shorter courses focusing on vocational skills is more cost effective than formal education centers. All these benefits will lead to reducing the unemployment rate, particularly among the youth which is considered to be a big challenge in the country.
- I believe that after secondary school, students should each choose their field and not just go for generality.
- Vocational colleges would be very helpful. Currently, high school students in Afghanistan are burdened with more than 16 to 18 subjects in their high school period. Most of these subjects do not help us in real life scenarios. It simply does not prepare us for the real world. It would be a great step to introduce

vocational colleges to the educational systems of our country.

- Yes, Afghan people, as I noticed, mostly prefer vocational schools due to the life challenges they face. It's because students are ready to start working and earn their own income after graduation from school, choosing occupations such as becoming a mechanic, plumber, electrician, etc. Students can easily open a small shop or work in a private company.
- I think more vocational schools are really helpful in Afghanistan because people can learn certain skills quickly and find jobs faster than the current long process of education and building a career.
- The establishment of more vocational schools and colleges throughout Afghanistan would be highly beneficial. Such institutions would offer individuals the opportunity to acquire specific skills directly applicable to their desired careers, enabling them to enter the workforce quickly and contribute to the country's economic development. By providing specialized training in fields aligned with industry demands, vocational education can bridge the skills gap and create employment opportunities. However, it is important to strike a balance between vocational and general education, as a solid foundation in literacy, numeracy, and critical thinking remains essential for comprehensive development. Integrating vocational training into the existing educational system and offering diverse educational pathways would be ideal, ensuring individuals receive both targeted skills and a well-rounded education.
- Yes, expanding vocational schools and colleges in Afghanistan could be beneficial for several reasons. Vocational education focuses on providing practical skills and knowledge directly relevant to specific careers, allowing individuals to enter the workforce more quickly. This approach is particularly valuable in

meeting the immediate needs of industries and addressing skill gaps. Vocational training can empower individuals with the skills required for various trades, enhancing their employability and contributing to economic development. Additionally, vocational education can be a practical alternative for those who may not be inclined towards or have the means for a traditional academic path. However, a balanced approach that also emphasizes foundational skills and general education can create a well-rounded workforce capable of adapting to evolving demands in the professional landscape.

Do you have a "career" mentor? If so, how did you meet this person and how is this person assisting you with your future career?

- No, I don't have any because this is not the norm in Afghanistan.
- Not at all, but there are career mentors that help students especially in the traditional way of learning the professions.
- No, I don't have a career mentor.
- No I don't.
- No.
- Unfortunately, no.
- No, I don't have a career mentor.
- I don't have a career mentor.
- I do have a career mentor and I met the person in a workshop event at university. The person helps me with the CV and job searching process.
- No.
- Unfortunately, I do not have a career mentor.
- I don't have a career mentor.
- Yes, I do have career mentors. I met them in my previous job or at the university, or they are my

relatives. The majority of them come from a background similar to mine, holding more senior roles and having been very successful in their careers. So, when I seek their advice, they share their experiences and guide me on how to efficiently achieve my targets.

- Yes, I have one. He always trains me on how to apply for jobs, build my skills, and provides guidance.
- I unfortunately do not have one, no career, no mentor.
- Yes. I met him at the airport, and he helped assist me with my school assignments.
- Not yet.
- I do not have a specific mentor for my decision-making purposes. However, when I am in doubt about making specific decisions, I seek guidance from individuals who have a wide range of expertise in that particular field.

Which career path are you interested in? Are there career opportunities for your specific field in Afghanistan?

- I am personally interested in the education section and this is available but the income is quite less.
- Computer Science. Yes, there are many.
- Well, there is a lack of career opportunities for a specific field so people are interested in any career path.
- I'm interested in journalism, but unfortunately after the Taliban takeover, this field seems too hard now. The primary role and responsibility of journalists is to reflect the truth to the society but nowadays you should act as a lobbyist for the de facto

administration. Sadly, I see there are almost no vacancy announcements in the field of journalism.

- I really love designing (men's suits- classic designs). Unfortunately no, that is why I want to move to other countries.
- I'm into FinTech, which is about using technology in finance. In Afghanistan, there might be some chances in this field, but it's not as common as in some other places. There could be opportunities, but there might not be as many as in some other countries.
- Researcher
- I consider Biotechnology and Intellectual Data science as my career path and I am interested in it. Opportunities for these paths are not in Afghanistan.
- Yes, in Management
- I am interested in teaching the English language and also I'm interested in studying psychology abroad. In Afghanistan, career opportunities are so few, especially for girls and women.
- The fields of finance and management attract my attention. Fortunately, there are more opportunities in these industries in Afghanistan.
- I am more interested in international development and hope that one day I will work for international organizations like the UN, USAID, and the World Bank as an expert, contributing to the improvement of livelihoods in the most needed countries.
- I am an engineer so I am interested in my field. There are few career opportunities for women, especially in engineering, and even fewer after bans on education and work for females.
- My major is Business Management. I want to start a career as an entrepreneur. My field has the capability to be influential in any location, including Afghanistan.
- Aviation, unfortunately no such opportunity in Afghanistan.

- Financial management. I am majoring in finance and think there are many career opportunities for me in the banks, government financial offices including the Ministry of Finance, and starting my own business.
- As a BBA graduate with 2 years of experience in management and program fields, I have a strong interest in the program field. Regarding opportunities in the program field in Afghanistan, there are several available, particularly in the private and NGO sectors. However, opportunities in the government sector seem to be limited.
- I am interested in pursuing a career in business because it offers various opportunities, and the business landscape is diverse. I can explore roles in areas such as entrepreneurship, finance, marketing, management, and international trade. Networking and building connections within the local business community, participating in industry events, and staying updated on market trends can be beneficial for my career growth. Additionally, considering the unique economic challenges and opportunities in Afghanistan, individuals in the business field may find meaningful roles in contributing to economic development, job creation, and sustainable business practices. Continuously developing my skills, staying informed about the business environment, and seeking mentorship can enhance my success in the business sector in Afghanistan.

Upon graduation from your current university, do you feel that you will have employment opportunities in Afghanistan? What is the labor market like in Afghanistan?

- I hope so, but as it seems the employment is difficult in Afghanistan, the labor market is down and there are less opportunities at the moment.
- Currently with a degree from my current university, it is not possible to have a job under the control of the Taliban.
- Yes , now the degrees and qualifications matter a lot for any job .
- Well, I believe that everyone can find their desirable job if they try and don't give up on their efforts.
- With the collapse of the Islamic Republic of Afghanistan, my dreams for my beloved country collapsed. I am not interested in working in my beautiful country under Taliban rule.
- The job market in Afghanistan is tough, especially in recent times. After graduating from my current university, finding work here might be really challenging. The situation in the job market is pretty difficult overall, with limited opportunities available.
- I will not have a career opportunity in Afghanistan. More so than the labor market, it is the government system in Afghanistan now that does not allow females to work or to acquire an education.
- The job market is currently not good in Afghanistan and most of the educated people are unemployed.
- No.
- Yes. However, the recent political changes in Afghanistan have negatively affected employment opportunities. Still, I am hopeful that receiving my degree from my current university will add more value to my career background, thus aiding in advancing within my current job/employer or securing a better position in other organizations. Obviously, my own efforts and hard work will remain key in developing my career further.
- Yes, there will be employment opportunities, different fields, different opportunities and better

days on the way. Actions are being taken to advocate for women's rights to employment.

- It can't be taken for granted, but in some cases it helps companies to understand that this university has credibility between people here and internationally. But the recruiters are focused on work experience and somehow it's difficult for recent graduates.
- I am optimistic about my future after graduation. If I come back to Afghanistan, there are tons of opportunities. Although the labor market is not stable and can be changed into economic chaos, I am sure business students can be employed and employ others in hard times.
- I acknowledge that there may be limited opportunities available to me, especially within NGOs and private companies. However, it is important to note that these opportunities are also constrained due to the prevalence of favoritism and nepotism in the recruitment process. Unfortunately, individuals who have personal connections within specific organizations often get shortlisted for positions even if they are not as qualified as other candidates like myself.
- Based on the current situation in Afghanistan. I do not feel that I will have employment opportunities in Afghanistan.

Discuss your personal experiences with the Taliban of today.

- The new generation is good but this does not mean they are better. They are better than their old version but still they don't respect humanity at all, and the main problem is that they use Islam religion to justify their own perspective. and this is not fair and good.
- I am speechless regarding them.

- Education is the most important thing for anyone but they put restrictions and bans on women.
- The situation became worse day by day. I don't know how to explain but I know this: it is the women who are always the victims, and this makes me feel really bad.
- Well, honestly I can't say a positive word. In short, I would say that when there is no freedom of speech, then there is no life. When there is no equal education and working opportunity for all, then it's impossible to live under such an Islamic dictatorship. When there is no logic, then there is no meaning of life at any cost. When there is no place for argument, then the dominant one is someone who has a fully reloaded rifle in hands.
- A terrorist is a terrorist and will be a terrorist forever.
- I had a few personal encounters with the Taliban. They did not seem bad at handling conflicts. The encounters I had were mainly on the streets. They seemed welcoming, especially if you spoke Pashto to them. I fled Afghanistan a few months later after the Taliban took over.
- I am afraid of the Taliban. My parents made me leave the country. I live in Pakistan. I constantly worry about my family in Afghanistan because the Taliban are persecuting Hazaras. For example, they are forcibly taking girls with them. My sister and cousins live there.
- I left Afghanistan on Aug 18, 2021. I actually did not have a close experience with the Taliban and their regime. But, I believe it must be a nightmare experience for Afghan girls with many useless and illogical restrictions.
- I have not had any experiences with them.
- We had to leave our house and lost some family members due to their affiliation with the previous government.

- They haven't made any changes from the past. They are the same people they were. They just say that they have changed from the past. They don't allow women and girls to have a higher education. They don't want to allow women to go to work outside. They banned everything for women.
- There are moments when I feel like this structure is destroying my life, and I sometimes don't want to breathe under this regime. I composed this thought in response to the Taliban's recent arrests of females in the marketplace or on the street. Life has gotten too complicated. For instance, one day, my brother and I went to a restaurant. When we left, the Taliban stood by us and asked where we were going and what the relationship was between us. He then checked our Tazkira ID and gave us permission to leave.
- I have been in Afghanistan for only two weeks after they came to power in 2021. Therefore, I don't have much to say about them as I was there for only a limited time after they took control of the country.
- The Taliban are not united with their opinions. Some of them are open minded while others are narrow minded. In general as we observe, they don't support females as independent humans with equal rights and opportunities.
- I fled the country when they took power.
- This time, the Taliban government is different from the previous as international countries are more involved.
- I lived only a few months in Afghanistan under the control of the Taliban. Life was really difficult. The possibility of threats was really high.
- I will compile it into one sentence: "The current regime is like a robotic toy, with our neighboring country holding the remote control, making Islam a burden on individuals, but hey, let's not forget that Islam is a great religion; it's just their harsh way of

implementation that has made it worse, and on top of that, bribery is reaching new heights in this regime."

- I don't really have a good experience with the Taliban of today. They have completely changed the life of Afghan people, especially the Afghan women and girls.
- The new generation is better but this does not mean they are perfect. They are better than their old version, but they still don't respect humanity at all, and the main problem is that they use the Islam religion to justify their own perspective which is not fair and good.
- I am speechless, I don't know what they are doing and what is their purpose.
- Well, honestly I can't say a positive word. In short, I would say that when there is no freedom of speech, then there is no life. When there is no equal education and working opportunity for all, then it's impossible to live under such Islamic dictatorship. When there is no logic, then there is no meaning of life at any cost. When there is no place for argument, then the person in charge is a tyrant who has a fully reloaded rifle in his hands.
- Unfortunately, there are no positive experiences with them. Twice when I was in Afghanistan, I was held at gun point, once when I was with my family and once with my friends.
- They are going to become more strict and they hate women.
- My brother and I were sitting in a car at the checkpoint when one of the Taliban people stopped the car and asked the driver why he had put the girl without a hijab in the car. He looked at us and said, "They are siblings." The Taliban said, "No, I'm asking why you permit her to sit in your car because she is not covering her face; otherwise, we will punish you." Girls are denied basic rights such as schooling.

Additionally, the Taliban does not allow picnics in parks or other public spaces like Bagha Babar, Qargha, and Bamyan.

- The Taliban don't have a common opinion. Some of them are good but some are very bad people. In general, as we've observed, they don't support females as independent humans with equal rights and opportunities.
- There is still personal enmity between their tribes. The issue is with old government people, although these people are not involved in each transaction. Corruption still exists at a high level in the government. People are suffering from the unemployment situation, because it's too difficult to find job opportunities during this period.
- I will provide a few examples of my experiences: Once, one of my friends was taken by them just because he had posted a story on his social media, which addressed the ban on girls' education and highlighted its cruelty. We attempted to rescue him, but we were asked to pay a specific amount for his release. Secondly, I was attending a government procurement bidding process. Upon reaching the location to bid for the project, we were advised to perform ablution first and then proceed with the bidding process.
- I don't really have a good experience with the Taliban of today. They have completely changed the lives of Afghan people, especially the Afghan women and girls.

How has the Taliban's return affected your work and home life?

- There are several problems. I'm afraid at my workplace as there is a fear of Taliban attack any moment. No one can easily talk about politics in the public areas. I used to teach at university but most of the students left the universities. The economic crisis made the people very hungry which caused problems and affected my business.

- It badly affected my education and life. It caused a gap in my education at Kabul University. Moreover, my teachers fled from Kabul to foreign countries so the quality of education there decreased. Also my family members are living in different countries now. We all are separated from each other.
- Working from home, and having no permission to go to work or to beauty parlors and elsewhere definitely affects my life badly, really badly.
- I lost my job and my income decreased after the Taliban takeover. The university doors shut on my sisters and they also lost jobs. I shifted my homes three times due to security and economic issues, and changed my physical appearance to look more like a devoted Muslim and many more.
- My brothers and sisters used to work. Now, none of them are working. Only my mother works (teacher). I spend all day at home because my mother doesn't want me to go outside, because she always says maybe something bad might happen to me.
- It obviously affected me a lot. For security purposes, we had to flee Afghanistan with my family. As things got intense in Pakistan, my family had to go back to Afghanistan.
- I couldn't go to my office when they took power and had to work online.
- Me and my family had to leave Afghanistan. I couldn't attend university.
- It changed everything.
- We had to close our business and leave the country.
- It affected us so much that everyone in my family became jobless and my sisters can't go to school.

- The return of the Taliban has an impact on numerous aspects of our lives; for example, it prohibits us from going to the park, working outside the home, learning, and leaving the house without a Mahram (a close male family member such as an older brother). In brief, Afghanistan is currently a jail for Afghan men and women alike.
- The return of the Taliban to power in August 2021 has profoundly affected my life in every aspect. At the national level, it has taken away my identity. I had never envisioned migrating and starting a new life in another country from scratch, where I would be considered a second-class citizen or face discrimination as a migrant. On the family level, it has disrupted our family unity. I haven't been able to see my parents and siblings for years, and we can't come together to support each other as we used to. Personally, I have lost my career path, my job, my personal freedom, and the ten years of savings I had accumulated through hard work in different organizations. Therefore, I lost many things...
- As they came to power I lost my job for being a female engineer.
- My father and I both lost our jobs. It basically turned our life's upside down. I fled the country and my father is still unemployed.
- Our company closed as the government collapsed, and I was unemployed after 15 August. During this period life was full of challenges.
- I left my family and home. After my evacuation to Iraq, my family left Afghanistan and never went back. The uncivil Taliban came to power like a wild animal escaping from the jungle.
- My father has lost his government job, and unfortunately, we are unable to advocate for our own rights. The situation has had a significant impact on our mental health, preventing us from enjoying any

social gatherings. It is disheartening to think about the various aspects of life that have been affected, including halted efforts at progress and the perception that our country is being exploited for the success of other nations.

- The return of the Taliban has significant implications for various aspects of my life, including potential changes in education, employment opportunities, and freedom of movement.

What has improved since the return of the Taliban? Please explain.

- The only thing is the overall security of the country. There is also less hope that it will remain the same as we experienced throughout Afghanistan's history.
- Nothing except poverty.
- Just security.
- Nothing has improved, but in fact, it has further worsened. The so-called security isn't good at all. I personally witnessed many people looted or killed by thieves and unknown gunmen. You still risk your life returning home after 08:00 PM.
- I don't know about others but for me NOTHING. They build only more Madrasas to educate more extremists.
- The centralization and the imposition of law. Taliban have not given any real importance to the warlords who looted and ravaged the country in the past four decades.
- Nothing has improved.
- I don't believe anything has improved. They ruined everything and violated many rights and laws.
- Security
- I do not believe there has been any improvement. However, overall all the warlords, criminals, thieves,

and kidnappers who were backed by the leaders of the country fled.

- Security has improved.
- The most important thing I should note is that the Taliban takes the collection of taxes from homes, shops, and other businesses that operate in Afghanistan far too seriously.
- With the return of the Taliban to power, security has improved. The people of Afghanistan are no longer witnessing hundreds of killings in a day. The level of corruption has significantly declined, and opium production has been cut off dramatically. There is no warlordism, no street robberies where people are killed for a mobile phone, car, or a few thousand Afghani, and there is no one to question it based on their province or political party affiliation. The entire country is now controlled by a single source of power, eliminating islands of power run by warlords. The rule of law has improved, applying to everyone regardless of their ethnicity. The implementation of development projects has become faster as there are no corrupt elements causing challenges. Despite the problems that have arisen, there have been many positive changes since the Taliban came to power. If I could explain it in one sentence, they have eradicated the microbe of warlordism that was suffocating the people.
- Rate of fraud and discrimination. Also, sexual harassment and insults.
- According to my family, nothing. Things have gotten worse. Earlier, only limited things were possible and done through corruption and money, nowadays anything can be done if someone has money. This includes things that are impossible to imagine.
- Some Development in the road construction sector.
- I don't see any improvement. All I see is backwardness and going back to the Medieval era.

- I cannot perceive any improvements under the current regime, and even if there are any, they appear to be driven by specific agendas benefiting other nations rather than our own.
- I don't see any improvements.

The Taliban's decision to ban older girls and women from education has received the most global attention. Is it possible for anyone – girl or boy – to receive a true education in Afghanistan?

- No. The education system is a joke.
- Possible but very difficult.
- No it is impossible. Girls are only allowed to study till 6th grade.
- I don't know.
- No, it is not.
- The fact is that not only girls and women are affected by the said ban but the boys' and men's education is also negatively impacted. The Taliban's overall focus is on building more Madrasas and Mosques rather than schools. They pay all their attention to Madrasas and Mosques and believe that the only path to success here and there is in religious education. So, in such cases, it isn't possible at all to learn a true and modern education.
- Under the previous government, boys used to go to schools, had rules, uniforms but now they don't care because they don't receive an education.
- It is possible for Afghan girls to receive some form of education but not true education within a systematic curriculum. Other forms of indoor education are currently ongoing in Kabul secretly.
- Not a complete education. Even if there are online and hidden classes, this type of education is standard and cannot help a lot.

- Great question, I do not believe Afghanistan had a quality education, especially in terms of high school. In the schools of Afghanistan, in each class there were only two to three people that got anything from the classes.
- It is difficult to receive true education in Afghanistan these days.
- The Taliban banned women's and girls' education. People in Afghanistan are increasingly afraid for their boys' education because the Taliban are attempting to influence students' minds and force them to think like them. Thus, I can affirm that everyone in Afghanistan will not receive a true education.
- The quality of education in Afghanistan, even before the Taliban came to power, was a challenge, and with the Taliban, it has deteriorated. For boys, it is still possible to some extent, as they are allowed to attend education centers. Unfortunately, for girls, it is completely banned, a decision by the Taliban that goes against Islamic rules and the narratives of Afghanistan. It's notable that in a few districts/provinces of Afghanistan, girls from a specific ethnicity are still allowed to go to schools up to high school, and the Taliban keep silent about it to maintain national unity and political agreements. Personally, I have been to those areas and am aware of this through my personal network. This makes me very sad as it raises inequality, with thousands and millions of girls being denied their very basic right to education.
- These days, it's tough for females.
- For boys, we still have hope that those that try their absolute best might learn something. But for women, I have to unfortunately say that there is nothing left.
- In every home there is a girl who suffers from such a decision. If this situation continues, many girls will grow up helpless and face many problems in the

future because of their lack of education. Especially when raising children, it becomes more difficult to help with their children's lessons and thus impacts their children's futures. If a mother is illiterate, an illiterate family will be born. She should accompany her children in any case. Unless the Taliban ends the ban on education for girls, both girls and boys will not receive true education as it affects boys' education methods, too.

- Unfortunately, no. There is no "true education" in Afghanistan as long as the Taliban and their extreme interpretation of Islam exist in the country.
- Definitely, there are already some possibilities available, but it is the government that is not enabling them. Firstly, the education system should be reformed by prioritizing science subjects and reducing the emphasis on general and Islamic subjects. Secondly, female instructors should be assigned to teach female students, ensuring smooth education for everyone.
- No, in this situation it is not possible.

Afghanistan received its independence before some other countries. However, Afghanistan continues to struggle. Why do you think Afghanistan is in the situation that it is in? What is the root cause?

- The geopolitical location of Afghanistan, the ethnic diversity, and the main point is that people are illiterate and uneducated.
- The root cause is disunity and hate between different groups of people.
- Gender discrimination.
- The root cause is not being united.
- I think the Afghan society should focus more on providing modern education rather than religious

education. Afghan society should adopt a secular approach while dealing with many societal issues. The education curriculum needs to be aligned with modern education and should account for graduating an open-minded student, not a religious student. I know these points can't be even discussed in Afghan society, but it's the bitter truth.

- I can talk about it all day long but in summary, Afghanistan's enduring struggles stem from a complex blend of historical conflicts, geopolitical rivalries, weak governance, ethnic divisions, economic hardships, and the impact of extremism. Decades of conflict, political instability, and interventions have hindered the country's development, perpetuating societal challenges and impeding progress. Addressing these root causes demands comprehensive efforts in fostering peace, strengthening governance, improving economic conditions, and combating extremism through unified national and international initiatives.
- The main reason is the extremism that almost all government administrations have used. Each administration that was overthrown from power in the last several decades was due to their extremist behavior, whether religious or not.
- The root cause is having an extremely centralized state in Afghanistan for two centuries.
- Lack of governance.
- Warlords and thieves.
- Afghan people don't have enough unity to live peacefully together.
- The most important thing, in my opinion, is that we are not a united people and that we have the mistaken belief that other countries will build our Afghanistan. Instead, we should have worked together to create a welcoming and prosperous country.
- There are several reasons behind the prolonged war in Afghanistan. Firstly, its strategic location has made it

a geopolitical hotspot, with both Western and Eastern
powers vying for influence due to its easy access to
China and Russia. Additionally, the presence of
valuable natural minerals and other resources further
intensifies global interests. Geopolitical issues in the
region have fueled competition among superpowers.
Equally significant is the issue of inadequate
education among the Afghan people, making them
susceptible to manipulation by extremists or foreign
intelligence agencies. Furthermore, there are elements
within Afghanistan including the warlords that
prioritize foreign interests, especially those of
neighboring countries, over the national interest. This
is evident in individuals who hold key positions in the
government but are concerned more with personal,
family, and ethnic advancement than the interests of
Afghanistan. The existence of a contentious border
with a country exporting extremism and terrorism has
perpetuated a regional cancer that affects both
Afghanistan and the wider world.

- In my opinion, neighboring countries interfere with
  Afghanistan's stability, with plans to prevent Russia
  from influencing Afghanistan. The issue is more with
  other countries rather than problems inside
  Afghanistan. Some examples include war between
  Pakistan and India, Iran's atomic activity, and
  shooting of neighboring nations by Russia to
  destabilize Afghanistan.
- The root cause is the intervention of powerful actors
  in our country's politics and leadership. We are
  banned from education, our national identity has been
  destroyed multiple times, and we have forgotten who
  we "Afghans" are. We are so busy with finding a loaf
  of bread that we are not realizing as a nation that we
  are being torn apart by external players and enemies.
- Because there is no mutual acceptance. Everyone
  goes to Afghanistan in the name of nation building,

however, every nation is thirsty for power. Prejudice is very high at the moment because all this is caused by ignorance.

- Afghanistan has been in the intersection of backwardness and modernity. There has been a continuous struggle between modernity and imported ideologies and thoughts.
- Some of the root causes are as follows: 1) Afghans have historically shown a weakness in politics. 2) Education has been given less priority throughout the history of Afghanistan. Even if a president supports education and modernization, they often face opposition from the people. 3) Favoritism and cultural chaos among individuals.
- Afghanistan's struggles stem from a combination of factors, including decades of conflict, political instability, the rise of the Taliban, economic challenges, and geopolitical influences. Prolonged conflict has left the country with weakened infrastructure and disrupted governance, while economic struggles, high poverty rates, and reliance on agriculture hinder sustainable development. The geopolitical significance of Afghanistan has made it a focal point for external interventions, further complicating internal dynamics. Addressing these challenges requires a comprehensive, coordinated effort involving the international community, regional stakeholders, and the Afghan people to promote stability, strengthen institutions, and foster long-term development.

What are your personal thoughts on girls not being able to go to school and/or work outside of the house? How has this impacted society?

- It has a direct impact on our society's mental health, on job creation and health responses. The people are worried for the future of their society and families.
- It is a big shame. We lack a diverse workforce in different areas such as women's health that can be best filled by women. Now they are replaced by some unqualified males.
- I don't have any comments; we are speechless
- If this situation continues, we will witness an illiterate generation and an Afghanistan which went 20 years back in time.
- Afghanistan's population is almost 50-50 male and female. I can't imagine that the 50% allowed to work will be able to solve all the challenges we face. To educate a girl means an educated sister, educated friend, educated life partner, educated mother... Certainly, you can't expect development in a country where half of the society is deprived of their fundamental rights to education and employment. There are millions of widows who are caretakers of their families in the absence (death) of their husbands. If you don't let them work outside their homes, then you undoubtedly make them beggars.
- Women are half of the society. Now half of our society is paralyzed.
- The ban has no religious reasoning behind it. It is merely a cultural issue that is being used politically. Hence, the first thing that must be done is to change society's mindset about the education of women.
- Afghan society will be radicalized.
- It has deactivated half of the society and its role.
- This decision has a great impact on society.
- I believe this has made Afghanistan go back 100 years compared to the rest of the world.
- This impacted so badly on the economy and improvement of society.

- Women and girls are prohibited from attending school and working, which has an impact on society. Children raised by educated mothers will also be educated, so uneducated mothers will not add value to their children's education. Women who do not work outside the home will be dependent on men and will tolerate abuse. As a result, we will accept whatever violence comes our way. Additionally, when we don't study, we become unaware of our rights and lose our value in society as people.
- Girls are prohibited from receiving education in Afghanistan due to the influence of a few extremist elements within the Taliban, especially within their leadership. To some extent, this issue has become politicized, partly in response to the pressure exerted on the Taliban, including sanctions imposed by the US and other Western countries. A potential solution lies in the intervention of enlightened members within the Taliban who consistently raise their voices against this discriminatory decision. Additionally, some pressure from the US, which still wields significant influence, could contribute to a positive change in this regard. Collaborative efforts involving internal advocates for change and external diplomatic influence might pave the way for the restoration of educational rights for girls in Afghanistan.
- Afghan society is going backwards, and we will go back to calamity.
- Currently half of our society is cut off from Education and work. I imagine our society as a human with half a body: one leg, one arm and half a face and brain. It is a devastating act by the Taliban, and it will never be acceptable for us. I have 5 sisters that were all educated and are at home since the Taliban has taken over the country.
- A girl or a woman is a stratum of a society. A house is not complete without a mother or a woman, and a

society is not complete without a daughter. If illiteracy is not prevented in the near future, a society full of illiterates will be created.

- I think that Afghanistan will remain in the vicious circle of history and never go forward. It would be a failed state with more than half of its population uneducated.
- However, the restriction on girls not being able to go to school or work outside of the house has had a detrimental impact on society. Denying girls access to education and employment opportunities limits their potential, stifles their personal development, and perpetuates gender inequality. It hinders the progress of society as a whole by depriving it of the diverse skills, talents, and contributions that women can bring. Additionally, it reinforces harmful societal norms and restricts the empowerment and autonomy of women, hindering social and economic growth.
- Restricting girls from attending school and working outside the house has detrimental effects on both individuals and society. Individually, it hampers personal and professional development, limiting economic independence and career opportunities. Societally, it perpetuates gender inequality, depriving communities of diverse perspectives and talents, hindering economic growth, innovation, and overall social progress. Encouraging gender equality in education and employment is crucial for building inclusive and prosperous societies.

From your perspective, what are the 3 major areas that the Taliban need to focus on?

- Stabilizing the nation's security. Economic Development and International recognition

- Women's rights. Economy. Changing their style of governance.
- Education, work and women's empowerment
- Education, Diplomatic positions, Accountability, Honesty, and Integrity with people
- 1) Equal modern educational opportunities for females and males. 2) Building and maintaining excellent relationships with all countries. 3) Equal working opportunities for both women and men.
- A fair election, economy, education.
- Education of women while understanding social norms, attempting to represent Afghanistan in the UN, and clarifying their neutral stance between superpowers.
- Letting other ethnic groups be included in the higher governmental positions. Removing restrictions on women and girls. Stop Hazara genocide.
- Education, security, and equality (gender, ethnic, religious).
- Education, Security, Economy.
- Economy, education, and freedom.
- Education, economy, and unity.
- Education: During Afghanistan's forty years of war, no one has had access to an education. Employment: There is no need for people to migrate to Pakistan or Iran in search of employment. Mining: There are several mines and minerals in Afghanistan.
- 1) National security and law enforcement: Ensure the country's security by engaging the public from diverse backgrounds in decision-making. Display no leniency towards warlords and corrupt elements that have been involved in looting the country over the past decades. 2) Education for girls and boys: Prioritize education for both genders to achieve human and economic development, ultimately curbing illegal migration. 3) Accelerated reconstruction and development projects, particularly those contributing

to the national economy, such as water management, highways, and initiatives that attract national and foreign investment. This can be accomplished by providing opportunities to professionals and the educated generation with technical expertise in designated areas. It is crucial to minimize the influence of extremist elements in critical decision-making processes.

- Women's education, water resource management, and economy
- 1) They should stop their extremism against women. 2) Create a democratic government and allow every Afghan to have equal opportunities. 3) Improve exterior politics and affairs and stop external factions from playing with our country.
- First and foremost education, then equity and freedom.
- First, they need to develop their own religious philosophy. Currently, the Taliban follow the dictates of Islamic scholars from other nations, which are not necessarily applicable to Afghanistan. Afghans have been Muslims long before other schools of Islam arose and we have our own beliefs. Second, the Taliban does not understand the evolving politics of this current era. Everything is changing, including relationships and alliances between nations. Our country's interests need to come first, and we should stay out of conflicts between other nations. If we want to ally with another country, we should follow what's in Afghanistan's best interests. Finally, education and freedom for Afghan women should be pursued. It is in Afghanistan's best interest for the entire population to be educated so that they are able to contribute to its economy.
- From my perspective, the three major areas that the Taliban need to focus on are: 1) Girls' Education and Female Employment: The Taliban should prioritize

and actively promote access to education for girls and ensure opportunities for female employment. By allowing girls to receive quality education and enabling women to participate in the workforce, the Taliban can foster gender equality, empower women, and contribute to the overall development of society. 2) Inclusive and Representative Governance: It is crucial for the Taliban to establish a government system that includes fair and transparent elections, where individuals can freely choose their leaders, including the president. By embracing democratic principles and ensuring inclusive governance, the Taliban can promote political stability, public participation, and trust in the government. 3) Economic Development and Infrastructure: The Taliban should focus on fostering economic growth and improving infrastructure within the country. By investing in key sectors such as healthcare, education, transportation, and communication, the Taliban can enhance the quality of life for the Afghan people, attract investments, and create job opportunities, leading to overall economic development and stability.

- For stability and development in Afghanistan, the Taliban should prioritize three key areas. Firstly, establishing an inclusive and representative government that incorporates diverse voices, including women and minority groups, is crucial for political stability. Secondly, focusing on economic reconstruction by addressing issues like unemployment, poverty, and economic diversification can contribute to long-term stability and improve the livelihoods of the population. Lastly, prioritizing education for all, regardless of gender, and upholding basic human rights, especially for women and minorities, is essential for social progress and international legitimacy. A comprehensive and balanced approach in these areas can contribute to the overall well-being of Afghanistan and its people.

On a scale of 1-10 with 10 being "*extremely satisfied*" and 1 being "*extremely dissatisfied*", how satisfied are you with the Taliban?

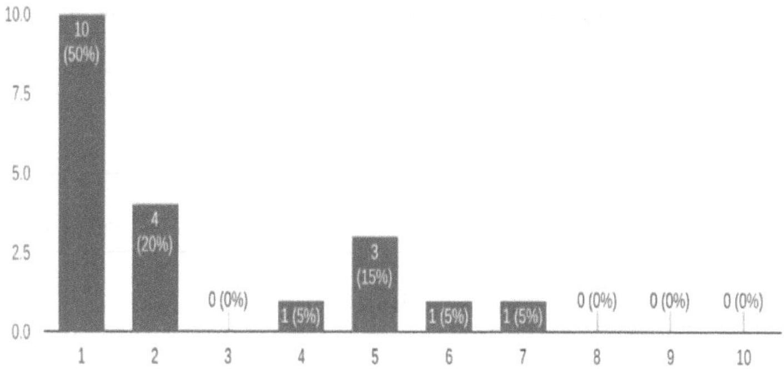

Please explain why you gave the score that you did regarding the Taliban.

- Because they are authoritarian, the people are not happy with them, and the Taliban are trying to impose rules which people did not like.
- It is a big downgrade for everyone living under their governance.
- If they give women rights then things will be changed. We have good security and no war any more.
- Because I am not satisfied.
- I see no development in the Taliban's regime. We witness one of the darkest eras in the contemporary history of Afghanistan. Afghanistan is now a backward country from all aspects. All the negative credit goes to the Taliban regime. I would have given

them ZERO points in case it was available in the option.

- If someone says time traveling is not possible, come and see. We went back to decades ago.
- The policies of the Taliban against women and the restrictions on different parts of the society are pulling Afghanistan into isolation. However, the country has a previously unseen security and centralized governance.
- Because the Taliban are terrorists.
- No education rights for Afghan women, not having security, and uneducated elders have all ruined Afghanistan.
- Because judging is difficult.
- The only benefit they had was to remove the warlords from the country, who prevented growth and security within the country. However, other than that, there are not any other benefits.
- We just have security.
- Because the Taliban has prohibited girls from attending school and women from working for non-governmental organizations, and the Taliban has terminated the majority of government employees. Indeed, the Taliban have discriminated against Tajik, Hazara, and other non-Pashtun people.
- Despite numerous challenges faced by the Taliban, some positive changes have occurred since they came to power. Improved security, reduced corruption, a decline in opium production, the removal of warlords and corrupt elements, and accelerated implementation of development projects are noteworthy achievements. Consequently, I would rate their performance as 6 out of 10, expressing hope for further improvements in the near future.
- All my answers add up to that score. My life and my family's life have been destroyed since the Taliban have come to the country. We became unemployed,

and my sister was banned from education. Everyone is sitting at home not being able to go out or do anything, not even educate themselves. What worse could happen to a family that wants a better future for themselves and their country?

- Because in this government, there has been progress and development, and especially the powerful warlords have disappeared.
- As I mentioned earlier, the Taliban are the most politically immature force in the world.
- As previously stated, the existing government resembles a robotic toy, with our neighboring country having control over its actions. They have made Islam burdensome for individuals, but it's important to remember that Islam itself is a remarkable religion. The negative impact arises from their harsh methods of implementation, which have exacerbated the situation. Furthermore, corruption has escalated to unprecedented levels within this regime.
- As an Afghan girl, my dissatisfaction with the Taliban stems from concerns about the potential impact on personal freedoms, women's rights, and educational opportunities. The restrictions on girls' education and limitations on women's participation in public life under Taliban rule in the past have raised worries about a regression in progress. Many Afghan women aspire for equal rights, access to education, and the freedom to make choices about their lives. The uncertainty surrounding the Taliban's stance on these issues can contribute to feelings of unease and dissatisfaction, reflecting a desire for a society that values inclusivity, gender equality, and individual freedoms.

Is it currently safe to travel to Afghanistan?

- Yes, as many foreigners are coming nowadays, and no, as there is a fear of arrest by Taliban specifically for those who are coming from foreign countries.
- No, it is not. Especially when you worked with foreigners or had any type of connection with them. It is dangerous.
- Yes, it is.
- Not safe for foreigners.
- Peace and safety lose its meaning when you don't have peace of mind.
- Completely! Currently, we see more foreigners walking and cycling on the streets of Kabul than there were before in armored vehicles.
- Not at all.
- No, because there is no security.
- Yes.
- If you have a foreign passport, it might be safe for you, but if you are a person who has worked with the previous government or the American government, it is not safe.
- Yes, it's safe to travel to Afghanistan and its provinces if you are a man, otherwise in most of the places women are not allowed to travel.
- The general public can travel there without any issues and in safety, but it is unsafe for individuals who oppose this regime. However, a lot of foreign tourists travel to Afghanistan these days, and I believe that they are all supporting the Taliban and want to show other countries that Afghanistan is now safe and everything is normal.
- Yes, I know many friends who left the country at the edge of collapse in 2021 or who are residents in foreign countries, including those who worked for the government or international organizations. Some of

them have since returned to Afghanistan and have been able to travel around safely.

- Yes, it is safe.
- Afghanistan is not safe for anyone. Taliban are unpredictable, no one is their ally, and none will remain their friend forever. Any single soldier of the Taliban can do anything to anyone. No one else would even notice or care about who did what to who. It is a country of no questions asked for them.
- Yes, for those people who are not involved in corruption and do not violate people's rights.
- No.
- Yes, it is safe to travel at any time anywhere in Afghanistan as compared to the previous government.
- The situation in Afghanistan is highly complex, and travel safety can change rapidly. Due to ongoing security concerns, political instability, and the potential for violence, It is not 100% safe.

Where would you like to see Afghanistan in 20 years?

- A developed industrial country with millions of tourists each year
- The most I can hope for is the same development as in the last months of Islamic Republic of Afghanistan so we can continue to grow from that point again.
- A country free of any restrictions, including the influence of any other country. Developed in technology, number one in education system and economy.
- Under the Taliban regime, Afghanistan in the upcoming 20 years will be similar to Saudi Arabia in 625 CE (approximately 1,400 years ago).

- Free of extremists. A fair country for everyone. A country where everyone sees themselves. And respect each other with their differences and rights
- A global economic power house.
- As bright and powerful as other countries in the world.
- Like other developed countries
- I want it to be a safe and stable country like the UAE.
- A place where everyone can live peacefully without any fear and frustration.
- I want Afghanistan to be entirely reconstructed and free of all conflicts. Education is accessible to everyone, regardless of gender. As a people, we want to be united. People will have employment, and our economy will grow well.
- A peaceful country where every citizen feels safe to travel around and has access to their basic needs, including quality education for both girls and boys. A country where each individual feels a sense of ownership and involvement in decision-making processes. A nation free of warlords and corrupt elements and their next generation, where there is no place for those who have exploited the country over the past decade. In this vision, personal freedom is respected, social safety is enhanced, and individuals are not threatened by street robberies. It's a country where differences in one's province, ethnicity, and political ideology do not divide its people; everyone remains a proud Afghan, working together towards a transparent and prosperous Afghanistan. I sincerely hope that my wish becomes a reality one day!
- If you ask how I wish to see it in 20 years, my biggest dream is to witness a whole generation of educated Afghans. I want to see my country heal, I want to see my people smile at each other. I want to see happiness and smiles and kindness among my people. I want our educational system to become so strong

that students do not need to pay thousands of dollars to private schools and universities. I want a democratic stable and safe country and government. I want us to become economically stable without any foreign aid. I want our country to be independent in each and every political decision.

- With this current situation, Afghanistan is at least 50 years behind the rest of the world.
- I want to see a politically, culturally, economically, and religiously independent Afghanistan where all citizens have equal rights and freedom in the next two decades.
- In 20 years, I envision Afghanistan as a fully advanced nation that has made tremendous progress in various fields. It would be wonderful to see Afghanistan hosting major international events such as the Olympics, FIFA World Cup, and even the Cricket World Cup. Beyond sports, I hope to see Afghanistan flourish in terms of technological advancements, scientific research, arts and culture, education, healthcare, and sustainable development. A peaceful and prosperous Afghanistan, known for its innovation and contributions to the global community, would be an incredible achievement.
- For the well-being of the Afghan people and the country's future, many individuals hope to see Afghanistan in a state of stability, peace, and prosperity in 20 years. This vision typically includes a thriving economy, inclusive governance, respect for human rights, and opportunities for education and employment for all, regardless of gender or background. Ideally, Afghanistan would be a nation where individuals can live in security, participate in the democratic process, and enjoy the benefits of social and economic development. The path to achieving these goals involves addressing various

complex challenges and fostering international collaboration.

Summary

This important chapter allowed Afghan students to provide their unique perspectives on the education system in Afghanistan based upon their experiences. The Afghan students are multilingual and represent many of the Provinces throughout Afghanistan. The interviewees provided valuable information for structuring the content within this book.

Chapter Seven Discussion Questions

1) From your perspective, how can this chapter be leveraged by government officials for making strategic education decisions?

2) What trends did you notice with the responses? Did you notice consistency in the responses or was there a lot of variation/disagreement?

3) Do you feel that the responses of the 20 participants from this study can represent the perspectives of most Afghans in Afghanistan?

4) What do you feel was the most important question and response?

5) Do you think men and women have different views of the Taliban?

8

CONCLUSION AND RECOMEMMENDATIONS

"The pen is mightier than the sword."
– Edward Bulwer-Lytton

*A*fghanistan has suffered for decades. Afghan leaders neglected the importance of education for all of its constituents, and as a result, the youth have been dealing with the political, economic, societal, technological, environmental, and legal consequences. Perhaps the reason is because *no one is going to give you the education you need to overthrow them*. There is and has been an education crisis in Afghanistan. Afghan leaders must understand that education is an investment and the return on investment (ROI) is stability, security, and success. Each day, the value of education increases and those without an education are left behind. Many years ago, a high school diploma was sufficient for obtaining a job that paid well enough to survive. Today, with global competition, a volatile economy, and high unemployment rates in Afghanistan, those without a college degree will have a more difficult time finding employment opportunities. The future may require even higher levels of self-efficacy and education of each person in a society. In certain areas of the world,

280

education is considered a luxury and only for the elite whereas in other parts of the world education is a necessity of life. The beauty of education is that it is the one thing in life that no one can take away from anyone else. Money can be taken away, power can be taken away, loved ones can be taken away, and even talent or skill can be taken away. Education will always endure with an individual and will help an individual make ethical decisions that are worthwhile. Being educated will open up many doors that can result in immediate success.

Many of the ongoing issues throughout Afghanistan can be associated with a lack of education. If this cycle continues, then this vicious cycle of poverty, instability, inequity, and dependency will never end. The authors of this book have underscored many areas of the education system in Afghanistan that need to be reformed with practical solutions. In this final chapter, additional recommendations and ideas will be shared.

A Brief Recap of the Book

Chapter 1 highlighted the dire state of education in Afghanistan since the end of King Amanullah's reign. Numerous national and international reports continue to show Afghanistan's educational shortcomings when compared to other countries. An important conversation was conducted with the Regional Director of *Read to Lead Afghanistan* on the importance of literacy projects throughout Afghanistan. Afghanistan must consider various new avenues of education, such as instruction in English and in the language of coding. Also, this chapter discussed the importance of females being able to obtain a quality education without any barriers based upon the teachings of Islam.

Chapter 2 focused on high school and the Kankor exam. The Kankor exam currently determines the fate of each student and is significantly flawed. A recommendation was made to not only change the Kankor exam, but also for university admissions to take a more holistic and comprehensive approach to reviewing each applicant's ability to succeed at an Afghan university. At the absolute minimum, university admissions should use high school GPA and a modified version of the Kankor exam. However, it is highly recommended for other components to be considered as outlined in the chapter. Furthermore, the standardization of curriculum and improvement in teacher training throughout Afghanistan should be a long-term goal.

Chapter 3 underscored the significance of undergraduate education and accreditation based upon international standards. Currently, the lack of educational resources and qualified instructors presents a challenge for higher education. The use of Community Colleges should be further explored in Afghanistan. Furthermore, a recommendation was made for students in primary school to start studying English as a foreign language so that by the time they are in high school, teachers can teach in English 25% of the time, and by the time that they start university, their university professors can teach in the English language at least 50% of the time because English is the language of the world. By learning English, Afghan students will have more job opportunities.

Chapter 4 provided suggestions for graduate education and, more specifically, Ph.D. programs. Afghanistan has just recently started offering a Ph.D. program in Farsi and Pashto literature. A country with limited PhDs will not have quality professors, scientists, or researchers. As a result, these important services will need to be outsourced to neighboring countries and Afghanistan will once again depend on others for assistance and guidance which typically leads to conflict, corruption, and chaos- including hidden agendas.

Chapter 5 emphasized the importance of vocational education for Afghans to help provide specific skills and training to prepare students for the workplace. Among other fields, education in the mining field can prove greatly successful when considering Afghanistan's mineral wealth. An important conversation was conducted with the Executive Director of *Code to Inspire*, which is currently providing Afghan women with vocational training in the coding field which is in high demand globally.

Chapter 6 stressed the need for online education in Afghanistan so that students throughout the country have access to quality education. Online education and its various elements continue to develop and are proven invaluable to breaking educational barriers. With girls unable to go to school after the 6th grade and women unable to attend classes at universities, online education can help bridge the gender gap. An important conversation was conducted with a subject matter expert regarding possible solutions for providing internet services to remote and rural areas of Afghanistan.

Chapter 7 illuminated the voices of 20 university-level Afghan students. This focus group provided unique perspectives and experiences that helped create the structure and content for this book.

Chapter 8 summarizes and reiterates the importance of education in Afghanistan. The most urgent educational priorities that need to be addressed are discussed, along with practical examples and solutions.

The Appendix consists of the full interviews that were either conducted and/or retrieved from online sources. Each subject matter expert provides a wealth of information based upon their vast experiences (Appendix A).

قطره قطره دریا می‌شه
"Drop by drop a river is formed."

Final Thoughts and Recommendations

On the surface, some people are easily fascinated by the tall buildings (not built to international codes and standards) and the glamorous wedding halls, but below the surface, an astute person will remember that Afghanistan and its people are struggling politically, economically, socially, psychologically, and technologically based upon years of educational neglect. This *Iceberg Effect* or *Titanic Effect* refers to the idea that there is often more to a situation or problem than meets the eye.

If a serious and collaborative effort is undertaken to improve the education system in Afghanistan, then it is imperative that international standards are taken into account. For example, implementing M.B.A. or D.B.A. programs in Afghanistan that are not accredited by one of the top three international business education accrediting agencies would be pointless. Afghan leaders can no longer put a band-aid on a broken bone and pretend as if the problem has been resolved. The education system in Afghanistan is currently broken and as a result, significant education reform is needed.

This book provided many recommendations that should be considered. Urgent educational priorities include: eradicating illiteracy in Afghanistan, eliminating gender apartheid in Afghanistan, the implementation and adoption of a certain amount of English instruction throughout Afghanistan, the need for servant leaders in Afghanistan, and implementing and investing in civic engagement projects throughout Afghanistan. These urgent recommendations are addressed in more detail below and need to be implemented as soon as possible because Afghanistan has been in a state of educational crisis for many decades.

Eradication of Illiteracy in Afghanistan

Helping someone learn to read and write effectively improves the future of everyone in society. Patrinos (2023) explains that it has been 50 years since the publication of Psacharopoulos and Hinchliffe's (1973) influential book *Returns to Education: An International Comparison*, "where they rigorously demonstrated what most teachers and educators already knew both from intuition and from experience: while education is much more than just an economic investment, the fact is that, in simple economic terms, education pays. Five decades of research – and the experience of many countries – have confirmed this time and again: investing in education is one of the best, if not the best investment a country can make to increase income and improve the material well being of its population. And yet, paradoxically, we are far from investing enough in education."

پنج دهه تحقیق و تجربه بسیاری از کشورها مکرراً تأیید کرده است: سرمایه‌گذاری در آموزش یکی از بهترین سرمایه‌گذاری‌هایی است که یک کشور می‌تواند برای افزایش درآمد و بهبود رفاه مادی مردم خود انجام دهد.

د پنځو لسیزو څیرونو او دغه راز د بیلابیلو هیوادونو تجربو په کراتو کراتو جوته کړی ده: د ښوونې او روزنې برخه کې پانګونه یو له غوره هغو پانګونو څخه ده، چی له لاری یی یو هیواد کولی شی د خپلو وګړو عاید لور او د مادي سوکالی ور په برخه کړي.

Literacy is critical to economic development as well as individual and community well-being. The economy is enhanced when learners have higher literacy levels. The program discussed by Samady (2014) has been stopped by the current government:

> The national program for eradication of illiteracy should be decentralized and conducted in cooperation with all governmental and non-governmental organizations, agencies, institutions, enterprises, development projects, and communities. Realistically, at present it seems unlikely that adequate resources could be mobilized for an accelerated national program of adult literacy. There are also social and cultural constraints for literacy programs especially for women. Furthermore, in 2012 only 58% of school age children were in basic education. The out-of-school children and young people will impact literacy efforts. Nevertheless, in addition to governmental measures, the communities and

voluntary groups could play an important role in literacy efforts. The non-governmental organizations and private sector should be engaged.

It is possible for a country to have a nearly 100% literacy rate. A literacy rate that hovers around 100% is seen in some dedicated countries around the world, including Azerbaijan and Cuba.

> **"Live as if you were to die tomorrow. Learn as if you were to live forever."**
>
> **- Gandhi**

A lofty goal for Afghanistan should be to have a nearly 100% literacy rate for the first time in its history. Afghanistan can learn from Cuba and its commitment to ending illiteracy in the country.

The Cuban Literacy Campaign (Campaña Nacional de Alfabetización en Cuba) was a huge step towards advancing equality and social development, to which education is key. According to Rey (2021), "In 1961 in Cuba, a quarter of a million volunteers, the brigadistas, who were mostly young women, went to every corner of Cuba to teach people to read and write. They packed their bags and set out for the remotest villages, many without electricity or running water. In a little over a year, literacy rates in Cuba went from only 60%-76% to almost 100%."

«در سال ۱۹۶۱ در کیوبا، یک چهارم میلیون داوطلبان، بریگادیست‌ها، که عمدتاً زنان جوان بودند، به منظور تدریس مردم در خواندن و نوشتن به سراسر کیوبا حتی به دورترین قریه‌ها و مناطق کشور که بسیاری بدون برق و آب بودند، رفتند. بنا بر تلاش‌های این زنان، در مدت کمی بیش از یک سال، میزان باسوادی در کیوبا را از فقط ۶۰-۷۶ فیصد به تقریباً ۱۰۰ فیصد رساندند.»

"کیوبا کې په ۱۹۶۱ د بریګېډیستا رضاکارانو د یو میلیوني ډلی څلورمه برخه چی اکثریت یې خوانی ښځی وی د کیوبا هر ګوټ ته لارل ترڅو خلکو ته لوستل او لیکل زده کړی. دوی زیاتره هغو کلیو او باڼډو او لېرو سیمو ته لارل، چی اکثرو کی بریښنا نه وه او د اوبو له کمښت سره مخ وو. د دغو ښنځو د هڅو له برکته، کیوبا کې د څه باندی یو کال په موده کی د سواد کچه له ۶۰-۷۶ سلنی څخه نږدی ۱۰۰ سلنی ته لوړه شوه."

Some other practical suggestions that Afghan leaders can consider include the following:

- <u>Imams Must Emphasize Literacy</u>: In Afghanistan, over 99% of the country is Muslim and on Fridays, Muslims attend a special Friday prayer known as Jum'ah prayer which also includes a sermon (khutbah). The weekly sermon by the Imam should consistently focus on the importance of literacy and education for everyone in Afghanistan. For example, in the Qur'an (Al-Alaq, 96:1), it is mentioned, *"Read! In the Name of your Lord, Who has created (all that exists).*

- <u>Free Textbooks</u>: Textbooks should be sponsored. The government should encourage entrepreneurs, philanthropists, and wealthy Afghans living in the West to come forward and contribute to this noble cause. Consequently, when more Afghans have access to the internet, the use of eBooks and free open education resources (OER) can be used because textbooks are becoming obsolete and as a result, old textbooks can easily be donated to other developing countries in a similar education crisis.

- <u>Child Labor Control</u>: Local law enforcement agencies, politicians, and community elders should work together to make sure no children are working in the streets. Children belong in school. One feasible solution for the government is to implement a welfare system that supports families who lack a guardian so that children are able to go to school.

- <u>Exposure to Parents</u>: The government should work on providing exposure to the parents on why education is vital for their kids. The awareness campaigns may be planned via social media, local TV channels, brochures, and village seminars.

- <u>Acquisition of Rewards</u>: The parents of children having a 90% or higher class attendance should be rewarded with government-issued food vouchers.

- <u>Free Vocational Training For Teenagers</u>: To attract the illiterate teenagers, the government should consider providing free vocational training. This training should be bundled with mandatory literacy education.

- <u>Special Focus on Female Literacy</u>: The government should work on the techniques to provide awareness to parents to let their daughters study at all costs. As Napoleon Bonaparte once said, "Give me an educated mother, I shall promise you the birth of a civilized, educated nation."

ناپلنون بناپارت زمان گفته بود: "اگر به من یک مادر تحصیلکرده بدهید، من به شما تولد یک ملت متمدن و تحصیلکرده را وعده می‌دهم"

ناپلیون بوناپارټ یو وخت ویلي و: "که ماته یوه باسواده مور راکرئ، زه تاسو ته د یو متمدن او باسواده ملت د زیږون ژمنه درکوم"

- <u>Prison Literacy</u>: The government cannot neglect the importance of prison literacy. Ethical, Islamic, and educational sessions should be scheduled to improve prison inmate literacy. Thousands of prisoners can become better citizens if they are provided the right amount of education.

- <u>Measurement of Literacy</u>: Some countries have very poor literacy measurement criteria. For example, if a person can write his/her name, then he/she is considered literate in some nations. The government should raise the bar of measurement and focus on improving the quality of education as well as achieving a higher literacy rate.

- <u>Mandatory Schooling Years</u>: A law must be passed that every individual must attend at least 10 - 12 years of education. This initiative must be linked with some citizen-specific benefits from the government so that minimum education is achieved.

- <u>Adequate Infrastructure</u>: The government should provide the infrastructure that is needed so that all students throughout Afghanistan are able to achieve their educational objectives in a safe environment. For example, the Williams Act established new standards and accountability mechanisms to ensure that all California public school students have textbooks and instructional materials and that their schools are clean, safe, and functional. It also took steps toward ensuring all students have qualified teachers. Consequently, the state of California in the US has specific laws, rules, and regulations that schools must follow. Some examples include:

  - All educational buildings should be planned in a way that maximizes safety, enrollment, and comfort while minimizing maintenance. These buildings must comply with federal, state, and local fire and structural safety codes.

  - When selecting a school site, the school district must consider things

like available acreage, enrollment,
population density, economic
feasibility, and bussing expenses.
All school sites must be a certain
distance from power lines, and the
district must also take into account
any potential environmental, traffic,
or industrial hazards in the vicinity.
The school site must be easily
accessible for pedestrians, waste
disposal, and emergency services,
and should be in a location that
encourages the usage of parks,
libraries, museums, and other
facilities.

- Classrooms must be adequate in
  number and size, according to the
  building's planned enrollment and
  curriculum. For grades 1-12, all
  classrooms must be at least 960
  square feet. Each classroom must
  have the appropriate outlets for
  networking and technology.

English Instruction in Afghanistan

As mentioned throughout this book, Afghanistan
can benefit from English instruction as long as the
traditional languages are not neglected. It is important to
recognize the economic potential of English — a
language of global business, trade, science, and
diplomacy. That is precisely why a balanced approach of
preserving Afghan cultural heritage and identity along

with embracing the English language is recommended for yielding the best results for modernization, independence, and eventually interdependence with the global community. Throughout primary school, Afghan students should learn English as a second language. In secondary school, English should become the mode of instruction in at least 25% of the curriculum or courses. At the university or post-secondary level, English should become the mode of instruction in at least 50% of the courses. The goal is for all Afghans to become multilingual.

Singapore represents a compelling case of successful bilingual education policy where English is taught as the first language alongside mother tongue languages. Singapore's bilingual education policy has been central to its economic transformation, positioning it as a global business hub while maintaining cultural identity (Lee & Phua, 2020). This policy has facilitated Singapore's remarkable economic growth, transforming it into a global business hub. Further, The Singaporean model underscores the potential of English proficiency to enhance economic opportunities without sacrificing cultural identity or linguistic diversity (Dorottya, 2023; Singapore's Global Schools for a Global Society). For Afghanistan, Singapore's approach suggests that integrating English education with robust support for native languages could maximize benefits while mitigating cultural preservation concerns.

In 2008, Rwanda made a bold shift from French to English as the medium of instruction in schools, aiming to integrate more closely with the East African Community and the global economy. Pearson (2016) details this transition, noting that Rwanda's policy shift to English as the medium of instruction was driven by economic and geopolitical considerations, necessitating significant investments in teacher training and educational resources. This transition highlights the importance of English for economic integration but also illustrates challenges, such as the need for teacher retraining and the adaptation of educational materials. Furthermore, Pearson (2016) emphasizes Rwanda's experience underlines the critical importance of careful planning and resource allocation in the effective implementation of a language policy shift, suggesting parallels that Afghanistan might consider in its context.

دل به دل راه داره
"Heart to heart, there is a way."

End Gender Apartheid in Afghanistan

The Taliban regime has decided to ban girls from continuing with their education after the sixth grade. The rationale for such an extreme decision is not clear. If it's a matter of public safety, then the focus should be on providing more effective law and order instead of punishing the entire female population. Perhaps the punishment for those who break the law should be more severe and as a result, crime will go down and public safety will not be an issue.

Isolating the females- nearly 50% of the population- of a country is not conducive of a healthy society and is considered gender apartheid. Farid and de Silva de Alwis (2023) discuss the severity of the issue by stating,

According to UNICEF, 3.7 million Afghan children are currently out of school, and 60% of those are girls. Despite a pledge to allow all girls to return to school by Spring 2022, the government has continued to keep most out of school. In March 2022, the Taliban government declared girls could return to primary school (grades one through six) but that secondary and high schools for girls would remain shut. In December 2022, the government announced an indefinite ban on university education for women and girls (as well as an order forbidding females from working for nongovernmental organizations (NGOs).

A civil society cannot function correctly and progress without all individuals contributing to it.
It should be noted that many households depend on both incomes to support their families. If women are unable to go to a university to study and are also unable to work, then how can a family afford to survive without having to send their young children to work in the streets? How will this vicious cycle of poverty end in Afghanistan? According to Farid and de Silva de Alwis (2023), Afghan female teachers who were interviewed reported "concern over the loss of rights and civil liberties for women. Many are experiencing economic hardship, as many have lost their jobs and are unable to contribute to their families' livelihoods" and "they emphasized that most of the girls prevented from going to school have no options for obtaining education by alternative means. They reported concern about adverse social consequences that might result, such as an increase in forced childhood marriages." This quandary must be

further analyzed and an equitable and feasible solution is needed. The Taliban have suggested that they are trying to find a solution to this problem but will not allow foreigners to interfere with their internal affairs. Abdul Ghaffar Khan (a.k.a. Bacha Khan 1890 - 1988) once said, *"If you wished to know how civilized a culture is, look at how they treat its women."*

پاچا خان گفته است: "اگر می‌خواهید بدانید که یک فرهنگ چقدر متمدن است، جایگاه برخورد آن را در مقابل زنان آن مطالعه کنید."

باچا خان ويلي: "که غواړی وپوهيږئ چی يو فرهنگ څومره متمدن دی؛ نو د ښځو پر وراندې يی چلند مطالعه کړئ"

A Conversation with Layma Murtaza - International Development Specialist

Layma Murtaza is an Afghan American International Development specialist with a focus on Central and South Asia and the MENA region. Her professional work and research has focused on development in Afghanistan for more than 12 years. She has worked for the Aga Khan Foundation, International Rescue Committee, International Organization for Migration and the Danish Refugee Council working on both emergency operations and long-term infrastructure and societal development outcomes. She has a Master of Arts in Global Public Policy focused on Forced Migration and Refugee Studies from the American University in Cairo and is currently completing her second Master's degree in International Development Management at the American University in Washington D.C. The entire interview can be found in Appendix A.

Authors: After the Taliban's renewed takeover of power in Afghanistan, was it foreseeable that women would be excluded from education?

> **LM:** When the Doha Peace negotiations between the United States and the Taliban began, fear ran through all sectors of Afghan society, because not only was the then-existing government sidelined in these discussions, but civil society, including women, was not part of the conversation to shape the settlement which all stakeholders would be happy with. The Afghan government was the only actor that held an internal Afghan women's jirga during the negotiation process, for women to attend, share their grievances, fears, hopes and wishes for their future. Once the deal was set, and the fall of Kabul happened in August 2021, the anticipated fear from Afghans across the world was that Afghans would return to a 1996 - 2001 era where human rights, and basic dignity for all, were ignored by the Taliban. One part of the fear was for women, because during 1996-2001, women were not allowed to go to school, or even leave the home without a mahram to run every day errands. The excuse at that time, in addition to Sharia law, was that it was unsafe, as Afghanistan had just ceased a civil war.
>
> Many human rights advocates and women activists domestically and abroad used social media, public demonstrations, and media

interviews to share their thoughts, analyses and fear through reports, traditional media, opinion editorials, social media, and meetings during to the Doha peace deal and have continued since the Taliban took over Afghanistan in August of 2021. All of this information is easily searchable online.

Authors: Is Afghanistan dealing with "gender apartheid?" What are your thoughts on the term and how it applies to the situation there? How does (or doesn't) it capture the essence of the challenges faced by Afghan women and girls?

LM: Gender Apartheid is a term that was first used by the Feminist Majority Foundation to launch a campaign to stop Gender Apartheid in Afghanistan in 1997, and is now being used again because the same themes and actions are happening again to women under Taliban rule. Gender Apartheid is essentially defined as the economic and social discrimination of individuals because of their gender or sex and is enforced by physical or legal practices. By this definition, Afghan women are living under Gender Apartheid for the following reasons:

1. The Taliban have restricted women from attending higher education, after grade six. This sharply contrasts with progress that was made during the last 20 years where Afghan girls and women had increased access and opportunity to education at all levels.

2. Women have been removed from the public sector, limiting employment to health-related professions or tailoring. This has significantly limited women's participation in the workforce and their ability to support not only themselves, but their families in a dwindling economic environment. The Taliban even dissolved the Ministry of Women's Affairs, signaling a disinterest in women rights and representation in the public sector.
3. Women are required to follow a strict dress code, and in some locations, this includes wearing the burqa. There are also movement restrictions without a male guardian or mahram, which severely limits their independence and access to public services like healthcare.
4. There have been reports of violence against women, including forced marriage and domestic violence that has increased since the Taliban have taken over. Women also face harsh punishments such as executions and public flogging.

These policies and practices can very well be argued to be a systematic effort to erase women's rights and visibility in society, fitting the very definition of gender apartheid.

Authors: Shortly after the Taliban imposed the ban on women attending institutions of higher education, Iran issued a statement saying it would accept Afghan women into its own universities - potentially an interesting option for many Afghan women academics. Not only is the culture in Iran similar to their own, it may also be more "acceptable" to return to Afghanistan after studying in Iran. What are your thoughts on this and what options do Afghan women have now? What can those who insist on their right to education do?

LM: Iran's offer to accept Afghan women into its universities following the Taliban's ban on women attending institutions of higher education is generous and is a trend among many countries offering both in-country and remote education opportunities for Afghan women. This is a positive step, but still complex as many Afghans may be seen to have a lower societal status and have been subject to discrimination and xenophobia by the government and host communities. This is something to note as a potential risk; however, I believe that many Afghan women would still choose to study abroad for the freedom they would feel in Iran, in contrast to Afghanistan under the Taliban. Another complexity is that Iran is also facing its own internal cultural revolution related to women and independence that may also pose a risk factor to stability in the country, or on the contrary, a space of solidarity that can be grown between both Afghan and Iranian activists.

Many other countries have offered educational opportunities to Afghan women such as the United States, the United Kingdom, Sweden, Switzerland, Australia, Kyrgyz Republic, and Bangladesh through online and in-person opportunities. These are all positive gestures but not nearly enough to accommodate all Afghan women seeking higher education, nor does it create a solution to the root issue of gender apartheid in Afghanistan.

Alternative options for Afghan women are to continue to explore scholarship and support programs that are remote/online-based and abroad. International organizations and NGOs offer funding opportunities that could help mitigate high travel and accommodation costs.

The International community needs to continue to not only support the increase of educational opportunities for women, but they also need to continue advocacy and international coalition pressure on the Taliban to allow women both their Islamic rights, as well as their basic human rights of education. The private sector should be included in discussions to leverage technology in Afghanistan to ensure that Afghan women have access to education, and this could include making sure there is internet reach throughout the entire country. Many rural populations still do not have access to the internet, which disconnects entire populations from accessing education.

هیچ گل بی خار نیست

"There is no rose without thorns."

Invest in Civic Engagement with a Focus on Edupreneurship

Throughout history, individuals have been faced with creating innovative solutions to solve predicaments that communities are facing. Civic engagement is an initiative or project taken on by individuals or groups, in which they develop and implement solutions to social, cultural, and/or environmental issues. Some examples of civic engagement include: social entrepreneurship, activism, political engagement, activism/advocacy, and community service. Under the extreme circumstances in Afghanistan, citizens must take action and create opportunities.

An outstanding example of a civic engagement initiative in Afghanistan is Freshta Karim's mobile libraries. Other countries have initiated similar strategies to help educate the youth. In the Philippines for example, children from indigenous fishing communities are learning to read and write thanks to floating boat schools. In Colombia, makeshift donkey libraries called Biblioburro take books to children in rural communities who otherwise wouldn't have access to reading materials. An interview was conducted with Freshta Karim (Founder and Executive Director of Charmaghz). The following excerpts of an interview were retrieved from *Girl Up India* (2023):

Could you tell us a little bit more about your initiative – "*Charmaghz*"?

> **FK:** Back in 2018, we initiated a project by transforming a public bus into a mobile library in Kabul on a snowy day. The project was made possible by the generous donations of our

friends. Today, we have expanded to 23 vibrant libraries, known as *Charmaghz*, which translates to *walnut* in Persian, and focus on literacy and numeracy skills for children. Despite the challenging circumstances in Afghanistan, our team has grown with 80% of the team being women. We are thrilled to mark our fifth anniversary this year.

The education system in Afghanistan, and Asia in general, often discourages questioning, promoting rote learning instead. At our libraries, boys and girls sit and read together. Later, society imposes notions of superiority and inferiority based on gender, taking away from children what should be theirs – the freedom to be themselves.

Our vision is to empower children in our country, giving them the agency to make decisions and change their circumstances.

We focus on literacy and mental health because these are vital for anyone to feel empowered and have control over their lives. Each of us possesses a level of power, often untapped, and by recognizing and utilizing this power, we can collectively bring about significant societal change.

If we believe in equality, then we should involve children and teenagers in designing any program or curriculum, especially when it concerns them. Otherwise, it's a top-down, undemocratic approach that disregards equality.

Many children worldwide lack access to libraries –
a basic resource that fosters creativity,
imagination, and knowledge. Reading allows us to
empathize with others, understand complex
emotions, and become less judgmental.
Governments, as decision-makers, must
recognize that learning extends beyond schools.
Rote learning can be incredibly dull. We owe it to
children and ourselves to make life more
interesting by addressing this issue.

*** A more detailed interview with Freshta Karim can be
found in Appendix A. The interview was conducted on
April 27, 2023 by Melissa McNeilly of *New Tactics in
Human Rights*.

Develop Servant Leaders in Afghanistan

Afghanistan needs servant leaders in all fields and
professions who are not concerned about authority,
salary, or status. Servant leaders serve their followers to
create a civil society and expect absolutely nothing in
exchange.

> **"The true heroes of the new millennium will be
> servant leaders, quietly working out of the
> spotlight to transform our world."**
>
> **-Ann McGee-Cooper**

Servant leaders empower their followers to achieve their full potential and possess referent power. As President John F. Kennedy exclaimed in one of his speeches to the people of the US: "*Ask not what your country can do for you, ask what you can do for your country.*"

چنان که رئیس جمهور جان اف کنیدی در یکی از سخنرانی‌های خود خطاب به مردم ایالات متحده گفت: "نپرسید که کشورتان برای شما چه کار کرده می‌تواند؛ بلکه بپرسید شما برای کشورتان چه کار کرده می‌توانید؟"

ولسمشر جان ایف کېنېدي په یوه وینا کی د متحده ایالاتو خلکو ته وویل: "مه پوښتنۍ چی هېواد مو ستاسو لپاره څه کولی شی، بلکی وپوښتنۍ چی تاسو د خپل هېواد لپاره څه کولی شئ؟"

An outstanding example of a servant leader in Afghanistan is Tetsu Nakamura (known as "Uncle Murad" by Afghans), a selfless Japanese medical doctor who worked for years to transform war-torn Afghanistan into a lush oasis. Dr. Tetsu Nakamura left his home in Japan in the 1980s to treat leprosy patients in Afghanistan and Pakistan. He later found, however, that severe drought was killing more people than his clinics could save. So he discovered a new calling: irrigation in Afghanistan. In the 2000s, adapting old Japanese techniques that required little technology, he helped villagers displaced by drought build a network of canals that has transformed an area of nearly a million residents. Unfortunately, Dr. Nakamura was gunned

down by unidentified armed men in Jalalabad,
Afghanistan on December 4, 2019.

A different example of a servant leader is Dr. Abdul Kayeum (1919 - 2012) who served as President of the Teachers Training Institute (1948 - 1952), Governor of the Helmand Province (1952 - 1962), Minister of Interior (1962-1965), and Minister of Education (1968 - 1971). In 2014, Dr. Kayeum's wife, Joan Kayeum, wrote a book titled *Afghan Patriot* about her late husband's life and career. Upon completing his doctoral degree in Education in 1948 from the University of Denver, he told his wife and friends that, "I'm a scholarship student from a poor country. I have a life-long debt to repay my people" (Kayeum, 2014, p. 9).

داکتر قیوم گفت: من یک محصل بورسیه از یک کشور فقیر هستم و این وام دایمی خود را باید به مردم خود پس پرداخت کنم.

داکتر قیوم وویل: زه د یو بی‌وزله هیواد د بورسیی زده کوونکی یم. زه له خپلو هیوادوالو دایمی پوروری یم او باید خپلو خلکو ته دا پور بیرته ادا کرم.

He worked strenuously to improve Afghanistan and contributed to the "Golden Age" of the country. He tried to end the nepotism and cronyism that he noticed in Afghanistan. For example, Dr. Kayeum "replaced governors who had little or no formal education, with professional young men who had at least a bachelor's degree and a minimum of four years of experience working in Afghanistan" (Kayeum, 2014, p. 23). When Dr. Kayeum's brother (Dr. Abdul Zahir) was appointed to the Prime Minister position of Afghanistan, Dr. Kayeum declined his brother's invitation to join him in the cabinet. "He felt that it would be politically and socially unwise for two brothers to occupy high posts in the same administration" and "it would be too reminiscent of the royal family's rule through nepotism as practiced years ago when the entire Cabinet and all the ambassadorial posts were held by family members: brothers, half brothers, and their sons" (Kayeum, 2014, p. 41).

As the Minister of Interior, Dr. Kayeum was able to reorganize the seven provinces in Afghanistan to 29 provinces so that the governors and sub-governors were more accessible to the people. He would say, "We need to reach the people so as to better serve them" (Kayeum, 2014, p. 21). As the President of the Teachers Training Institute, "he took pride in improving the curriculum, raising the standards of the Institute, and opening the gates for both students and faculty to obtain scholarships for higher studies abroad" (Kayeum, 2014, p. 11). As the Minister of Education, Dr. Kayeum tripled the number of elementary and secondary schools in the provinces. This inspiring and selfless servant leader showcased humility, persuasion, integrity, foresight, stewardship, empathy, valued people, developed other leaders, and helped build community throughout his tenure – all of which are characteristics of a sophisticated servant leader.

Servant leadership emphasizes that leaders should be attentive to the concerns of their followers and empathize with them; they should take care of them and nurture them (Northouse, 2004, p. 309). Being able to deliver a warm style of leadership and paying attention to others are key elements of gaining the trust and respect of your peers. The importance of paying attention is to show people that you care, and the best way to do this is to pay attention to what they're doing, how they're feeling, who they are, and what they like and dislike. "Paying attention demands that you put others first" (Kouzes & Posner, 2003, p. 79).

Servant leadership should become a part of the primary and secondary curriculum in Afghanistan so that students can learn and develop their servant leadership skills and traits at a young age. As a matter of fact, Islam teaches Muslims to be servant leaders. Servant leadership is about behavior first. According to one hadith, Prophet Muhammad (PBUH) mentions the following: "Verily, each of you is a shepherd, and each of you is responsible for the well being of your flock" (Sahih al-Bukhari, 7138). Some of the characteristics of a servant leader are: empathy, empowerment, building community, stewardship, trust, appreciation, valuing people, humility, integrity, and foresight. Servant leaders are known for positively influencing and motivating their peers and recognizing their achievements. From this outgoing and compassionate behavior, it is very easy for peers and colleagues to open up and communicate how they feel about specific situations. Servant leaders will respect everyone's opinion, even if someone challenges the status quo. "Learning to understand and see things from another's perspective is absolutely crucial to building trusting relations and to career success" (Kouzes & Posner, 2003, p. 79). Servant leaders treat people better than they would like to be treated. "You express joy in seeing others succeed, you cheer others along, and you offer supportive coaching, rather than being a militant authority figure who is out patrolling the neighborhood" (Kouzes & Posner, 2003, p. 77).

Servant leaders are followed because people trust and respect them, rather than just the skills they possess. Leadership is both similar to and different from management. Management relies more on planning, organizing, and controlling. Leadership relies on some management skills too, but more so on qualities such as integrity, honesty, humility, courage, commitment, sincerity, passion, confidence, wisdom, determination, compassion, and sensitivity. Most people don't seek to be leaders. Those who want to be a leader can develop leadership ability. It is important to understand that "as you take the role of a caring leader; people soon begin relating to you differently" (Kouzes & Posner, 2003, p. 77).

Summary

The 21st century is full of options, competition, and choices. Afghan leaders will have to make important and difficult choices that will have an impact on their entire country and its future. However, one of the most important decisions will be to figure out how to provide educational opportunities for all of its citizens. This book provided many practical solutions to this ongoing conundrum.

خپله لاسه کله لاسه

"The labor of one's own hand is beautiful."

The people of Afghanistan are intelligent and resilient and if they are given equal opportunities without interference, they will innovate and flourish. Even under the most unfortunate circumstances, Afghans continue to innovate. Some notable recent examples include: Afghanistan's first supercar (the Mada 9) created by Muhammad Raza Ahmadi, and as a different example, the Afghan External Fixation device for the knee and elbow, which is a new orthopedic device created by Dr. Mohammad Wardak.

As such, education is the means to success in Afghanistan. As Aristotle mentioned many years ago, *"The roots of education are bitter, but the fruit is sweet."*

همانطور که ارسطو سال‌ها پیش گفته بود: "ریشه‌های تعلیم و تربیه تلخ است، اما میوه آن شیرین است."

لکه چي ارسطو دپر کاله وراندي ويلي و، "د زدهکړي ريښني ترخي دي، خو مپوه یی خوږه ده."

Chapter Eight Discussion Questions

1) Why is it important to focus on eradicating illiteracy in Afghanistan? What are the short term and long term implications?

2) Why is it important to eliminate gender apartheid in Afghanistan? What are the short term and long term implications?

3) Why is it important to implement and adopt a certain amount of English instruction throughout Afghanistan? What are the pros and cons?

4) What are the benefits of having more servant leaders in Afghanistan? What are some examples of how servant leadership is deeply rooted in Islam?

5) Why is it important to invest in civic engagement projects throughout Afghanistan? What are some civic engagement projects that can benefit the people of Afghanistan?

6) Based on the information and suggestions given in this book, what do you think is a realistic first step in implementing education reform in Afghanistan?

Bibliography

Abdulbaqi, M. (2009). High education in Afghanistan. *Policy Perspectives*, 6(2), 99-117.

Adams, J. (1984). *Transforming work*. Alexandria, VA: Miles River Press.

Advameg, Inc. (2011). *Countries and their cultures: Afghanistan*. Retrieved from http://www.everyculture.com/A-Bo/Afghanistan.html#ixzz1EWqSu0ga

Afghanistan Constitution. (1964). Retrieved from https://digitalcommons.unl.edu/cgi/viewcontent.cgi?article=1005&context=afghanenglish

Afghanistan. (2007). *Cultural Appreciation Booklet*. Retrieved from http://www.mod.uk/NR/rdonlyres/DC510C8E-C58C-4DC7-B6EE-86A69F709A12/0/afghanistan_cultural_appreciation_booklet.pdf

Agarwal, S., & Mital, M. (2009). An exploratory study of Indian university students' use of social networking web sites: Implication for the workplace. *Business Communication Quarterly*, 72(1), 105-110.

Ahiakpor, J. (1985). The success and failure of dependency theory: The experience in Ghana. *International Organization*, 39(3), 535-552.

Akin-Little, K.A., Eckert, T.L., Lovett, B.J., & Little, S.G. (2004). Extrinsic reinforcement in the classroom:

Bribery or best practice. *School Psychology Review*, 33(3), 344-362.

Ali, O. (2014). *Cheating and Worse: The university entry (kankur) exams as a bottleneck for higher education.* Retrieved from https://www.afghanistan-analysts.org/en/reports/economy-development-environment/cheating-and-worse-the-university-entry-kankur-exams-as-a-bottleneck-for-higher-education/

Ali, O., Milstein, G. & Marzuk, P. (2005). The Imam's role in meeting the counseling needs of Muslim communities in the United States. *Psychiatric Services, 56*(2), 202-205.

American Association of Community Colleges. (2024). Retrieved from www.aacc.nche.edu.

Arora, R., & Maheshwary, A. (2023). *In Conversation with Freshta Karim.* Retrieved from https://girlup.org/voices/in-conversation-with-freshta-karim

Aryan, B. (2010). *From Kabul to the Academy: Narratives of Afghan Women's Journeys to and Through U.S. Doctoral Programs.* Morgridge College of Education, Denver, CO. Available from ProQuest Dissertations and Theses database.

Austin, R., Nolan, R., & O'Donnell, S. (2009). The technology manager's journey: An extended narrative approach to education technical leaders. *Academy of Management Learning & Education*, 8(3), 337-355.

Azuma, Y., & Grossman, H. (2008). A theory of the informal sector. *Economics & Politics*, 20(1), 62-79.

Babcock, L. (2008). What happens when women don't ask? *Negotiation*, 11(96), 1- 4.

Bamik, H. (2019). Restructuring the Kankor examination format: A feasible solution for the existing issues with the current Kankor examination in Afghanistan. *Humanitarian and SocioEconomic Sciences Journal*, 2(13), 12- 29.

Banner, D.K. (1995). Conflict resolution: A re-contextualization. *Leadership and Organization Development Journal*, 16(1), 2-4.

Barakat, A.M. (2014). Public and Private Teacher Training Colleges in Afghanistan. Retrieved from https://www.diva-portal.org/smash/get/diva2:813283/FULLTEXT01.pdf

Batabyal, A. & Seung J. (2007). Corruption, bribery, and wait times in the public allocation of hoods in developing countries. *Review of Development Economics*, 11(3), 507-517.

Beall, A. (2022). *The CSU will no longer use SAT and ACT scores in admissions. But what does that mean for applicants?* https://www.calstate.edu/csu-system/news/Pages/Explained-Admissions-Without-the-SAT-or-ACT.aspx

Beckman, D. & Menkhoff, L. (2008). Will women be women? Analyzing the gender difference among financial experts. *Kyklos*, 61(3), 364-384.

Bhagat, V. (2024). *12 Best Countries to Outsource Software Development*. Retreived from https://www.pixelcrayons.com/blog/software-development/best-countries-to-outsource-software-development/

Blank, I. (2008). Selecting employees based on emotional intelligence competencies: Reap rewards and minimize risk. *Employee Relations Law Journal*, 34(3), 77-85.

Bolles, R. (2009). *What Color is Your Parachute?2009: A Practical Manual for Job-Hunters and Career-Changers*. CA: Ten Speed Press.

Bolman, L.G., & Deal, T.E. (2003). *Reframing Organizations* (3rd ed.). San Francisco: Jossey-Bass.

Brint, S. & Karabel, J. (1989). *The diverted dream: community colleges and the promise of educational opportunity*. New York: Oxford University Press.

Brown, A.L., Campione, J.C., & Dapy, J.D. (1981). Learning to learn: On training students to learn from texts. *Educational Research*, *10*(2), 14-21.

Burka, J., & Yuen, L. (1983). *Procrastination*. Cambridge, MA: Perseus Books.

Cabrera, E. (2009). Fixing the leaky pipeline: Five ways to retain female talent. *People and Strategy*, 32(1), 40-45.

Cannon, C. (2001). *Does education increase moral development? A re-examination of the moral reasoning abilities of working adult learners.* Doctoral Dissertation. Nova Southeastern University.

Chang, S.H., & Smith, R.A. (2008). Effectiveness of personal interaction in a learner centered paradigm distance education class based on student satisfaction. *Journal of Research on Technology in Education,* 40(4), 407-426.

Ciccarelli, S., & Meyer, G. (2006). *Psychology.* NJ: Pearson Prentice Hall.

Code to Inspire. (2023). Retrieved from https://www.codetoinspire.org/

Cohen, A. & Brawer, F. (1996). *The American Community College* (3rd ed.). San Francisco: Jossey Bass Publishers.

Cohen, A. (1995). *Projecting the Future of Community Colleges.* (ERIC Document Reproduction Center No. ED 388 351).

Collier, V. (1989). How long: A synthesis of research on academic achievement in a second language. *TESOL Quarterly, 23,* 509-531.

Conchas, G. (2008). *Education as a Tool for Breaking the Cycles of Poverty.* Retrieved from https://www.tc.columbia.edu/articles/2008/november/ education-as-a-tool-for-breaking-the-cycles-of-poverty/

Cook, R., Ley, K., Crawford, C., & Warner, A. (2009). Motivators and inhibitors for university faculty in distance and e-learning. *British Journal of Educational Technology*, 40(1), 149-163.

Cooper, T. (1998). *The Responsible Administrator* (4th ed.). San Francisco, CA: Jossey-Bass.

Cornwall, J. (2009). Becoming a Classroom Facilitator - Entrepreneurship Education Newsletter. *The Entrepreneurship Educator*. Retrieved from: newsletter@planningshop.com.

Correia, A., & Davis, N. (2008). Intersecting communities of practice in distance education: The program team and the online course community. *Journal of Distance Education*, 29(3), 289- 306.

Covella, G.A., McCarthy, V., Kaifi, B., & Corcoran D. (2017). Leadership's role in employee retention. *Business Management Dynamics*, 7(5), 10-25.

Craig-Henderson, K. & Brown-Sims, M. (2004). An investigation of African American college students' beliefs about anti-Middle Eastern hate crime and victims in the wake of September 11th. *The Western Journal of Black Studies,* 28(4), 511-517.

Dastoor, B., Roofe, E., & Mujtaba, B. (2005). Value orientation of Jamaicans compared to students in the United States of America. *International Business and Economics Research Journal,* 4(3), 43-52.

Daulay, H.P. (2017). *Islamic Education in Indonesia.* Retrieved from https://mpsi.umm.ac.id/files/file/291_%20ISLAMIC%

20EDUCATION%20IN%20INDONESIA%20A%20H istorical%20Analysis.pdf

De Maria, W. (2008). Cross cultural trespass: Assessing African anti-corruption capacity. *International Journal of Cross Cultural Management,* 8(3), 317-341.

Denhardt, R. (1993). *Theories of Public Organization.* Belmont, CA: Wadsworth.

Deniz, M., Tras, Z., & Aydogan, D. (2009). An investigation of academic procrastination, locus of control, and emotional intelligence. *Educational Science: Theory and Practice*, 9(2), 623-632.

Derrick, M.G. & Carr, P. B. (2008). *Global Learning and Education. HRM Review.* Retrieved from www.iupindia.org

Desai, M., Hart, J., & Richards, T. (2008). E-learning: Paradigm shift in education. *Education,* 129(2), 327-334.

Diaz-Rico, L.T. & Weed, K.Z. (2005). *The Cross-Cultural, Language, and Academic Development Handbook: A complete K-12 reference guide.* Boston, MA: Allyn-Bacon.

Dirks, D. & Parlove, S. (2003). *Islam our Choice.* Beltsville, Maryland: Amana Publications.

Dos Santos, T. (1970). The structure of dependence. *American Economic Review*, 60(2), 231-236.

Drury, R. (2003). Community Colleges in America: A historical perspective. *Inquiry*, 8(1), 1-6.

Drury, R.L. (1999). *Entrepreneurship education in the Virginia Community College system.* Doctoral dissertation on entrepreneurship education in Virginia's Community College System.

Eastmond, D. (1998). Adult learners and Internet-based distance education. *New Directions for Adult and Continuing Education, 78*, 33-41.

Echazu, L., & Bose, P. (2008). Corruption, centralization, and the shadow economy. *Southern Economic Journal, 75*(2), 524- 537.

Egbu, C. (1999). Skills, knowledge and competencies for managing construction refurbishment work. *Construction Management and Economics, 17*(1), 29-43.

Egéa-Kuehne, D. (1999). Twenty-Five Years of Le Grand Concours. *The French Review, 73*(2), 224–251._

Ellis, J.K., & Fouts J.T. (1994). *Research on School Restructuring*. Princeton Junction, NJ: Eye on Education, Inc.

Elobeid, D. E., Kaifi, B. A., & Lele, U. (2016). Corporate social responsibility in higher education institutions: The experience of the College of Business and Economics at Qassim University. *International Leadership Journal, 8*(1), 120–144.

Emadi, H. (2005). *Culture and customs of Afghanistan.* Westport, CT: Greenwood Press.

Entezar, M. E. (2007). *Afghanistan 101: Understanding Afghan culture.* Bloomington, IN: Xlibris.

Esposito, J. (1992). *The Islamic Threat: Myth or reality?* New York: Oxford University Press.

Ewans, M. (2002). *Afghanistan: A Short History of its People and Politics*. NY: HarperCollins Publishers.

Faiz, A. (2013). *Rule of Law Experts in Afghanistan: A Socio-Legal History of the First Afghan Constitution and the Indo-Ottoman Nexus in Kabul, 1860-1923*. Doctoral Dissertation from University of California, Berkeley.

Farid, N., & de Silva de Alwis, R. (2023). *Afghanistan Under the Taliban: A State of Gender Apartheid*. Retrieved from https://www.princeton.edu/events/2023/afghanistan-under-taliban-state-gender-apartheid

Farrokhi-Khajeh-Pasha, Y., Nedjat, S., Mohammadi, A., Rad, E., Majdzadeh, R., Monajemi, F., Jamali, E., & Yazdani, S. (2012). The validity of Iran's national university entrance examination (Konkoor) for predicting medical students' academic performance. *BMC Med Education*, 12(60), 1-8.

Fortner, B. (2005). U.S. universities sign distance learning education contract with India. *Civil Engineering*, 75(11), 28-35.

Franken, A., Edwards, C., & Lambert, R. (2009). Executing strategic change: Understanding the critical management Elements that lead to success. *California Management Review*, 51(3), 49-73.

Freeman, Y., & Freeman D. (2000). *Closing the Achievement Gap*. Thousand Oaks, CA: Heinemann Publishing.

Freire, P. (1993). *Pedagogy of the City*. New York, NY: Continuum.

Friedman, T.L. (2005). *The World is Flat: A Brief History of the Twenty-First Century*. New York: Farrar, Straus, and Giroux (1st edition).

Gardenswartz, L., Rowe, A., Digh, P., & Bennett, M. F. (2003). *The Global Diversity Desk Reference: Managing an International Workforce*. San Francisco, CA: Pfeiffer.

Gerhart, B. (2008). Cross cultural management research: Assumptions, evidence, and suggested directions. *International Journal of Cross Cultural Management*, 8(3), 259-274.

Gerner, M. (2007). *Psychotherapy in Kabul*. Retrieved from http://www.qantara.de/webcom/show_article.php/_c-478/_nr-562/i.html

Gibson, S., Harris, M., & Colaric, S. (2008). Technology acceptance in an academic context: Faculty acceptance of online education. *Journal of Education for Business*, 83(6), 355-359.

Girl Up India. (2023). In Conversation with Freshta Karim. Retrieved from https://girlup.org/voices/in-conversation-with-freshta-karim

Gladwell, M. (2002). *The Tipping Point*. New York: Little, Brown and Company.

Gladwell, M. (2008). *Outliers: The Story of Success*. New York: Little, Brown and Company.

Glesne, C. (2006). Becoming *Qualitative Researchers: An Introduction*. Boston: Pearson/Allyn & Bacon.

Goddard, T., Ali, M., & Frideres, J. (2018). The long journey for Afghan Teacher Training Colleges: Accreditation and quality assurance. *Comparative and International Education / Éducation Comparée et Internationale*, 47(1), 1-19.

Godlas, A. (2003). Hadith and the Prophet Muhammad. Retrieved from http://www.uga.edu/islam/hadith.html

Google Classroom. (2024). *Where teaching and learning come together*. Retrieved from https://edu.google.com/workspace-for-education/classroom/

Graham, S. (2008). *Culturally Proficient Inquiry: A Lens for Identifying and Examining Education Gaps*. San Francisco, CA: Crowin Press.

Groschl, S. (2008). *Diversity Management in Europe: A viewpoint*. *HRM Review*, December 2008. Retrieved from: www.iupindia.org

Grote, R. (2004). *Separation of Powers in the New Afghan Constitution*. ZaoRV, 64, 897-915. Zeitschrift für ausländisches öffentliches Recht und Völkerrecht (ZaöRV).

Hannum, W.H., Irvin, M.J., Lei, P., & Farmer, T.W. (2008). Effectiveness of using learner-centered principles on student retention in distance education courses in rural schools. *Distance Education*, 29(3), 211-229.

Harris, L. (2002). Achieving a balance in human resourcing between employee rights and care for the individual. *Business & Professional Ethics Journal*, 21(2), 45-60.

Harzing, A. (2006). Response styles in cross-national survey research: A 26-country study. *International Journal of Cross Cultural Management, 6*(2), 243-266.

Hayford, M. (2007). Using supply, demand, and the Cournot model to understand corruption. *Journal of Economic Education*, 38(3), 331-340.

Henke, H. & Russum, J. (2000). Factors influencing attrition rates in a corporate distance education program. *Education at a distance, 14* (11), Article 03. Retrieved from http://www.usdla.org/ED_magazine/illuminactive/ NOV00_Issue/ story03.htm

Herda, E. (1999). *Research Conversations and Narrative: A Critical Hermeneutic Orientation in Participatory Inquiry.* Westport, Connecticut: Praeger Publishers.

Hernandez, D.J. (2011). *Double Jeopardy: How Third-Grade Reading Skills and Poverty Influence High School Graduation.* Retrieved from http://ippsr.msu.edu/research/double-jeopardy-how-third-grade-reading-skills-and-poverty-influence-high-school-graduation

Himanshu, R. (2009). Gender differences: Ingratiation and leader member exchange quality. *Singapore Management Review*, 31(1), 63-72.

Hofstede, G. (2001). *Culture's Consequences: Comparing Values, Behaviors, Institutions, and Organizations Across Nations (2nd ed.).* Thousand Oaks, CA: Sage.

Hogan, D. (2014). *Why is Singapore's school system so successful, and is it a model for the West?* Retrieved from https://theconversation.com/why-is-singapores-school-system-so-successful-and-is-it-a-model-for-the-west-22917

Hoodfar, H. (2007). Women, religion, and the Afghan education movement in Iran. *Journal of Development Studies, 43*(2), 265-293.

Horowitz, J. (2021). *The Taliban are sitting on $1 trillion worth of minerals the world desperately needs.* Retrieved from https://www.cnn.com/2021/08/18/business/afghanistan-lithium-rare-earths-mining/index.html

Huang, Kuo-Ying and Mujtaba, B. G. (2009). Stress, task, and relationship orientations of Taiwanese adults: An examination of gender in this high-context culture. *Journal of International Business and Cultural Studies, 3,* 1-12.

Hubler, S. (2021). *Why Is the SAT Falling Out of Favor?: The University of California will no longer use SAT and ACT scores in admissions decisions. Critics say the tests put less wealthy students at a disadvantage.* Retrieved from https://www.nytimes.com/2020/05/23/us/SAT-ACT-abolish-debate-california.html

Hunter, M.C. (1987). Beyond reading, Dewey: What's next? A response to Gibboney. *Educational Leadership, 44,* 51-54.

Ishii, S. & Bruneau, T. (1994). Silence and Silences in Cross-Cultural Perspective: Japan and the United States. In L. A. Samovar & R. E. Porter (Eds.), *Intercultural communication: A reader (7th ed.)* (pp. 246-251). Belmont, CA: Wadsworth.

Islamic Education. (2023). *Retrieved from* https://mpsi.umm.ac.id/files/file/291%20ISLAMIC%20EDUCATION%20IN%20INDONESIA%20A%20Historical%20Analysis.pdf

Jack, A. & Parkin, B. (2024). *Afghan women and girls flock online* to evade Taliban curbs on female education. Retrieved from https://www.ft.com/content/3ac4860f-02dc-4015-88af-e2be74c9d1b9

Jackson, M.J., & Helms, M.M. (2008). Student perceptions of hybrid courses: Measuring and interpreting quality. *Journal of Education for Business,* 84(1), 7-12.

Jackson, T., Hill, S., Tamangani, Z., & Chipanbira, F. (2000). The management of people and organizations in South Africa and Zimbabwe: A cross-cultural study. *Management Research News,* 23(2), 98-100.

Jago, A. (1982). Leadership: Perspectives in theory and research. *Management Science,* 28(3), 315–336.

James, E. H., & Wooten, L. P. (2006). Diversity crises: How firms manage discrimination lawsuits. *The Academy of Management Journal,* 49(6), 1103-1118.

Jenkins, J., Khanfar, N., & Kaifi, B. (2017). Coping with changing business models in medicine: A case study. *Journal of Business Studies Quarterly*, 8(4), 123-131.

Johansen, T. M. (2005). Applying individual psychology to work with clients of the Islamic faith. *Journal of Individual Psychology*, 61(2), 174-184.

Johnson, G.M., & Bratt, S.E. (2009). Technology education students: e-tutors for school children. *British Journal of Educational Technology*, 40(1), 32-41.

Kaifi, B.A. (2008). The power of education in international economic development. *Sitara Magazine*, 1(5), 16-17.

Kaifi, B.A. (2008). King Amanullah Khan: A transformational leader. *Sitara Magazine*, 1(4), 48- 50.

Kaifi, B.A. (2008). Democratic Imperialism: Islamization vs. Democratization. *Arab Studies Quarterly*, 30(3), 73-74. Book Review.

Kaifi, B.A. (2009). *21ˢᵗ Century Leadership in Healthcare*. Pages 90-100. Chapter Twelve in the Pharmaceutical Technician Laboratory Manual by Sandeep Bansal. Jones and Bartlett Publications, Boston.

Kaifi, B.A. (2009). *A Critical Hermeneutic Approach to Understanding Experiences of Selected Afghan-American Leaders post-9/11 in the Bay Area*. Doctoral Dissertation. University of San Francisco.

Kaifi, B.A. (2009). Islam voices across cultures: Venues for leadership and understanding. *Journal of Sufism/An Inquiry*, 14(4), 19-22.

Kaifi, B.A. (2009). The 21st century glass ceiling: An inquiry on Afghan-American leaders in the workforce. *Fortune Journal of International Management*, 6(1), 57-72.

Kaifi, B.A., Mujtaba, B.G., & Xie, Y. (2009). Future Afghan-American leaders' perception of their role in economic development in Afghanistan: A study of gender differences and willingness to return to the motherland. *Journal of Diversity Management*, 4(3), 35-46.

Kaifi, B.A., Williams, A., & Mujtaba, B.G. (2009). Online college education for computer-savvy students: A study of perceptions and needs. *Journal of College Teaching Methods and Styles*, 6(10), 1-15.

Kaifi, B.A. (2009). *The Impact of 9/11 on Afghan-American Leaders*. Bloomington, IN: Xlibris.

Kaifi, B.A. (2009). What color is your parachute? *Journal of Applied Management and Entrepreneurship*, 14(4), 72-75. Book Review.

Kaifi, B.A., & Aslami, W. (2009). *Managing Diversity: Afghan-Americans and the Aftermath of the Twin Towers Tragedy. Journal of Diversity Management*, 4(4), 31-37.

Kaifi, B.A., & Mujtaba, B.G. (2009). Diversity management in the post-9/11 educational workplace: An inquiry on how much instructors know and understand about Islam. *Pakistan Management Review*, 45(4), 38-57.

Kaifi, B.A., & Mujtaba, B.G. (2009). Workforce discrimination: An inquiry on the perspectives of Afghan-American Professionals. *Journal of Business Studies Quarterly,* 1(1), 1-15.

Kaifi, B.A., Mujtaba, B.G., & Williams, A. (2010). The feasibility of distance education for cyber-savvy students. *Journal of Quarterly Review and Distance Education,* 10(4), 347-350.

Kaifi, B.A., & Mujtaba, B.G. (2010). A Study of management skills with Indian respondents: Comparing their technical, human and conceptual scores based on gender. *Journal of Applied Business and Economics,* 11(2), 129-138.

Kaifi, B.A., & Mujtaba, B.G. (2010). Transformational leadership of Afghans and Americans: A study of culture, age and gender. *Journal of Service Science and Management,* 3(1), 151-158.

Kaifi, B.A. (2010). Eastern and western management skills: Comparing the scores of Indians and Americans. *Fortune Journal of International Management,* 7(1), 1-12.

Kaifi, B.A. (2010). Eastern Indian women in management: A study of their skills, behaviors, and traits. *International Leadership Journal,* 2(3/4), 3-21.

Kaifi, B.A. (2010). *Managing Your Future: An Educational Guide.* Davie, Florida. ILEAD Academy. ISBN: 978-1-936237-03-6.

Kaifi, B.A. (2010). Strengths based leadership. *Journal of Applied Management and Entrepreneurship*, 15(1), 139-141. Book Review.

Kaifi, B.A., & Mujtaba, B.G. (2010). Transformational leadership and the impact of socialization in the Afghan culture: A study of behavioral differences based on gender, age, and place of birth. *International Leadership Journal*, 2(2), 33-52.

Kaifi, B.A. (2010). The state of business schools: Educational and moral imperatives for market leaders. *Journal of Business Studies Quarterly*, 1(2), 75-76. Book Review.

Kaifi, B.A. (2010). The way we're working isn't working. *Journal of Applied Management and Entrepreneurship*, 15(4), 116-120. Book Review.

Kaifi, B.A., & Noori, S.A. (2010). Organizational management: A study on middle managers, gender, and emotional intelligence levels. *Journal of Business Studies Quarterly*, 1(3), 13-23.

Kaifi, B.A., & Noori, S.A. (2010). Servant leadership in organizations: A study on Afghan-Americans. *Journal of Innovations*, 5(1), 59-64.

Kaifi, B.A., & Noori, S.A. (2011). Organizational behavior: A study on managers, employees, and teams. *Journal of Management Policy and Practice*, 12(1), 88- 97.

Kaifi, B.A., & Noori, S.A. (2011). The best of both worlds: A quantitative study on Afghan-Americans, culture, and servant leadership. *International Leadership Journal*, 3(1), 90-100.

Kaifi, B.A. (2011). Everyone communicates, few connect: What the most effective people do differently. *Journal of Applied Management and Entrepreneurship*, 16(1), 131-133. Book Review.

Kaifi, B.A. (2011). Shine: Using brain science to get the best from your people. *Journal of Applied Management and Entrepreneurship*, 16(4), 126-128. Book Review.

Kaifi, B.A. (2011). Sun Tzu for women: The art of war for winning in business. *Journal of Applied Management and Entrepreneurship*, 16(3), 102-104. Book Review.

Kaifi, B.A., & Mujtaba, B.G. (2011). Eastern Indian and Afghan women in management: A quantitative inquiry on their leadership proficiencies and propensities. *International Journal of Business Management*, 6(3), 3-11.

Kaifi, B.A., Aslami, W.A., Noori, S.A., & Korhummel, D. (2011). A decade after the 9/11 attacks: The demand for leaders with emotional intelligence and counseling skills. *Journal of Business Studies Quarterly*, 2(2), 54-67.

Kaifi, B.A., & Mujtaba, B.G. (2012). Awareness of Islam in the post-9/11 American workplace: A study of educational instructors' comprehension. *American Journal of Islamic Social Sciences*, 29(4), 46-62.

Kaifi, B.A., Khanfar, N.M., Nafei, W.A., Kaifi, M.M. (2012). A multi-generational workforce: Managing and understanding millennials. *International Journal of Business and Management*, 7(24), 88-93.

Kaifi, B.A., & Mujtaba, B.G. (2012). The emergence of a new era of management: The leadership traits and skills of eastern Indian and Afghan women. *Tecnia Journal of Management Studies*, 6(2), 1-9.

Kaifi, B.A., & Do, Q. (2012). Critical concepts applied to leadership in energy and environmental design: Insights from Karen Maggio. *Journal of Applied Management and Entrepreneurship*, 17(2), 97-103.

Kaifi, B.A., & Medenhall, S. (2012). Strategic leadership applied to retail management: Joe Contrucci discusses the 21st century dynamic workforce. *Journal of Applied Management and Entrepreneurship*, 17(4), 103-109.

Kaifi, B.A. (2013). *Capitalism in a Developing, Dependent, and Divided Nation: Afghanistan's Conundrum*. Pages 39-48. Chapter 4 in Capitalism and its Challenges across Borders. ILEAD Academy, Davie, Florida. ISBN: 978-1-936237-08-1.

Kaifi, B.A. (2013). *Organizational Behavior: Managing and Leading Organizations*. Tamarac, FL: Llumina Press. ISBN: 978-1-62550-006-9.

Kaifi, B.A. (2013). The rise of the naked economy: How to benefit from the changing workplace. *Journal of Business Studies Quarterly*, 5(2), 260-261. Book Review.

Kaifi, B.A., Khanfar, N.M., Nafei, W., & Kaifi, M.M. (2013). The need for human resource managers to maximize performance: A study on the perceptions of business students on job performance. *Journal of Management and Sustainability*, 3(4), 103-109.

Kaifi, B.A. (2014). A Millennial in IT Management. A conversation with Michael Sabado. *Journal of Applied Management and Entrepreneurship*, 19(1), 102-109.

Kaifi, B.A. (2014). *Afghanistan's Conundrum: Capitalism in a Dependent Nation*, pp. 29 - 37, Chapter 4 in "Capitalism and its Challenges Across Borders". Edited by Bahaudin G. Mujtaba. Florida: ILEAD Academy.

Kaifi, B.A. (2014). *Human Resource Management: An Applied Approach*. Tamarac, FL: Llumina Press. ISBN: 978-1-62550-188-2.

Kaifi, B.A. & Aslami, W. (2014). *Women and Islam in Afghanistan*. Pages 71-82. *Chapter 4* in Gender, Education, and Employment Developments in South Asia. ILEAD Academy, Davie, Florida. ISBN: 978-1-936237-11-1.

Kaifi, B.A., & Tarin, Y. (2014). Learning from the CEO of Electro Imaging Systems, Inc. A conversation with Qasim Tarin. *Journal of Applied Management and Entrepreneurship*, 19(2), 126-132.

Kaifi, B.A., Khanfar, N., Noor, A., & Poluka, L. (2014). Business students' commitment to corporate social responsibility: A study based upon gender, generational affiliation, and culture. *Journal of Business and Management Research*, 3(3), 34-42.

Kaifi, B.A., & Aslami, W. (2014). Women and education in Afghanistan. A leadership dilemma. *Journal of Business Studies Quarterly*, 6(2), 18-27.

Kaifi, B.A., Kang, H., & Corcoran, D. (2015). Afghan-Americans' understanding, perception, and commitment to corporate social responsibility in Afghanistan: A study based upon gender, generational affiliation, and leadership experience. *Open Journal of Law and Ethics,* 1(3), 17-23.

Kaifi, B.A. (2017). An Interview with Edreece Arghandiwal, CEO of Jurni: A millennial entrepreneur who is making an impact by capitalizing on technology. *Journal of Applied Management & Entrepreneurship,* 22(2), 103-109.

Kaifi, B.A., Khanfar, N., & Swigart, P. (2017). Learning from a General Manager of Ford: Tooran Popal shares his leadership experiences, strategies, and ambitions. *The Journal of Applied Management and Entrepreneurship,* 22(3), 76-80.

Kaifi, B.A. (2021). *Health Care Administration: A Quantitative Research Study on Afghan American Nurses, Leadership, and Acculturation Factors.* Breezeway Books. ISBN: 978-1625506139.

Kaifi, B.A., Mujtaba, B., & Mujtaba, M. (2022). The impact of acculturation on the leadership style of Afghan-American registered nurses working in the US healthcare system. *Public Organization Review,* 22, 173-191.

Kaifi, B.A., Mujtaba, B.G., Mujtaba, M.G., & Younos, F. (2023). Assessing the leadership orientation of Afghan American registered nurses based on acculturation factors. *Journal of Cultural Leadership Studies,* 4(4), 95-118.

Kamgar, J. (2003). *The History of Education in Afghanistan. Kabul.* Maiwand Publication Company.

Karadjova-Stoev, G. & Mujtaba, B.G. (2009). Strategic human resource management and global expansion lessons from the Euro Disney challenges in France. *International Business and Economics Research Journal*, 8(1), 69-78.

Karahalios, M. & Mujtaba, G.B. (2006). Women, disabilities, technology, and the reconstruction of Afghanistan. *Society of Afghan Engineers Journal*, 3(1), 38-47.

Karlsson, P. & Mansory, A. (2008). *Islamic and Modern Education in Afghanistan: Conflictual or Complementary?* Unpublished doctoral dissertation, Institute of International Education, Stockholm. Retrieved from http://www.netreed.uio.no/articles/Papers_final/Karlsson_Mansory.pdf

Katz, R. L. (1955). Skills of an Effective Administrator. *Harvard Business Review*, 33(1), 33-42.

Kayeum, J. (2014). *Afghan Patriot: Dr. Abdul Kayeum.* Independently Published, Las Vegas. ISBN: 1096634538.

Kearney, E. (2008). Age differences between leader and followers as a moderator of the relationship between transformational leadership and team performance. *Journal of Occupational & Organizational Psychology*, 81(4), 803-811.

Kegan, R. (1994). *In Over Our Heads.* Cambridge, MA: Harvard University Press.

Kennedy, W.J., Heinzman, J., & Mujtaba, B. G. (2007). The Early Organizational Management Theories: The

Human Relations Movement & Business Ethical Practices Pioneered by Visionary Leader Mary Parker Follett. *Journal of Business and Economics Research,* 5(3), 27-36.

Kennedy, W.J. (2003). A Study of the Moral Reasoning Skills of Proactive and Reactive Organizational Management. Doctoral Dissertation. Nova Southeastern University.

Khademian, A. (2002). Working with Culture. Washington, D.C.: CQ Press.

Khanfar, N.M., Harrington, C., Alkhateeb, F., & Kaifi, B.A. (2013). Cultural differences in leadership styles of pharmacist preceptors. *Journal of Business and Management Research,* 2(1), 1-17.

Kim, P. (2004). Conditional morality? Attitudes of individuals toward racial profiling. *The American Behavioral Scientist,* 47(7), 879-895.

Knouse, S.B. (2009). Targeted recruiting for diversity: Strategy, impression management, realistic expectations, and diversity climate. *International Journal of Management,* 26(3), 347- 353.

Kotter, J.P. (1996). *Leading Change.* Boston, MA: Harvard Business School Press.

Kouzes, J., & Posner, B. (2003). *Encouraging the Heart.* San Francisco, CA: Jossey-Bass.

Lamberton, L.H., & Minor, L. (2010). Human Relations (4th ed.). Boston, MA: McGraw Hill.

Lantz, P. (2008). Gender and leadership in healthcare Administration: 21st century progress and challenges. *Journal of Healthcare Management*, 53(5), 291-301.

Lawrence-Lightfoot, S. (2000). *Respect*. Cambridge, MA: Perseus Books.

Lee, C. L., & Phua, C. P. (2020). Singapore bilingual education: One policy, many interpretations. *Journal of Asian Pacific Communication*, 30(1-2), 90-114.

Leithwood, K., & Louis, K.S. (2004). *Learning Leadership Project: How Leadership Influences Student Learning*. New York: The Wallace Foundation.

Ling, Y., Simsek, Z., Lubatkin, M.H., & Veiga, J.F. (2008). Transformational leadership's role in promoting corporate entrepreneurship: Examining the CEO-TMT interface. *Academy of Management Journal*, 51(3), 557-576.

Livengood, J. & Stodolska, M. (2004). The effects of discrimination and constraints negotiation on leisure behavior of American Muslims in the post-September 11 America. *Journal of Leisure Research*, 36(2), 183-208.

Lopez-Fernandez, M., Martin-Alcazar, F., & Romero-Fernandez, P. (2009). Key factors in the access to managerial posts. *Journal of General Management*, 34(4), 39-50.

Loucks, S. F. & Zacchei, D. (1983). Applying our findings to today's innovation. *Educational Leadership, 41*, 28-31.

Magnet Schools of America. (2021). Retrieved from http://www.magnet.edu/about/what-are-magnet-schools

Mandel, M. (2009). Economics: The Basics. Boston, MA: McGraw-Hill.

Mansory, A. (2012). An Exploratory Study of Private Teacher Training Colleges (TTCs). Kabul: Teacher Education Directorate.

Martin, K., Cullen, J., Johnson, J., & Parboteeah, K. (2007). Deciding to bribe: A cross-level analysis of firm and home country influences on bribery activity. *Academy of Management Journal*, 50(6), 1401-1422.

Marzano, R. (2005). *School leadership that works.* Alexandria, VA: Association for Supervision and Curriculum Development.

May, C. D. (2008). Taliban not sentimental. *The Gainesville Sun*, 9A, September 29, 2008.

McCarthy, N. (2016). The Countries With The Most Doctoral Graduates. Retrieved from https://www.forbes.com/sites/niallmccarthy/2016/12/19/the-countries-with-the-most-doctoral-graduates-infographic/amp/

McGee, S. (2023). Why the Soviet Union Invaded Afghanistan. Retrieved from https://www.history.com/news/1979-soviet-invasion-afghanistan

McGrath, M.E., & McGrath, C.K. (2009). Decide Better for College. Addison, TX: Motivation Publishing.

McNeilly, M. (2023). *Afghanistan's Mobile Libraries: A Conversation with Freshta Karim*. Retrieved from https://www.newtactics.org/conversation/afghanistans-mobile-libraries-conversation-freshta-karim

Mead, R. (2005). *International Management: Cross-cultural Dimensions* (3rd ed.). Malden, MA: Blackwell Business.

Menchaca, M.P. & Bekele, T.A. (2008). Learner and instructor identified success factors in distance education. *Distance Education*, 29(3), 231-252.

Mernissi, F. (1987). *Translated by Mary Jo Lakeland. The Veil and the Make Elite*. New York: Addison-Wesley Publishing.

Milton-Edwards, B. (2005). *Islamic Fundamentalism Since 1945. New York: Routledge.*

Mobley, S. (2002). The Study of Lawrence Kohlberg's Stages of Moral Development Theory and Ethics: Considerations in Public Administration Practices. Doctoral Dissertation. Nova Southeastern University.

Morrison, A., & Glinow, M. (1995). *Women and Minorities in Management.* Chapter 28 in The Leader's Companion by J. Thomas Wren, pp. 168- 181. NY: The Free Press.

Muhonen, S. (2017). *Teacher Voice: In Finland, it's easier to become a doctor or lawyer than a teacher — Here's why.* Retirieved from https://hechingerreport.org/teacher-voice-in-finland-its-easier-to-become-a-doctor-or-lawyer-than-a-teacher-heres-why/

Mujtaba, B.G., & Mujtaba, L. (2004). Diversity awareness and management in adult education. *Journal of College Teaching and Learning,* 1(3), 65-75.

Mujtaba, B.G., Preziosi, R., & Mujtaba, L. (2004). Adult learning, assessment, and the extraordinary teacher. *Journal of College Teaching and Learning,* 1(4), 29-37.

Mujtaba, B.G., & Mujtaba, L. (2004). Creating a healthy learning environment for student success in the classroom. *The Internet TESL Journal.* Retrieved from http://iteslj.org/Articles/Mujtaba-Environment.html

Mujtaba, G.B. (2005). Market-based leadership skills for public and private sector capacity development in Afghanistan. *Society of Afghan Engineers Journal,* 2(1), 39-52.

Mujtaba, B.G. (2005). Management and leadership developments in Afghanistan: An interview with Sayed Tayeb Jawad, Afghanistan's Ambassador to the United States. *Journal of Applied Management and Entrepreneurship,* (10)4, 81-92.

Mujtaba, B.G. (2005). Faculty development practices in distance education for success with culturally diverse students. *International Business and Economics Research Journal,* 4(4), 1-13.

Mujtaba, B.G. (2006). *Privatization and Market-Based Leadership in Developing Economies: Capacity Building in*

Afghanistan. Llumina Press and Publications, Tamarac, Florida.

Mujtaba, B.G., & Preziosi, R.C. (2006). *Adult Education in Academia: Recruiting and Retaining Extraordinary Facilitators of learning*. 2nd Edition. Information Age Publishing. Connecticut.

Mujtaba, B.G., & McAtavey, J. (2006). Performance assessment and comparison of learning in international education: American versus Jamaican students' learning outcomes. *The College Teaching Methods & Styles Journal*, 2(3), 33-43.

Mujtaba, B.G., & Scharff, M.M. (2007). *Earning a Doctorate Degree in the 21st Century: Challenges and Joys*. ILEAD Academy Publications; Florida, USA.

Mujtaba, G.B. (2007). Empowering the workforce to deliver superior value through the development of a customer-oriented culture in developing countries. In the *Global Economy: Challenges in Developing and Transition Economies*; edited byMina Baliamoune-Lutz, Alojzy Z. Nowak, and Jeff Steagall; Volume 2, pages 339-372. ISBN: 978-83-89069-20-7. Warsaw-Jacksonville, United States.

Mujtaba, B.G. (2007). *Afghanistan: Realities of War and Rebuilding (2nd edition)*. ILEAD Academy, LLC, Davie, Florida; United States.

Mujtaba, B.G. (2007). *The Ethics of Management and Leadership in Afghanistan (2nd edition)*. ILEAD Academy. Davie, Florida USA.

Mujtaba, B.G. (2007). *Situational Leadership for Developing a Productive Culture from Ground Zero in Afghanistan.* In the Global Economy: Challenges in developing and transition economies; edited by Mina Baliamoune-Lutz, Alojzy Z. Nowak, and Jeff Steagall; volume 2, pages 210-230. ISBN: 978-83-89069-20-7. Warsaw- Jacksonville, United States.

Mujtaba, B.G., & Kaifi, B.A. (2008). Afghan and American professionals' leadership orientation toward tasks and relationships: Are there tendencies toward convergence or divergence? *Fortune Journal of International Management,* 5(1), 107-125.

Mujtaba, B.G. & Kaifi, B.A. (2009). *Dependency and Bribery Linkages in Afghanistan: A Study of Business Ethics in the Afghan-American Population.* Proceedings of the Academy of Business Disciplines Conference, Ft. Myers Beach, Florida. November 5th -7th, 2009.

Mujtaba, B.G. & Kaifi, B.A. (2010). An inquiry into eastern leadership orientation of working adults in Afghanistan. *Journal of Leadership Studies,* 4(1), 36-46.

Mujtaba, B.G., & Kaifi, B.A. (2010). Business ethics and morality in Afghanistan. *Business and Professional Ethics Journal,* 29(1-4), 32- 63.

Mujtaba, B.G., & Kaifi, B.A. (2011). Management skills of Afghan respondents: A comparison of technical, human and conceptual differences based on gender. *Journal of International Business and Cultural Studies,* 4(1), 117-129.

Mujtaba, B.G. (2014). *Capitalism and its Challenges across Borders (edited)*. Florida: ILEAD Academy.

Mujtaba, B.G., Kaifi, B.A., & Lawrence, E. (2023). Safety mandates, legal requirements, and management practices to provide employees with a safe and healthful work environment. *International Journal of Occupational and Environmental Safety*, 7(2), 1-19.

Mujtaba, B.G., & Kaifi, B.A. (2023). Safety audit considerations for a healthy workplace that puts people before profit and OSHA compliance. Health Economics and *Management Review*, 4(1), 11-25.

Mujtaba, B.G. (2024). *Women's Education in Afghanistan: An interview with Dr. Abdul Qayum Safi, author of "One life: An Afghan Remembers."* YouTube link: https://youtu.be/WVnfgmjyBOA

Munck, R. (1999). Dependency and imperialism in the new times: A Latin America perspective. *The European Journal of Development Research*, 11(1), 56-74.

Munene, J. C., Schwartz, S. H., & Smith, P. B. (2000). Development in sub-Saharan Africa: Cultural influences and managers' decision behavior. *Public Administration and Development, 20*(4), 339-351.

Nafei, W. & Kaifi, B.A. (2013). The impact of organizational cynicism on organizational commitment: An Applied Study on Teaching Hospitals in Egypt. *European Journal of Business and Management*, 5(12), 133-147.

Nafei, W.A., Kaifi, B.A, & Khanfar, N. M. (2012). Organizational learning as an approach to achieve outstanding performance: An applied study on Al-Taif University, Kingdom of Saudi Arabia. *Journal of Advances in Management and Applied Economics*, 2(4), 13-40.

Nafei, W.A., Khanfar, N.M., & Kaifi, B.A. (2012). Leadership styles and organizational learning: An empirical study on Saudi Banks in Al-Taif Governorate Kingdom of Saudi Arabia. *Journal of Management and Strategy*, 3(1), 2-17.

Neely, L., Niemi, J. & Ehrhard, B. (1998). *Classes going the distance so people don't have to: Instructional opportunities for adult learners. T.H.E. Journal, 26*(4). Retrieved from https://thejournal.com/Articles/1998/11/01/Classes-Going-the-Distance-So-People-Dont-Have-To-Instructional-Opportunities-for-Adult-Learners.aspx?admgarea=Features1&m=1&Page=5

NEXA. Afghanistan. (2024). Retrieved from https://nexa.gov.af/fa/about-us

Nieves, R., Mujtaba, B. G., Pellet, P., & Cavico, F. J. (2006). Culture and universal professional values in global organizations: Is there a divergence or convergence of cultural values? *Journal of Diversity Management*, 1(1), 31-38.

Northouse, P. G. (2010). *Leadership: theory and practice (5th edition)*. Los Angeles: Sage Publications.

Norton, P., & Hathaway, D. (2008). Exploring two teacher education online learning designs: A classroom of one or many? *Journal of Research on Technology in Education*, 40(4), 475- 495.

Notar, C., Herring, D., & Restauri, S. (2008). A web-based teaching aid for presenting the concepts of norm referenced and criterion referenced testing. *Education*, 129(1), 119-124.

Nyumba, T., Wilson, K., Derrick, C., & Mukherjee, N. (2018). The use of focus group discussion methodology: Insights from two decades of application in conservation. *Methods in Ecology and Evolution*, 9(1), 20-32.

O'Donnell, L. (2022). *The Taliban Have Picked Up the Resource Curse.* Retrieved from https://foreignpolicy.com/2022/07/11/afghanistan-taliban-mining-resources-rich-minerals/

Oyserman, D., Coon, H. M., & Kemmelmeier, M. (2002). Rethinking individualism and collectivism: Evaluation of theoretical assumptions and meta-analysis. *Psychological Bulletin*, 128(1), 3-72.

Parcheta, N., Kaifi, B.A., & Khanfar, N.M. (2013). Gender inequality in the workforce: A human resource management quandary. *Journal of Business Studies Quarterly*, 4(3), 240-248.

Patrinos, H.A. (2023). *Education, economics and public policy.* Retrieved from https://hpatrinos.com/2023/12/13/an-investment-in-knowledge-pays-the-best-interest/

Pearson, P. (2016). *Language Policy in Rwanda: Shifting Linguistic and Educational Landscape*. Doctoral Dissertation. Georgia State University.

Peek, L. (2005). Becoming Muslim: The development of a religious identity. *Sociology of Religion,* 66(3), *215- 242.*

Perraton, J. (2007). Evaluating Marxian contributions to development economies. *Journal of Economic Methodology,* 14(1), 27-46.

Poluka, L., & Kaifi, B.A. (2015). Performance coaching within the telecommuting industry. *Journal of Applied Management and Entrepreneurship*, 20(4), 49-65.

Poole, D. (2000). Student participation in a discussion-oriented online course: A case study. *Journal of Research on Computing in Education,* 33(2), 162-77.

Postrel, S. (2009). Multitasking teams with variable complementarity: Challenges for capability management. *Academy of Management Review,* 34(2), 273-296.

Pounder, J. (2008). Transformational leadership: Practicing what we teach in the management classroom. *Journal of Education for Business*, 84(1), 2-6.

Psacharopoulos, G., & Hinchliffe, K. (1973). *Returns to Education: An International Comparison.* Jossey-Bass Publications.

Pudlowski, E.M. (2009). Managing human resource cost in a declining economic environment. *Benefits Quarterly,* 25(4), 37- 43.

Putz, C. (2015). *Fixing the Salang Pass Tunnel*. Retrieved from https://thediplomat.com/2015/10/fixing-the-salang-pass-tunnel/

Qur'an. (1999). Translation of the holy Qur'an. Riyadh: Tahrike Tarsile Qur'an.

Rahman, S., & Yang, L. (2009). Skill requirements for logistic managers in China: An empirical assessment. *IIMB Management Review*, 21(2), 140-148.

Rainey, H. G. (2003). *Understanding and Managing Public Organizations* (3rd ed). San Francisco, California: Jossey-Bass.

Rath, T. & Conchie, B. (2009). *Strengths Based Leadership*. NY: Gallup Press.

Reading Partners. (2013). *Do prisons use third grade reading scores to predict the number of prison beds they'll need?* Retrieved from https://readingpartners.org/blog/do-prisons-use-third-grade-reading-scores-to-predict-the-number-of-prison-beds-theyll-need/

Reich, R. (2002). *I'll Be short: Essentials for a decent working society*. Boston, MA: Beacon Press.

Rey, K.S. (2021). *Rosa Hernández Acosta on the Cuban Literacy Campaign*. Retrieved from https://daily.jstor.org/rosa-hernandez-acosta-on-the-cuban-literacy-campaign/

Rhodes, J., Walsh, P., & Lok, P. (2008). Convergence and divergence issues in strategic management – Indonesia's experience with the balanced scorecard in

HR management. *The International Journal of Human resources Management,* 19(6), 1170-1185.

Richards, C. & Ridley, D. (1997). Factors affecting college students' persistence in online computer-managed instruction. *College Student Journal,* 31, 490-495.

Ricoeur, P. (1992). *Oneself as Another.* Chicago: University of Chicago Press.

Roblyer, M. (1999). Is choice important in distance learning? A study of student motives for taking Internet-based courses at the high school and community college levels. *Journal of Research on Computing in Education,* 32(1), 157-71.

Rossman, M. (2000). Andragogy and distance education: Together in the new millennium. *New Horizons in Adult Education,* 14(1), 3-9.

Sadat, M.H. (2004). Modern education in Afghanistan. *Lemar-Aftaab.* Retrieved from http://afghanmagazine.com/2004_03/articles/educatio n.shtml

Sakhi, H., & Nabizadah, A.A. (2015). *Kankor Post-Examination MIS.* Kabul University, Kabul.

Samady, S.R. (2001). Modern education in Afghanistan. *Prospects,* 31(4), 587-602.

Samady, S.R. (2013). *Changing profile of education in Afghanistan.* Retrieved from https://www.pedocs.de/volltexte/2013/7798/pdf/Sam ady_2013_Education_Afghanistan.pdf

Scarborough, J. (1998). *The origins of cultural differences and their impact on management*. Westport, CN: Quorum Books.

Schwartz, S.H. (1999). Cultural value differences: Some implications for work. *Applied Psychology, 48*(1), 23-47.

Sekandari, N. (2007). *Parenting in Afghan families: The influence of war experience*. The California School of Professional Psychology, Allied International University, San Francisco, CA. Available from ProQuest Dissertations and Theses database.

Shaomin, L., & Ming, O. (2007). A dynamic model to explain the bribery behavior of firms. *International Journal of Management*, 24(3), 605-618.

Sherzad, A. (2016). *Using Descriptive Analytics for the Improvement of National University Entrance Exam: A case study in the Context of Kankor in Afghanistan*. Retrieved from https://arxiv.org/ftp/arxiv/papers/1612/1612.01378.pdf

Shin, M. & Lee, Y. (2009). Changing the landscape of teacher education via online teaching and learning. *Techniques: Connecting Education & Careers*, 83(9), 32-33.

Singapore's Bilingual Policy. (2023). *Bridging Cultures and Driving Progress*. MCC Corvinák. Retrieved from https://corvinak.hu/en/velemeny/2023/09/07/singapores-bilingual-policy-bridging-cultures-and-driving-progress
Singapore's Global Schools for a Global Society. (n.d.). Asia Society. Retrieved from https://asiasociety.org/global-cities-education-network/singapores-global-schools-global-society

Singham, M. (2003). The achievement gap: Myths and reality. *Phi Delta Kappan*, 84(8), 586 -591.

Smith, R.O. (2008). The paradox of trust in online collaborative groups. *Distance Education*, 29(3), 325-340.

Smith-Evans, P. (2004). *A Study of Cognitive Moral Development Theory and Moral Maturity of African-American Business Professionals*. Doctoral Dissertation. Nova Southeastern University.

Survey of Earned Doctorates (2022). Retrieved from https://ncses.nsf.gov/surveys/earned-doctorates/2022

Sutherland, W., Dicks, L., Everard, M., & Geneletti, D. (2018). Qualitative methods for ecologists and conservation scientists. *Methods in Ecology and Evolution*, 9(1), 7-9.

Tajaddini, R., & Mujtaba, B.G. (2009). Stress perceptions and leadership orientation of Malaysians: Exploring their similarities and differences with Americans. *Chinese Business Review*, 8(8), 26-42.

Tan, C. & Ng, P.T. (2011). Functional differentiation: A critique of the bilingual policy in Singapore. *Journal of Asian Public Policy*, 4(3), 331–341.

Tanner, S. (2009). Indomitable Afghanistan. *Military History, August/September Issue, 26 -35*.

Tapper, N. (2001). Pashtun nomad women in Afghanistan. *Asian Affairs*, 8(2), 163-170.

Tatum, B. (1997). *Why are the Black Kids Sitting Together in the Cafeteria?* NY: Basic Books.

Tensey, R. & Hyman, M. (1994). Dependency theory and the effects on advertising by foreign-based multinational corporations in Latin America. *Journal of Advertising, 23*(1), 27-42.

Terry, N. (2001). Assessing enrollment and attrition rates for the online MBA. *T.H.E. Journal, 28* (7), 64-68.

The World Bank. (2023). Gender Data Portal – Afghanistan. Retrieved from https://genderdata.worldbank.org/countries/afghanistan/

Tzabbar, D. (2009). When does scientist recruitment affect technological repositioning? *Academy of Management Journal, 52*(5), 873-896.

UNICEF – Afghanistan. Retrieved from https://www.unicef.org/afghanistan/education#:~:text=An%20estimated%203.7%20million%20children,women's%20role%20in%20the%20society.

U.S. Army. (2004). The study of a nation. Retrieved from http://www.atsc.army.mil/crc/iso6a10l/AfghanistanCountryStudyC.pdf

Vecchio, R., Justin, J., & Pearce, C. (2008). The utility of transactional and transformational leadership for predicting performance and satisfaction within a path-goal theory framework. *Journal of Occupational and Organizational Psychology, 81*(1), 71-82.

Velasco, A. (2002). Dependency theory. *Foreign Policy, 133*, 44-46.

Veracierto, M. (2008). Corruption and innovation. *Economic Perspectives*, 32(1), 29- 40.

Vogl, F. (2007). Global corruption: Applying experience and research to meet a mounting crisis. *Business & Society Review*, 112(2), 171-190.

Wadud. A. (1999). *Qur'an and Woman: Rereading the Sacred Text from a Woman's Perspective.* NY: Oxford University Press.

Wahlstedt, A., Pekkola, S., & Niemela, M. (2008). From e-learning space to e-learning place. *British Journal of Educational Technology*, 39(6), 1020-1030.

Walker, T. (2018). *Where Do Teachers Get the Most Respect?* Retrieved from https://www.nea.org/nea-today/all-news-articles/where-do-teachers-get-most-respect

Walumbwa, F., Avolio, B., & Zhu, W. (2008). How transformational leadership weaves its influence on individual job performance: The role of identification and efficacy beliefs. *Personnel Psychology*, 61(4), 793- 825.

Weatherby, J. N., Arceneaux, C., Evans, E. B., Long, D., Reed, I., & Novika-Carter, O.D.
 (2009). *The Other World: Issues and Politics of the Developing World* (8th ed.). New York, NY: Pearson.

Wood, S. (2022). *Is High School Class Rank Still Important?* Retrieved from https://www.usnews.com/education/k12/articles/is-high-school-class-rank-still-important

World Bank. (2023). *Connecting for Inclusion: Broadband Access for All.* Retrieved from https://www.worldbank.org/en/topic/digitaldevelopment/brief/connecting-for-inclusion-broadband-access-for-all

Wu, X., & He, J. (2009). Paradigm shifts in public administration: Implications for teaching in professional training programs. *Public Administration Education, 69,* 21-28.

Wyld, D. (2008). How do women fare when the promotion rules change? *Academy of Management Perspectives,* 22(4), 83-85.

Yetton, P., & Crouch, A. (1983). Social influence and structure: Elements of a general theory of leadership. *Australian Journal of Management,* 8(2), 15-26.

Younos, F. (2002). *Gender Equality in Islam.* Bloomington, IN: Authorhouse.

Zellen, E. (2011). Zarbul Masalha: 151 Afghan Dari Proverbs. Karwan Press. ISBN: 978-1475093926.

Author Biographies

Belal A. Kaifi, Ph.D., Ed.D., M.P.A., M.B.A., has been working in the field of education for 20 years. As a result, Dr. Kaifi has acquired invaluable experience teaching high school students, community college students, vocational/technical college students, and university students at the undergraduate and graduate levels. With such comprehensive teaching experiences (ranging from high school to graduate programs), Dr. Kaifi is the ideal candidate to offer unbiased recommendations to enhance the current and future goals of the education system in Afghanistan.

As a Fulbright Scholar, Dr. Kaifi has experience teaching international students in Afghanistan and Saudi Arabia. Furthermore, Dr. Kaifi has over 10 years of combined academic leadership experience in higher education and has served as a Dean, Associate Dean, Department Chair, Faculty Lead, Program Director, and Program Coordinator at various academic institutions.

Dr. Kaifi completed his post-doctoral studies in Business Administration at the University of Florida. He completed his first doctoral degree in Education and Leadership from the University of San Francisco and his second doctoral degree in Healthcare Administration at the American InterContinental University. Dr. Kaifi holds a master's degree in Public Administration and a second master's degree in Business Administration. He completed his bachelor's degree in Business Administration. Dr. Kaifi also earned a specialized teaching credential in Business and Finance for Career and Technical Education (CTE) programs. Based upon his graduate level training and work experience, Dr. Kaifi is academically and professionally qualified to teach in the following academic departments: Education, Business Administration, Healthcare Administration, and Public Administration.

Dr. Kaifi has extensive experience teaching in traditional classrooms and in online settings. Dr. Kaifi has 15 years of experience with educational consulting and has helped hundreds of students with their educational endeavors. While visiting Afghanistan in 2005, Dr. Kaifi created a Community Based Education (CBE) English Language Learning (ELL) course for 10 students. Dr. Kaifi spent time in Kabul, Afghanistan in 2015 teaching students at Dunya University. In 2019, Dr. Kaifi and his team launched the *Institute of Management, Education, and Arts Development* (imead.org) to provide free self-study micro courses to students in Afghanistan. In 2022, he joined the faculty of the American University of Afghanistan.

In the US, Dr. Kaifi has taught at: University of the Pacific, California State University - East Bay, Saint Mary's College of California, American River College, Carrington College, Franklin University, Mountain House High School, and several online universities.

Dr. Kaifi is the author of five books and has published over 50 peer reviewed research articles. His research focuses on Afghan Americans, leadership, and the future of Afghanistan.

Mohammad Haris Azimi, M.I.R., M.B.A., has garnered over 15 years of experience in the field of education. During this time, he has imparted invaluable knowledge to high school students, as well as to university students at the undergraduate level in Afghanistan, and has conducted training for the younger generation through short-term courses using various platforms. With his extensive teaching background in Afghanistan, Mr. Azimi is well-equipped to provide recommendations for improving the current and future educational objectives in the country.

As an influential education activist, Mr. Azimi has actively taught local students in Afghanistan. Additionally, he possesses decades of combined academic leadership experience in higher education and has held administrative and program coordinating positions with both national and international NGOs and academic institutions.

Mr. Azimi earned his first Master's degree in International Relations (M.I.R.) from Kardan University in Kabul and his second Master's degree in Business Administration (M.B.A.) from the American University of Afghanistan (AUAF) based in Doha, Qatar. He completed a specialization in Diplomacy and Peacebuilding and has completed cross-certified courses in International Public Law and Policy Analysis from Ruhr University of Bochum, Germany. Furthermore, he obtained his bachelor's degree in Arabic literature from Kabul University.

With extensive international commerce experience and business-related travel to multiple countries, Mr. Azimi currently owns a travel agency while also engaging in volunteer work. He leads a committee for business conflict resolution, addressing local business issues in Kabul. Through his international travels, Mr. Azimi has become proficient in four foreign languages: English, Urdu, Arabic, and Chinese, in addition to his fluency in native languages (Dari and Pashto). He has held senior positions in Administration, Communications, Outreach, and served as a board member for NGOs in Kabul, Afghanistan. In 2019, Mr. Azimi was part of the team that launched the *Institute of Management, Education, and Arts Development* (imead.org) to provide free self-study micro-courses to students in Afghanistan.

In Kabul, Mr. Azimi has taught at Peshgam Institute of Higher Education and Naiestan Institute of Higher Education, and has worked with PAE, TetraTech, and IRD International NGOs, as well as RDP and TLO National NGOs.

Mr. Azimi has conducted research on Islamic Tasawwuf, specifically Tareqa Chishtiya, and has authored several unpublished papers.

Appendix

Appendix A

Conversations With Afghan Professionals

A Conversation with Mashal Hamidi - Regional Director of Read to Lead Afghanistan

Mashal is the Regional Director of Read to Lead Afghanistan. Mashal earned her degree in Sociology at Adelphi University and graduated in honors as a Levermore Global Scholar. She has been working with R2L since its inception in 2017, but was doing significant humanitarian work prior to that.

Authors: Please explain what *Read to Lead Afghanistan* is all about.

> **MH:** Read to Lead (R2L) Afghanistan, was founded in 2017 and began as a grassroots organization based in Kabul, Afghanistan works one on one with child workers in Kabul in ensuring school enrollment through sports, literacy, art and mentorship programs. The idea behind R2L was primarily based on the importance of books. During one of our trips to Afghanistan, we realized that a book per child will save the future. R2L provides the children with sports uniforms, coaches, mentors, books, school supplies, winter clothes and other necessities. Our children are often the main breadwinners of their family, making approximately 100-200 AFG a day (1.50 to 2.50 dollars). Most are exposed to drug and substance abuse through their parents which create a vulnerable and unstable environment and force them to work. Read to Lead Afghanistan is committed to supporting children who are exploited as child workers in Kabul. We not only work with children but their families as

well in ensuring access to healthcare, financial opportunities, and sustainability. Currently, with the restrictions placed by the new regime, we've pivoted our efforts more towards sustainable aid and emergency relief.

Authors: What is the goal of Read to Lead Afghanistan?

MH: The goal is to ensure children are no longer working on the streets at risk to vulnerable situations. Our Streets to School initiative consists of recreational, art and sponsorship programs. Essentially, we aim to create as many literacy opportunities as possible through the establishment of schools and courses. Sustainability is vital in all of our projects and we try to work within the parameters the current government permits us to.

Authors: Discuss the "Read With Me" Program.

MH: "Read With Me" also known as با من بخوان encourages peer to peer collaboration in encouraging each other to read. Read to Me is a storytelling program where children are required to read and discuss books taken out from our library. The goal is to enhance their literacy and speaking skills through engagement with their peers and mentors.

Through "Read With Me" we encourage school attendance by providing school supplies, school uniforms and books to educational facilities to ease the financial burden of families. Within the past year, Read to Lead provided over 1,300 children with either uniforms, school supplies or books through Read to Me. Our in house library is open to our participants even when school is not in session. We aim to promote life-long learning and tackle inequality through the passion for books.

Authors: From your perspective, why do you believe reading is so important for Afghan children?

MH: We believe that the greatest friend one can have is a book. The ability to read from a tender age as a child encourages ambition and can prevent the growing population of child laborers. Reading enriches emotional awareness and fosters development in youth. Children are not meant to be on the streets making a dollar a day. They belong in classrooms where they are able to focus on enhancing their cognitive development via reading and education.

Authors: The Read to Lead Vision statement mentions the following: "We works towards creating better opportunities for working children and orphans by implementing accessible programs to ensure higher literacy rates, improved mental health and stable households. We support those struggling to support their families in hopes of creating a stronger generation." What will it take to achieve this vision?

MH: Resources. The only way to achieve any of this is having an abundance of resources and a trusted team on the ground. As of August 2022, it's been incredibly challenging to function with full autonomy given the restrictions placed by the current government. We are trying our best to work within the guidelines that have been provided to us by the Directorate of Non Governmental Organizations.

Authors: Your work is commendable. Based upon your experiences in Afghanistan, what stats, trends or

patterns have you noticed in regards to illiteracy and poverty? How important is early reading intervention?

MH: During one of our first trips to Kabul, we came to the realization that children were forced to grow up incredibly fast in Afghanistan. Mental health issues were rampant. Majority of these children were a product of broken homes where either their fathers were killed in war, parents were drug addicts, or they were simply neglected by their families. Some families have no choice but to send off their children (some as young as 4) to become child street laborers. This is where we noticed a pattern of low self esteem, self doubt, temper tantrums, and fear of abandonment. These children were let down by the people who were supposed to care for them and nurture them. Making matters worse, society made this seem normal. The words of one student still haunt me, "these drug addicts ruined our country. If they went to school, maybe we could've rebuilt it."

Authors: From your experiences, which provinces need the most help and why? Please give some examples.

MH: Rural provinces have the greatest disadvantage. They lack infrastructure, resources, adequate electricity and water. We've seen students in Paktia sitting on dirt as makeshift classrooms. However, none of these impediments have barred them from picking up a book or aiming to be the number one student in their class. Afghan people are tenacious and if a couple of hurdles aren't going to stop them from gaining an education, then we have no excuse in being the resource in helping them get to the pinnacle.

Authors: Can you please discuss some of Read to Lead's outcomes or accomplishments since 2017? Can you also discuss some disappointments or obstacles that Read to Lead has faced?

MH: Thinking back, we are so proud of who we are as an organization. We are small and in our own words, "super grassroots". Every single one of our projects and accomplishments are possible because of our community here in the United States, particularly the Afghan community in NYC. Our donors have rarely hesitated to assist in a fundraising effort, food distribution, or emergency response. Since 2017, we have removed about 100+ children from the streets of Kabul and have placed them in school. One of our students, Jamshed, used to weigh people on the street and make less than a dollar a day. His father was a drug addict, and his mother was unable to work. We noticed his talent as an artist. He belonged in a classroom with a sketchpad and paint. Just by comparing photos, you notice how much he changed physically as a person. His confidence flourished. He was able to do what he loved and provide for his family via the stipend Read to Lead Afghanistan Organization provided. He eventually became one of our teachers and taught art classes at our facility. This is the power of giving a child a chance and allowing them hone into their talent. For Jamshed, his book was his sketchpad. He was even recognized by local networks and Arg palace. We created English language, art, and computer classes. We have heavily aided the needy, especially widows. During the month of Ramadan, we provide Iftar for 30 days. Our Winter Campaign is a major focus as we distribute blankets, coats, hats, shoes, gloves, heaters and food supplies. We have responded to urgent emergency situations such as the earthquakes in Paktika, Khost, and Herat.

Our team has provided medical supplies, clothing, and food. During COVID, we worked with the Rabia Balkhi Hospital, Wazir Akbar Khan,and Jamhooryat Hospital to provide masks, hand sanitizer, gloves,and heaters. We have also created water wells at Lycee Zarghona, Lycee Rabia Balkhi, mountains near Darlaman and in Kunduz (by a school and mosque). We have worked with Alaudin and Tayeh Maskan Orphanages to provide food and clothing for the children. We have supported the families of 130 widows and enrolled their children in school. Currently, we have launched a vocational program for widows—Female Artisan Program. We have enrolled 10 women and have provided them with sewing machines and materials to create winter blankets. Their revenue stream is provided by our donors who purchase the blankets and then we distribute them to the needy as a part of our winter campaign.

Authors: Do you have a personal anecdote that you will always remember and that keeps you motivated? If so, please explain.

> **MH:** Afghan people don't need our pity. We should never deem ourselves as "saviors." Providing a lending hand is part of the human condition. This should be normalized and not glorified.

Authors: Since many children are being forced to work throughout Afghanistan instead of going to school, what mechanisms can a government implement to address this unfortunate phenomenon?

> **MH:** There needs to be a serious implementation of making school mandatory for children and this needs to be enforced by the government. Education should not be considered an afterthought or option within

Afghan society. The building blocks of a sustainable economy starts with education as the foundation. Budget and resources need to be allocated. I know so many brilliant minds who are willing to return back to Afghanistan and assist in driving these efforts. However, as mentioned before this has become increasingly difficult.

Authors: Do you think vocational schools are more appropriate for young children to be able to immediately apply their skills to specialized jobs for more stable employment?

> **MH:** At this point, any type of education is vital in maintaining enrichment of mind and to prevent them from becoming street laborers.

Authors: The Taliban are back in power and controversial. What are your experiences with running Read to Lead during Ashraf Ghani's regime compared to your experiences with the current Taliban regime?

> **MH:** As a female founded organization, it was definitely easier to run our organization during Ashraf Ghani's presidency. It definitely was not a walk in the park and obtaining something as simple as a document was a challenge only because the government wanted to function in a particular manner. As you may know, women do not have many rights with the Taliban regime. Gaining recognition from the new regime was important for us as we did not want to let our people down.

Authors: Since the return of the Taliban, have you noticed more or less children going to school and/or off the streets working?

MH: Absolutely. It is heartbreaking seeing young girls having to stop their education past the 6th grade. We've had to make some tough decisions, but the safety of our staff and children is of utmost importance to us. There has been less children on the streets as the current government is trying to diminish child workers, but it also does not mean they are in school.

Authors: From your vast experiences, is education the key to a unified, progressive, and independent nation? Please explain.

MH: Absolutely. A nation without education will not progress in any way. Educating young girls and women is the pillar of advancement of society— especially Afghanistan.

*****

Dr. Farid Younos is a retired Professor of Cultural Anthropology and Islamic Philosophy at California State University, East Bay. Dr. Younos completed his doctoral degree in Education (International and multicultural Education) from the University of San Francisco.

Authors: One of the reasons the Taliban gave for issuing the education ban was that female university students did not follow the strict dress code and sometimes made their way to the universities without a male chaperon. This, they say, contradicts their interpretation of Sharia law. Why is it that Islamic law is interpreted differently in other Islamic countries?

FY: Religion is a liberal field of study. It is not 2 + 2 = 4. Everyone has their own understanding and interpretation. However, the majority of Muslim

scholars are against the Taliban's understanding of
Islam.

**Authors: Are you hopeful that women's rights in
Afghanistan will take a turn for the better in the future?
In recent years, Saudi Arabia has made some progress
with women's rights.**

> **FY**: Women and men in Islam have equal civic rights
> in Islam. I don't think the Taliban will change. This is
> because the Taliban came to power based upon their
> own ideology. Those who possess an ideology don't
> change.

**Authors: Based upon your many years of research and
understanding of Islam, what does Islam teach about
education and women's rights?**

> **FY**: The foundation of Islam is knowledge. The first
> aya revealed was "to read". Later the Prophet (peace
> be upon him) said that the first thing God created was
> the pen. Hence the foundation of this Deen is
> learning for both genders. The Quran says: "Oh my
> Lord advance me in knowledge" in surah Ta-Ha;
> 20:114. This verse is very much universal and applies
> to both men and women. Fatima al-Fihri was a
> Muslim woman from Tunisia who founded the first
> known university more than 1,000 years ago: the
> University of al-Qarawiyyin in Fez, Morocco.

*****

Dr. Marina Aminy is an Associate Vice Chancellor at the
Foothill-De Anza Community College District, and the
Executive Director of the California Virtual Campus, a state-
wide initiative to help students accelerate completion of their
educational goals through access to high-quality online

368

courses and programs across the 116 California Community Colleges (CCC). Marina has over 20 years of experience in education, and previously served as a dean, director, and full time faculty member at both the CSU and California Community College levels. She holds a BA, MA and PhD in Education from UC Berkeley.

Authors: Is online education trusted? Are courses online interactive and engaging?

> **MA:** This question alone would need its own book. Of course, the answer is that it strongly depends on the faculty member, the services available, and the policies of the institutions. The preparation and professional development of the faculty member is paramount, as is the course design (to ensure quality and accessibility). The policies of the institution around regular substantive interaction (RSI) are critical as well to ensure interactivity in that online classroom. Furthermore, the institution's ability to provide wraparound services for online students will also impact success, such as the availability of online tutoring, counseling, and other services.

Authors: What impact will Artificial Intelligence (AI), ChatGpt, and other similar Apps have on online education? Will plagiarism become a larger issue in the future? Will the use of these types of Apps prevent students from learning and being successful in the workplace?

> **MA:** This is a question a lot of our colleges are currently grappling with. Generative AI is certainly a major disrupter in the classroom (online or not), and students, faculty and institutions are in the midst of some very critical conversations around how to respond. In general, policies and clear guidance are

needed for faculty and students on the ethical and appropriate use of AI in the classroom. I would also add we need policies for use of AI in faculty publications toward tenure and retention, scholarly work, classroom materials, and curriculum. There needs to be a conversation around equity as well, since students can have access to "better" AI if they pay a fee, versus the free versions available to the public. Do these varying levels of access in turn impact the resources and quality of work that students can produce? I truly believe that AI can be a powerful tool for education rather than a scary unknown; however, to fully realize its potential, we must pull together and respond thoughtfully and in student-centered ways. For example, using plagiarism or AI detectors as a "response" to AI can be very harmful due to the prevalence of false flags and rather futile as AI improves and deterrents like those become less effective. I would like to see, instead, that we use more authentic assessments and project-based learning in the classroom – which are much harder to replicate with AI. Let the AI question serve as a challenge to all faculty and administrators to fundamentally rethink their approaches to learning, assessments, and supporting students in the classroom.

Authors: How does online education break barriers?

MA: Online Education provides access as a key element. This means it helps the student who is disabled and cannot come to a physical campus, the student who has two young children and cannot afford childcare, the student who cannot afford the parking fees or gas needed to drive to campus, and the student who may be caring for a sick parent or family member. These are the students who have traditionally been locked out of education because they cannot easily come to a physical campus. Online education provides an avenue for these students to learn and have a seat at the table. One of my favorite online content creators on LinkedIn is Jessica Lopez, a student at a local community college. She was born with no legs and arms, so it's clearly difficult for her to travel and physically navigate a college campus. She speaks at length about the transformative value of online education in her life, and how access to a computer and online courses have allowed her to get a degree, have a job, and live a fulfilling life where she contributes to society in meaningful ways.

Authors: What will the future of online education look like?

MA: The future of online education will certainly incorporate AI, but we don't know for sure just how this will look. It will be flexible, student-centered, and driven by student needs rather than institutional needs. Moreover, boundaries will increasingly blur for students' experiences. The BAs being offered by community colleges is just a first step. I oversee the California Virtual Campus, or CVC, which allows for cross-enrollment across California's 116 colleges. Whereas before a student at a small CC had no choice but to wait for an online course to be offered by their home institution, today that student has access to the online inventory of dozens of other colleges. The CVC Exchange basically removes the walls between colleges and allows students to enroll in courses at any of the state's 116 colleges. This happens in a matter of minutes, and our platform takes care of all the details like admissions, records, transcripts and other business processes. We ask: why should the student have to keep filling out applications each time they need a class outside of their college? Basically, we cut a lot of the red tape for students to be able to enjoy a seamless experience. That's the future – a marketplace of education and learning experiences at the students' fingertips.

Authors: With students and teachers becoming increasingly comfortable with technology, what are the pros and cons to online education?

> MA: I've already discussed some of the pros, but the potential challenges could be identity management. Colleges are struggling at times to ensure that students are who they say they are. There are some nefarious activities (usually from non-students) who pose as online students to fraudulently access student financial aid. Also, some disciplines like mathematics are slow to join the online offerings because of the lack of effective proctoring solutions for online courses. AI is bringing a whole other element of concern around academic honesty.

Authors: Is it true that schools are increasingly seeking teachers/professors with online skills?

> MA: I would say this is a definite yes, and colleges are now looking for certification or evidence of the ability to teach online. The CVC has a professional development unit (called the Online Network of Educators or @ONE for short) where we offer training and certification for the system's faculty and staff. Many colleges also have their own in-house training and badging programs as well.

Authors: How does online education impact the pedagogical side? Such as assessment, collaboration,

and engagement that's hard to reproduce, basically the in-classroom experience?

> **MA**: Colleges have been measuring the success and retention rates of online courses versus their traditional counterparts, and there has been a gap there for years. Students in on-campus courses tended to do better and stay in their courses longer than online students in the same courses. However that gap has been quickly closing in the past few years as we get better at teaching online. It will be important to monitor the gap across ethnic groups to ensure that it's closing for all students in an equitable manner. Furthermore, there are a number of quality rubrics for course design that support improved pedagogy, including the CVC @ONE's Online Course Quality Rubric, Quality Matters, and the SUNY system's OSCQR rubric.

Authors: Based upon your vast experiences, can online education promote student-centric and equity-minded education?

> **MA**: Yes.

Authors: According to current research, about 15-20% of Afghanistan have access to the internet. What can be done for the rest of the population to have access to quality online education?

> **MA**: This is an unfortunate circumstance of war, displacement, and foreign interference and occupation in Afghanistan. A critical prerequisite to online education is broadband access so that students can get online. In fact, internet access or lack thereof isn't just an issue for Afghanistan; there are colleges here in California that also struggle with this due to

the remote nature of their geography and location.
Hotspots could work, but would also rely on existing
infrastructure. It's unfortunate that worldwide
solutions like Elon Musk's Starlink are used politically
rather than for humanitarian reasons in places like
Afghanistan and Palestine where the citizenry
desperately need this access for both economic and
educational opportunities.

**Authors: As an Afghan American with significant
experience in education, what are your thoughts,
suggestions, or recommendations when you see the
following stats regarding Afghanistan:**

- An estimated 3.7 million children are out-of-school in
  Afghanistan – 60% of them are girls (UNICEF,
  2023). The gap in adult literacy between men (52.1%)
  and women (22.6%), is larger (29.5%) than the gap of
  the South Asia aggregate, 15.7. Adult literacy rate is
  the percentage of people ages 15 and above who can
  both read and write with understanding a short simple
  statement about their everyday life.

MA: Historically we know that the literacy rates of
women and girls in a nation are a precursor to their
ultimate success or demise. A key recommendation I have
is for the US to immediately discontinue the crippling
freezing of assets for Afghanistan as well as the sanctions
and embargo that was imposed on Afghanistan since
unexpectedly withdrawing their forces from Afghanistan
a couple of years ago and leaving power to the Taliban.
While the Taliban were not democratically elected, and
they come with their own set of concerns, the part that
the US can control are the sanctions and assets. By
releasing these, there is a greater chance that schooling
can restart in Afghanistan and some of these statistics can
be bridged. The economic sanctions are predominantly

hurting the citizens of Afghanistan rather than the leaders at this time.

- After spending 4 years in primary school (elementary school), around 65% of Afghan students have only fully mastered Grade 1 Language curriculum and less than half of them mastered Grade 1 Mathematics curriculum. Most Afghan principals (97%) were not knowledgeable of their schools' performance, in terms of teacher absence, teacher content knowledge, and learning outcomes.

MA: Again, the sanctions make it impossible to provide any support, travel, collaboration or training to the staff and administrations at the schools. My first recommendation is to lift these sanctions, normalize relations and ties with the Taliban (and therefore have opportunities to collaborate and influence what is happening in the country) and begin to rebuild schools and training.

- In the US, a student's high school GPA is very important when applying to college. However, in Afghanistan, high school GPA is irrelevant when applying to a public college. It all comes down to one exam (Kankor). What are your thoughts on this? Do you agree with this? Is this equitable?

MA: The reliance on that one exam is a dated historical and cultural norm in Afghanistan, and the US also had similar norms in the past (many European countries still do). Many institutions in the US still depend on high-stakes standardized tests such as the ACTs and SATs for admission, not recognizing the enormous benefit of test prep companies and access to preparation that benefit wealthier students. Basically, what I'm saying is that the US has its own set of inequitable testing practices. For

many years, the SATs have been a barrier to keep poorer
students (and many students of color) out of prestigious
institutions; wealthier students had the benefit of training,
test preparation, coaching and practicing for their SATs
with strategies that have been shown to dramatically
improve scores. Afghanistan can only offer more paths
and varied assessments with the right resources, training
and access to outside knowledge.

*****

Mansoor Haidari emerges as a distinguished professional,
boasting a cumulative 15 years of expertise in the dynamic
realms of cyber security and network protection, notably
through his service in the U.S. Army Intelligence. Mansoor's
skillset is characterized by a practical understanding of threat
analysis, network defense, and the implementation of
pragmatic security measures. His involvement in linguistic
analysis, coupled with hands-on experience in collection and
analytical techniques, underscores a versatility that resonates
with the rapidly changing landscape of cyber security.
Mansoor's career is underscored by a commitment to hands-
on excellence in cyber security and network protection, and
his dedication extends to addressing the unique challenges
faced by individuals in regions with limited access to
education as well as reliable internet services. As he advances
the mission of the U.S. Army Intelligence, Mansoor remains a
valuable contributor in the ongoing battle to secure sensitive
information and digital assets against irregular adversaries as
well as evolving cyber threats, ensuring inclusivity and
security for all. Mansoor completed his Bachelor of Science
degree in Computer Science (Network and Security) at the
University of the Pacific and is currently pursuing a Master's
degree in Information and Cyber Security at UC Berkeley. He
is an employee at the Lawrence Livermore National
Laboratory (LLNL) in the United States of America.

Authors: How can all of Afghanistan have access to the internet - even in the most remote and rural areas? Based upon my research, the generally accepted method is to invest a lot of capital in getting a developing nation onto a major fiber optic backbone, either terrestrial or undersea (e.g., most African coastal nations are on a backbone that rings the continent). However, planning and deploying an undersea cable can take a decade or more, and the cost is enormous. The lifespan of a cable is typically around 25 years. Terrestrial cable is less costly but might be challenging due to Afghanistan's terrain. It may also be possible to bring it in wirelessly from a neighboring country, as Haiti has done from the Dominican Republic (and even that is an alternate path to an existing fiber optic route), however that is severely limited in capacity.

MH: Providing internet access to remote and rural areas in Afghanistan comes with a lot of challenges that need to be assessed and considered. For example, network infrastructure limitations, landmark or geographical barriers, social and economic factors –all need to be examined. From the network perspective at this stage Afghanistan has two options which are wireless mesh networks or TV White Space (TVWS) Technology. I will explain each option but there are some other options that we will discuss.

Option # 1 is Wireless Mesh Networks which consist of interconnected nodes that communicate with each other to extend network coverage. Each node in the network serves as a router, relaying data to other nodes until it reaches a gateway that connects to the internet. Execution only considers deploying wireless mesh networks in remote areas of Afghanistan could help overcome infrastructure challenges. Nodes can be strategically placed to create a network that covers vast regions, even in rugged terrain. The use of solar-powered nodes can enhance sustainability in areas with unreliable power sources.

This approach can be very beneficial and is cost-effective, scalable, and adaptable to the geographical challenges of Afghanistan since Afghanistan is a mountaineer country. It can be quickly deployed and expanded, making it suitable for remote locations.

Option # 2 is TV White Space (TVWS) Technology which is the inactive or unused space found between channels actively used in the UHF and VHF spectrum. TVWS frequency spans from 470 MHz - 790 MHz Currently, TVWS radios are being deployed in rural communities by ISPs (Internal Service Provider) to provide broadband.

Spectrum in the VHF and UHF bands, originally reserved for analog television broadcasts. This spectrum can be repurposed for wireless communication without interfering with existing television signals.

It is very easy to deploy, and the technology is using frequencies that are not in use for TV broadcasting. TVWS signals can cover longer distances and penetrate obstacles better than higher-frequency signals, making them suitable for remote and rural areas. Access points using TVWS technology can be strategically placed to create a network.

TVWS technology is effective for reaching remote areas with limited existing infrastructure. It requires fewer base stations compared to traditional wireless technologies, making it a cost-effective solution. It is the best method that can provide connectivity over challenging terrains.

While thinking about creating or establishing internet connectivity in a remote and rural area of Afghanistan requires systematic approach from international community, local population, infrastructure, technology equipment, Afghan telecommunication ministry involvement and sustainability.

The lack of enthusiasm of Afghanistan's neighboring countries to support certain projects stems from concerns over Afghanistan's rapid advancements in telecommunication infrastructure and a robust internet network. The fear among neighboring nations is that Afghanistan's technological progress may pose an economic threat to their own economies. The worry is that Afghanistan's enhanced capabilities could lead to increased competition, potentially impacting market dynamics and economic interests in the region. This apprehension has contributed to a lack of support for certain initiatives, highlighting the complex interplay of economic interests and geopolitical considerations among neighboring countries in the region.

The self-provisioning of internet services in Afghanistan carries both positive and potentially concerning intelligence and cyber effects. On the positive side, a well-developed internet infrastructure could significantly enhance national security by improving communication among government agencies and bolstering the military's capabilities. Moreover, it has the potential to stimulate economic growth, fostering innovation and connectivity with global markets, thereby contributing to increased stability. Additionally, a robust internet network can enhance governance through improved transparency and efficient public services. However, concerns arise from the potential negative effects, such as the heightened risk of cyber espionage, terrorist groups exploiting advanced communication channels, and the increased susceptibility to disinformation campaigns and cyber-attacks. Neighboring countries may also worry about the geopolitical impact and economic competition, raising questions about regional dynamics and cross-border regulatory challenges. Navigating these complexities requires open communication, trust-building measures, and collaboration on cybersecurity initiatives to address shared concerns and foster regional stability. From an intelligence standpoint, ongoing monitoring and assessment of these developments are crucial for understanding the evolving cybersecurity landscape in the region.

In the pursuit of establishing resilient internet connectivity in remote and rural areas, an exhaustive plan has been meticulously crafted. Commencing with an in-depth Needs Assessment, the focus spans the complexities of population density, geographical nuances, existing infrastructure, and the socio-economic landscape. Identifying pivotal stakeholders, ranging from local communities to governmental bodies, NGOs, and potential private partners, is vital.

The following phase revolves around smart Technology Selection, where we analyze and choose technologies aligned with the unique demands uncovered during the needs assessment. Notably, our emphasis lies on scalability and adaptability, with a keen eye on wireless mesh networks and TV White Space technology, well-suited for challenging terrains.

Infrastructure Development takes center stage thereafter, meticulously planning the deployment of base stations, access points, and requisite equipment. Leveraging existing infrastructure minimizes costs, and our commitment to sustainability is evident in the incorporation of solar-powered solutions to address power challenges in remote locales.

Navigating the regulatory landscape is a strategic imperative, as we collaborate closely with local and national regulatory authorities to secure permissions and licenses, ensuring strict adherence to pertinent regulations to preempt any legal impediments.

This project will need dedication to Community Engagement, involving locals in a cooperative relationship where their needs and concerns are not just heard but form the foundation of this project approach. Training programs disseminate knowledge on the transformative benefits of internet access. Significantly, community involvement is ingrained in the maintenance and sustainability of the infrastructure.

Partnerships is the bedrock of this project strategy in order to forge alliances with local governments, NGOs, and private sector entities, pooling resources, expertise, and funding. Exploring collaborative opportunities with international organizations and donor agencies amplifies our impact.

Thorough Monitoring and Evaluation mechanisms are instituted to continually assess network performance and community impact, propelling iterative improvements. Host user and maintainer commitment to sustainability extend to Maintenance and Support, where we cultivate a model that engages local communities, trained technicians, or service providers. Exploring revenue streams, such as offering affordable internet services or collaborating with local businesses, fortifies the sustainability of our endeavor.

Every area plan should be tailored to the specific conditions of each community and its topography, characteristic dynamic, recognizing the imperative of ongoing collaboration with local stakeholders as the key player to the initiative's achievement and enduring sustainability. To stand up this kind of network infrastructure, physical and traditional security are very important to protect data privacy and safeguard.

Authors: We recently learned that "Afghanistan and China will be connected to a fiber optic network via Wakhan port. Apparently the Ministry of Communications and Information Technology is working on the implementation of the Wakhan corridor project and is also undertaking programs to be connected to the fiber optic networks in Tajikistan and Kyrgyzstan through the Silk Route fiber optic network." What are your thoughts on this and what are the pros and cons?

MH: The Wakhan Corridor is a narrow strip of territory in northeastern Afghanistan that extends to China's Xinjiang region. The area and its people were abandoned by both countries for years with no support and humanitarian assistance. In recent years, there have been discussions and plans to enhance network connectivity and other infrastructure projects in this region, including the possibility of a fiber optic network. The Silk Route fiber optic network is part of broader regional connectivity initiatives, and various countries in Central and South Asia have been exploring ways to improve communication and trade links between Afghanistan, China, Pakistan, Kyrgyzstan, and Tajikistan.

When it comes to infrastructure projects that are funded by other countries, there are always potential pros and cons associated with projects like the connectivity initiatives between Afghanistan, China, Pakistan, Tajikistan, and Kyrgyzstan through the Wakhan corridor. Keep in mind that the success or challenges of such projects can depend on various factors, and perspectives may differ based on individual and geopolitical considerations.

Potential Pros:

 Improved Connectivity: The development of a fiber optic network can and will enhance communication infrastructure, promoting better connectivity and communication between the involved countries. Fiber optic is the future of all communication and network connectivity.

Trade and Economic Opportunities: Enhanced connectivity can facilitate trade and economic opportunities by streamlining the movement of goods and services across borders of the neighboring countries. This can contribute a lot to economic development and regional cooperation.

This project can have geopolitical improvement that strengthens ties between countries and can have geopolitical implications, fostering cooperation and stability in the region.

Technological Advancement can implement advanced communication infrastructure and can contribute to technological advancement and innovation in the involved countries.

Potential Cons:

Security Concerns: The region, including the Wakhan corridor, may have security challenges. Infrastructure projects could be vulnerable to security risks, potentially affecting their implementation and operation.

Cost and Funding: Large-scale infrastructure projects often require significant investment. Ensuring adequate funding and managing costs effectively can be challenging and may pose financial risks.

Political Instability: Political instability in any of the involved countries could pose challenges to the successful implementation and operation of such projects.

Environmental Impact: Construction and development projects can have environmental consequences. Assessing and mitigating potential environmental impacts is crucial to sustainable development.

Dependency and Influence: Connectivity projects can lead to increased economic and political dependency between countries, which may have both positive and negative implications.

It's important to note that the success of such projects depends on careful planning, collaboration, and addressing potential challenges. Additionally, the perspectives on these initiatives may vary among stakeholders, and the broader geopolitical context can influence their outcomes. For the most accurate and current information, it's advisable to refer to official sources and expert analyses.

Authors: Is Starlink the solution? Based upon my research, Starlink has the potential to revolutionize connectivity in developing countries. By leveraging its satellite network, Starlink can bring high-speed internet to remote areas, bypassing the need for costly ground infrastructure.

MH: In the recent year, Starlink, a satellite internet collection project developed by SpaceX, has shown potential improvement to address connectivity challenges in remote, warzone, and developing areas. Starlink's objective is to provide high-speed, low-latency internet access through a constellation of small satellites in low Earth orbit.

Starlink benefits:

Worldwide Coverage: Starlink has the potential to offer internet services globally, reaching remote and underserved areas where traditional infrastructure is challenging to deploy.

Low Latency: The low Earth orbit configuration of Starlink satellites is designed to reduce latency, making it suitable for activities such as online gaming and video conferencing.

Quick Deployment: By relying on satellite technology, Starlink can potentially be deployed more quickly than traditional terrestrial infrastructure, which involves laying cables and building ground-based infrastructure.

The satellite constellation can be expanded to accommodate increasing demand, allowing for scalability in providing internet services.

However, it's important to note that as with any technology, there are challenges and considerations:

Cost: While Starlink may bypass the need for extensive ground infrastructure, the cost of satellite technology and user terminals could be a limiting factor for some individuals or communities.

Starlink Environmental Concerns: The large number of satellites in low Earth orbit has raised concerns about light pollution and space debris. SpaceX is working to address these concerns through measures like darkening satellites and implementing collision avoidance systems.

Regulatory Challenges: Different countries have various regulatory requirements for satellite internet services. Navigating these regulations can be a challenge for widespread global deployment.

Competition: Starlink faces competition from other satellite internet providers and emerging technologies, which may influence its market penetration and success but one thing about Startlink that stands out compared to other providers is risk. Starklink's CEO is willing to take risks to support countries in need during times of war.

Starlink, has potential to provide reliable and high-speed internet access, could play a role in supporting education initiatives, including those aimed at empowering Afghan women. Improved internet connectivity can have several positive impacts on education in various ways:

Access to Online Learning Resources with High-speed internet access allows individuals, including women in Afghanistan, to access a wealth of online educational resources. This can include online courses, educational videos, and interactive learning platforms that facilitate self-paced learning.

Remote Learning Opportunities in Afghanistan where access to traditional educational institutions may be limited, especially in rural or conflict-affected areas, internet connectivity can enable remote learning opportunities to those female students. This is particularly relevant in contexts where physical attendance at schools may be challenging.

Having reliable internet can contribute to Skill Development. The internet can provide opportunities for skill development and vocational training. This is important for empowering women with the skills they need to participate in the workforce and contribute to their communities.

Higher Education Opportunities Improved connectivity can facilitate access to higher education opportunities, enabling women to pursue advanced degrees or certifications through online programs and courses.

Access to Information The internet is a powerful tool for accessing information on a wide range of subjects. This can contribute to the empowerment of women by providing them with knowledge and information that may be otherwise difficult to obtain.

However, it's important to note that the success of such initiatives depends on various factors, including:

Affordability and pricing the cost of accessing internet services and devices should be affordable to ensure widespread adoption, especially in areas with economic challenges. I believe it should be free or one of the world's renowned nonprofit organizations should take charge of helping with the cost.

Cultural Considerations: In certain cultural contexts, there may be challenges and sensitivities related to the use of technology, particularly for women. Addressing these cultural considerations is essential for the success of educational initiatives.

Security and Privacy: Ensuring the security and privacy of individuals, especially in conflict-affected regions, is crucial. This includes considerations for the safety of women accessing online education.

While Starlink and similar initiatives can contribute to addressing connectivity challenges, a comprehensive approach involving collaboration between government agencies, non-governmental organizations, and the private sector is often necessary to address the broader challenges in promoting education, especially for women, in regions like Afghanistan.

Authors: From my understanding, Nigeria became the first African country to access the Starlink satellite broadband service. Do you have any information or stats on this? Has it been successful?

MH: The project was developed by SpaceX; the aerospace company founded by Elon Musk. The project aims to provide high-speed, low-latency internet access to underserved and remote areas around the world. Starlink operates a growing constellation of small satellites in low Earth orbit.

Currently there isn't much information on how the network is doing but there was an article published in the Business Insider titled "SpaceX's Starlink is active in Africa for the first time" on January 31, 2023. SpaceX's Starlink satellite internet service has become operational in Nigeria, marking the first African country to receive the service. The announcement was made on Twitter (now known as X) by the company. Nigeria's Minister of Communications and Digital Economy, Isa Ali Pantami, expressed gratitude to SpaceX for the deployment. Elon Musk, CEO of SpaceX, had previously announced Starlink's expansion into Africa in the preceding year. Despite operating in numerous countries with over a million users, Musk acknowledged that Starlink was not profitable to SpaceX.

An article authored by Francis Hook on November 3, 2023 explores the entry of SpaceX's Starlink satellite internet service into Africa. Initially met with enthusiasm, the service has encountered challenges related to pricing and regulatory considerations in markets such as Nigeria, Rwanda, Malawi, Kenya, Mozambique, and Zambia. The article highlights the disparity in pricing across countries, emphasizing higher terminal costs and variable monthly access fees.

The pricing strategy in Africa appears to target lower monthly costs compared to developed markets, aligning with the region's economic landscape. However, the relatively high equipment costs pose a barrier to widespread adoption. The article suggests that, with the current pricing structure, Starlink may only serve a niche market comprising remote businesses and high-income individuals, particularly in uncovered rural areas and specific urban segments.

Regulatory hurdles, including adherence to local ownership laws and licensing requirements, are discussed as additional challenges. Starlink's phased entry into key markets like Kenya and Nigeria involves navigating diverse regulatory landscapes and addressing issues such as taxation, employment, and payment channels. The article underscores the importance of regulatory bodies ensuring a level playing field for existing operators while considering access gaps in rural areas.

Looking ahead to 2024, the article anticipates a refining of Starlink's pricing strategy and a clearer go-to-market approach as it enters more African markets. It suggests that greater pricing harmony and simplified distribution partnerships could emerge, potentially leading to increased accessibility for consumers and businesses. The article speculates that, as Starlink accumulates more customers, prices may decrease, allowing the service to disrupt the market further.

In the mid-to-long term, the article envisions potential market disruption and expanded reach for Starlink, especially as terminal costs decrease, and monthly access fees become more competitive. It concludes by highlighting the broader impact Starlink and similar services could have, beyond connectivity, by playing a significant role in areas like conservation, agriculture, and humanitarian assistance, aligning with evolving discussions on the climate crisis.

According to an article by HarlemSolicitor, the impact of Starlink on Nigerian education has been notably positive, creating numerous opportunities for the delivery of online educational content to students in remote and underserved areas. Prior to Starlink, a significant portion of students lacked access to educational materials, but with the introduction of Starlink, they are now able to avail themselves of these resources. The improved connectivity has facilitated greater accessibility to educational content, thereby enhancing the learning experience for students in previously disadvantaged regions.

Authors: Do you agree with the following, "Satellite internet service has become increasingly popular in recent years, offering a viable alternative to traditional broadband connections. However, despite its advantages, there is one major problem that plagues satellite internet service: limited bandwidth and data caps. However much they've evolved, satellite internet doesn't compare to the speed of cable or fiber optics internet. Download speeds for cable range from 10 to 500 Mbps." What are your thoughts on this regarding Afghanistan's dire situation where fiber optics may not be a plausible solution?

MH: In my opinion, the statement accurately highlights the challenges associated with satellite internet service, particularly limited bandwidth and data caps. Satellite internet has indeed become more popular in areas where traditional broadband connections like cable or fiber optics are not readily available, making it a viable alternative in certain situations.

In the context of Afghanistan's situation, where deploying fiber optics infrastructure might be challenging due to various reasons such as geographical terrain, security concerns, or economic constraints, satellite internet can offer a practical solution. While it may not match the speed of cable or fiber optics, it can still provide internet access in areas where other options are not feasible.

However, it's essential to recognize that deploying satellite internet, or any technology for that matter, might be more straightforward in a peaceful country with robust security measures in place. The current situation in Afghanistan presents numerous obstacles, including ongoing conflicts and security challenges, making the implementation of any infrastructure a complex endeavor.

In regions with difficult terrain or areas affected by conflicts, satellite internet can be a crucial tool to bridge the digital divide and connect people to the online world. Despite its limitations, the reliability and accessibility of satellite internet make it a valuable option in such challenging circumstances.

While acknowledging the limitations of satellite internet compared to cable or fiber optics, it is important to consider the practicality and feasibility of deploying alternative technologies in regions facing unique challenges, such as Afghanistan. Satellite internet can play a crucial role in providing connectivity where other options may not be readily achievable, even though the current situation in Afghanistan adds an additional layer of complexity.

Authors: Satellite broadband holds exciting possibilities, providing improved access to digital opportunities for those previously left behind and offering reliable communication channels during critical times. As

technology continues to evolve, the future of internet connectivity will likely involve a hybrid approach, with satellite broadband complementing traditional terrestrial networks to create a more connected and inclusive world. What should we be prepared for in the future in the US?

MH: Honestly, there is no precise answer – Safeguarding Active Transmission protection and mitigating risks during critical times with Satellite Broadband is not going to be possible with a lot of bad actors around. From Cyberspace and Cybersecurity perspectives we need to understand that technology is transforming and bad actors are developing new theories to exploit vulnerabilities to attack users.

Although we understand that reliable communication during critical times is a fundamental necessity, the integration of satellite broadband offers promising solutions. However, as we embrace this technology, it is crucial to recognize and address hypothetical risks that could and can compromise communication reliability during critical moments.

Satellite broadband is undoubtedly a crucial communication lifeline, but its singular dependence may expose vulnerabilities that adversaries could exploit. Unforeseen issues such as satellite malfunctions, space debris, or solar interference could disrupt connectivity precisely when it is most critical.

Weather conditions pose a significant threat to satellite signals during crucial moments. Storms, heavy rainfall, or atmospheric disturbances may affect signal strength and reliability, necessitating robust solutions to mitigate these weather-related risks.

Critical events often trigger a surge in communication demand, potentially leading to congestion in satellite broadband networks. Heightened usage may result in delays or interruptions, emphasizing the need for proactive network capacity planning and management.

Satellite signals are susceptible to intentional or unintentional electromagnetic interference. Deliberate jamming or unintentional interference from nearby electronic devices could compromise reliability, requiring countermeasures to maintain connectivity during critical periods.

Regardless of expanding satellite constellations, there may still be areas with limited coverage. In remote or challenging regions, the risk of communication blackouts during critical times remains, necessitating strategic planning for comprehensive coverage.

Satellite communication often introduces higher latency compared to terrestrial networks. While efforts are underway to reduce latency, critical applications such as real-time decision-making or emergency response may still be impacted, prompting the need for optimization strategies.

Mitigation Approaches are necessary:

Implementing diverse communication channels, including a mix of satellite and terrestrial options, can mitigate the risk of a single point of failure and enhance overall reliability.

Investing in satellite systems designed to withstand adverse weather conditions ensures consistent performance during storms or other atmospheric challenges.

Employing dynamic network management tools can optimize bandwidth allocation, minimizing the impact of network congestion during critical events.

Today we have a lot of bad actors that are using Jamming technology to distribute internet or signal connectives. We need to deploy anti-Jamming Technologies.

Deploying anti-jamming technologies can protect satellite signals from intentional interference, enhancing the security and reliability of communication.

Continuously expanding and strategically planning satellite constellations to ensure comprehensive coverage, especially in critical regions, minimizes the risk of communication blackouts.

As we leverage satellite broadband for reliable communication during critical times, a proactive approach to identifying and mitigating risks is vital. Addressing issues related to infrastructure dependence, weather resilience, network congestion, interference, coverage limitations, and latency concerns fortifies our communication networks, ensuring they remain robust and dependable in the face of unforeseen challenges.

Authors: Based upon my research, companies are using LEO (Low Earth Orbit) Satellites in Afghanistan. However, affordability remains a barrier for widespread adoption. Is this accurate? If so, what can be done to make this affordable for all people throughout Afghanistan?

MH: To enhance accessibility to satellite services for the entire population of Afghanistan, a viable approach involves the allocation of funds by the Afghan government or international organizations specifically dedicated to satellite infrastructure development. This endeavor may encompass financial mechanisms such as subsidies, grants, or collaborations with private entities, aimed at mitigating the overall cost of satellite services.

An effective strategy entails fostering collaboration between the Afghan government and private companies through Public-Private Partnerships (PPPs) for the development and deployment of satellite infrastructure. Such partnerships distribute the financial responsibilities, establishing a sustainable framework for satellite services. To incentivize private sector involvement, the Afghan government could consider offering tax cuts or other relevant incentives. Financial support from non-governmental organizations (NGOs), international entities, and donor countries can significantly contribute to the deployment of satellite infrastructure in Afghanistan. These contributions play a crucial role in alleviating financial constraints and facilitating the successful implementation of satellite technology.

Engaging the local population within communities is pivotal for generating demand and garnering support for satellite services. Educational initiatives about the advantages of satellite technology can stimulate interest and foster increased utilization. A surge in demand may result in economies of scale, potentially leading to a reduction in overall costs.

Collaborative efforts between countries, international organizations, and private enterprises are essential for leveraging resources, sharing expertise, and collectively addressing challenges associated with satellite deployment, especially in challenging environments such as Afghanistan. Tailoring strategies to the specific context and challenges of Afghanistan, including security considerations and existing infrastructure limitations, is imperative for the successful adoption of affordable satellite technology.

Drawing inspiration from successful models, such as Japan's advanced internet infrastructure, the Afghan government can adopt relevant telecommunications policies to achieve its goals. Japan's consistent investments in broadband access, promotion of high-speed internet services, and encouragement of technological innovation serve as valuable benchmarks for Afghanistan's own aspirations in this domain.

Authors: Is there a way to get free internet for all of Afghanistan? For example, Tech giants including Microsoft have pledged to help populations hobbled by poor internet services to "leapfrog" into an era of online connectivity, with satellites set to play a key role as rival firms send thousands of new generation transmitters into low level orbit.

MH: I love your passion with this question but it is nearly impossible to become a reality in today's highly capitalistic world. Nothing is going to be free of charge someone must pay to acquire service or establish an infrastructure. Let's for a minute think and consider your proposal. Mission to provide free internet for an entire nation, such as in the case of Afghanistan, encounters overwhelming challenges that render the goal nearly impossible. The magnitude of this undertaking becomes apparent when considering the substantial financial investments required, involving not only the initial setup but also the continuous operational costs. Procuring the necessary funds for such an extensive project is a formidable task, necessitating contributions from various sources.

Manpower and security concerns further compound the complexity of the initiative. The deployment and maintenance of an expansive internet infrastructure demand a skilled workforce, adding to the project's costs and posing logistical challenges. Additionally, ensuring the security of the internet service against cyber threats requires constant vigilance, updates, and modifications, contributing to the overall intricacy of the endeavor.

Furthermore, achieving free internet for an entire country is not merely a technological challenge but a socio-political one. Collaboration with governments, international organizations, and local stakeholders is essential for success, and navigating the diverse interests and regulations of these entities can be a formidable task.

While major technology companies and organizations may contribute to such initiatives, the sheer scale and complexity make it unlikely for free internet to be universally provided without some form of cost-sharing or collaboration. The goal might shift towards making internet services more affordable and accessible, acknowledging the inherent challenges that hinder the realization of completely free internet on a national scale will be impossible.

Authors: Are there any environmental issues with the following - Elon Musk's Space X and Starlink are also putting thousands of satellites into an orbit between 400 and 700 kilometers (250 to 430 miles) above Earth. What are the implications to having so many satellites in orbit?

MH: Welcome to 2024 that any possibility can become impossible with a single person's view.

The deployment of thousands of satellites by SpaceX for Starlink and other projects raises environmental concerns, particularly regarding light pollution and its interference with astronomical observations. Additionally, the increasing number of satellites in low Earth orbit raises the risk of collisions and contributes to the space debris problem. Proper end-of-life disposal and efforts to mitigate frequency spectrum interference are crucial steps in addressing these issues. The environmental impact of rocket launches, which release pollutants and greenhouse gasses, further adds to the overall environmental footprint of satellite deployment.

Environmental activists are particularly concerned about the impact of satellite deployments on astronomy due to increased light pollution. They emphasize the need for responsible practices to mitigate space debris and advocate for sustainable rocket launch technologies to reduce the environmental footprint. Transparency, international cooperation, and regulations are seen as essential to ensuring environmentally responsible satellite deployment. The focus is on balancing technological advancements with the preservation of dark skies and minimizing ecological consequences in the evolving space industry.

The deployment of satellite constellations, exemplified by SpaceX's Starlink, has sparked concerns among environmental activists. Despite the promising prospect of providing free internet access to underserved areas, these activists raise environmental issues related to light pollution, the risk of collisions and space debris, and the overall environmental impact of rocket launches. The ongoing debate revolves around finding a balance between the potential benefits of expanded internet access and responsible practices to minimize ecological consequences and ensure sustainable space exploration. The challenge lies in addressing connectivity needs while considering the environmental impact of deploying and maintaining satellite networks. Ongoing collaboration and responsible practices are deemed essential to minimize the environmental impact of satellite activities in orbit.

Activists heavily rely on the internet as their primary platform for disseminating their perspectives and ideas, even though they may harbor some reservations about it. The internet serves as an indispensable tool for environmental activists, enabling global communication and the exchange of ideas that would otherwise be challenging without this digital medium.

Authors: Why is it so important to bridge this gap in Afghanistan? How can having access to the internet help Afghanistan develop and prosper? Can you give some examples (education, healthcare, government services, etc.)?

MH: Access to the internet can play a pivotal role in the development and prosperity of Afghanistan across various sectors, with education standing out as one of the most critical domains.

Online Learning the internet facilitates access to online educational resources, courses, and materials, thereby bridging educational gaps, especially in remote areas where traditional educational infrastructure may be lacking.

E-Learning Platforms can provide educational opportunities to a wider audience, allowing students to access diverse subjects and receive instruction from teachers beyond their immediate geographic location. Currently, several organizations within Afghanistan provide Islamic education classes via e-learning platforms, mostly for students outside Afghanistan, including those in the U.S. and Europe.

Educational Portals The creation of centralized online portals for educational information can assist students, teachers, and parents in staying informed about curricula, exams, and educational policies.

In the jurisdiction of healthcare, which is notably deficient in Afghanistan, the internet can play a transformative role.

Internet connectivity enables the implementation of telemedicine services, facilitating remote consultations, diagnosis, and treatment. This proves particularly beneficial in areas with limited access to healthcare facilities.

Health Information Access online platforms can disseminate health information, preventive measures, and updates on diseases, contributing to better health outcomes by improving awareness and promoting healthy practices.

Government services can also be significantly enhanced through the adoption of digital technologies.

E-Government Services Implementing e-government services can streamline administrative processes, reduce corruption, and enhance the accessibility of government services to the public.

Online Civic Engagement: The internet can facilitate citizen engagement in governance through platforms for feedback, participation in decision-making processes, and access to government information.

Benefits for the employment or job sector:

Remote Work Opportunities: The internet allows individuals to participate in the global job market through remote work opportunities, creating employment options and fostering economic growth, particularly in regions where local job opportunities may be limited.

Entrepreneurship and Online Businesses: Access to the internet enables individuals to initiate and expand online businesses, fostering entrepreneurship and contributing to economic development.

Addressing the digital literacy gap in Afghanistan, particularly in rural areas where a significant portion of the population lacks understanding of the digital world. The establishment of organizations equipped to provide educational services on digital literacy is imperative, with a primary focus on aiding individuals in comprehending the intricacies of the digital territory and recognizing its vital role in shaping the future.

It is essential to underscore the myriad opportunities that digital skills bring, unlocking doors to diverse job opportunities. However, alongside these prospects, it is crucial to acknowledge the challenges that arise when individuals do not grasp the significance of this digital transformation. This lack of understanding can lead to issues hindering the effective implementation of digital initiatives and impeding the overall progress of the community.

To address this issue comprehensively, initiatives should be meticulously designed to not only impart digital skills but also emphasize the broader implications and benefits of engaging with the digital world. Awareness campaigns, community workshops, and accessible educational programs can play a pivotal role in bridging this knowledge gap and fostering a collective understanding of the transformative potential of the digital age. Ultimately, empowering the people of Afghanistan with digital literacy is not merely about job opportunities; it is about enabling them to actively participate in shaping a more connected and sustainable future. Continuous training like the U.S. and other countries are necessary to make sure the process is working and successful.

*****

Dr. Marina Aminy is an Associate Vice Chancellor at the Foothill-De Anza Community College District, and the Executive Director of the California Virtual Campus, a state-wide initiative to help students accelerate completion of their educational goals through access to high-quality online courses and programs across the 116 California Community Colleges (CCC). Marina has over 20 years of experience in education, and previously served as a dean, director, and full time faculty member at both the CSU and California

Community College levels. She holds a BA, MA and PhD in Education from UC Berkeley.

Authors: Is online education trusted? Are courses online interactive and engaging?

> **MA:** This question alone would need its own book. Of course, the answer is that it strongly depends on the faculty member, the services and the policies of the institutions. The preparation and professional development of the faculty member is paramount, as is the course design (to ensure quality and accessibility). The policies of the institution around regular substantive interaction (RSI) are critical as well to ensure interactivity in that online classroom. Furthermore, the institution's ability to provide wraparound services for online students will also impact success, such as the availability of online tutoring, counseling, and other services.

Authors: What impact will Artificial Intelligence (AI), ChatGpt, and other similar Apps have on online education? Will plagiarism become a larger issue in the future? Will the use of these types of Apps prevent students from learning and being successful in the workplace?

> **MA:** This is a question a lot of our colleges are currently grappling with. Generative AI is certainly a major disrupter in the classroom (online or not), and students, faculty and institutions are in the midst of some very critical conversations around how to respond. In general, policies and clear guidance are needed for faculty and students on the ethical and appropriate use of AI in the classroom. I would also add we need policies for use of AI in faculty publications toward tenure and retention, materials,

and curriculum. There needs to be a conversation around equity as well, since students can have access to "better" AI if they pay a fee, versus the free versions available to the public. Do these varying levels of access in turn impact the resources and quality of work that students can produce? I truly believe that AI can be a powerful tool for education rather than a scary unknown; however, to truly realize its potential, we must pull together and respond thoughtfully and in student-centered ways. For example, using plagiarism or AI detectors as a "response" to AI can be very harmful due to false flags and rather futile as AI improves and deterrents like those become less effective. I would like to see, instead, that we use more authentic assessments and project-based learning in the classroom – which are much harder to replicate with AI. Let the AI question serve as a challenge to all faculty and administrators to fundamentally rethink their approaches to learning, assigning work, and supporting students in the classroom.

Authors: How does online education break barriers?

MA: Online Education provides access as a key element. This means it helps the student who is disabled and cannot come to a physical campus, the student who has two young children and cannot afford childcare, the student who cannot afford the parking fees or gas needed to drive to campus, and the student who may be caring for a sick parent or family member. These are the students who have traditionally been locked out of education because they cannot easily come to a physical campus. Online education provides an avenue for these students to learn and have a seat at the table. One of my favorite online content creators on LinkedIn is Jessica Lopez,

a student at a local community college. She was born
with no legs or arms, so it's clearly difficult for her to
travel and physically navigate a college campus. She
speaks at length about the transformative value of
online education in her life, and how access to a
computer and online courses have allowed her to get
a degree, have a job, and live a fulfilling life where she
contributes to society in meaningful ways.

**Authors: What will the future of online education look
like?**

MA: The future of online education will certainly
incorporate AI, but we don't know for sure just how
this will look. It will be flexible, student-centered, and
driven by student needs rather than institution needs.
Moreover, boundaries will increasingly blur for
students' experiences. The BAs being offered by
community colleges is just a first step. I oversee the
California Virtual Campus, or CVC, which allows for
cross-enrollment across California's 116 colleges.
Whereas before a student at a small CC had no choice
but to wait for an online course to be offered by their
home institution, today that student has access to the
online inventory of dozens of other colleges. The
CVC Exchange basically removes the walls between
colleges and allows students to enroll in courses at
any of the state's 116 colleges. This happens in a
matter of minutes, and our platform takes care of all
the details like admissions, records, transcripts and
other business processes. We ask: why should the
student have to keep filling out applications each time
they need a class outside of their college? Basically, we
cut a lot of the red tape for students to be able to
enjoy a seamless experience. That's the future – a
marketplace of education and learning experiences at
the students' fingertips.

Authors: With students and teachers becoming increasingly comfortable with technology, what are the pros and cons to online education?

MA: I've already discussed some of the pros, but the potential challenges could be identity management. Colleges are struggling at times to ensure that students are who they say they are. There are some nefarious activities (usually from non-students) where they pose as online students to fraudulently access student aid. Also, some disciplines like mathematics are slow to join the online offerings because of the lack of effective proctoring solutions for online courses. AI is going to bring a whole other element of concern around academic honesty.

Authors: Is it true that schools are increasingly seeking teachers/professors with online skills?

MA: I would say this is a definite yes, and colleges are now looking for certification or evidence of the ability to teach online. The CVC has a professional development unit (called the Online Network of Educators or @ONE for short) where we offer training and certification for the system's faculty and staff. Many colleges also have their own in-house training and badging programs as well.

Authors: How does online education impact the pedagogical side? Such as assessment, collaboration, and engagement that's hard to reproduce, basically the in-classroom experience?

MA: Colleges have been measuring the success and retention rates of online courses versus their traditional counterparts, and there has been a gap

there for years. Students in on-campus courses tended
to do better and stay in their courses longer than
online students in the same courses. However that
gap has been quickly closing in the past few years as
we get better at teaching online. It will be important
to monitor the gap across ethnic groups to ensure
that it's closing for all students in an equitable
manner. Furthermore, there are a number of quality
rubrics for course design that support improved
pedagogy, including the CVC @ONE's Online
Course Quality Rubric, Quality Matters and the
SUNY system's OSCQR rubric.

**Authors: Based upon your vast experiences, can online
education promote student-centric and equity-minded
education?**

MA: Yes.

**Authors: According to current research, about 15-20% of
Afghanistan have access to the internet. What can be
done for the rest of the population to have access to
quality online education?**

MA: This is an unfortunate circumstance of
war, displacement, and foreign interference in
Afghanistan. A critical prerequisite to online
education is broadband access so that
students can go online. In fact, internet access
or lack thereof isn't just an issue for
Afghanistan; there are colleges in California
that also struggle with this due to the remote
nature of their geography and location.
Hotspots could work, but would also rely on
existing infrastructure. It's unfortunate that
worldwide solutions like Elon Musk's Starlink

are used politically rather than for humanitarian reasons in places like Afghanistan and Palestine where the citizenry desperately need this access.

Authors: As an Afghan American with significant experience in education, what are your thoughts, suggestions, or recommendations when you see the following stats regarding Afghanistan:

- An estimated 3.7 million children are out-of-school in Afghanistan – 60% of them are girls (UNICEF, 2023). The gap in adult literacy between men (52.1%) and women (22.6%), is larger (29.5%) than the gap of the South Asia aggregate, 15.7. Adult literacy rate is the percentage of people ages 15 and above who can both read and write with understanding a short simple statement about their everyday life.

MA: Historically we know that the literacy rates of women and girls in a nation are a precursor to their ultimate success or demise. A key recommendation I have is for the US to immediately discontinue the crippling freezing of assets for Afghanistan as well as the sanctions and embargo since they unexpectedly withdrew their forces from Afghanistan a couple of years ago and left power to the Taliban. While the Taliban were not democratically elected, and they come with their own set of concerns, the part that the US can control are the sanctions and assets. By releasing these, there is a greater chance that schooling can restart in Afghanistan and some of these statistics can be bridged.

- After spending 4 years in primary school (elementary school), around 65% of Afghan students have only fully mastered Grade 1 Language curriculum and less than half of them mastered Grade 1 Mathematics curriculum. Most Afghan principals (97%) were not knowledgeable of their schools' performance, in terms of teacher absence, teacher content knowledge, and learning outcomes.

MA: Again, the sanctions make it impossible to provide any support, travel, collaboration or training to the staff and administrations at the schools. My first recommendation is to lift these sanctions, normalize relations and ties with the Taliban and begin to rebuild schools and training.

- In the US, a student's high school GPA is very important when applying to college. However, in Afghanistan, high school GPA is irrelevant when applying to a public college. It all comes down to one exam (Kankor). What are your thoughts on this? Do you agree with this? Is this equitable?

MA: The reliance on that one exam is a dated historical and cultural norm in Afghanistan, and the US also had similar norms in the past (many European countries still do). Afghanistan can only offer more paths and varied assessments with the right resources, training and access to outside knowledge.

*****

An outstanding example of social edupreneurship in Afghanistan is Freshta Karim's mobile libraries. A podcast interview was conducted with Freshta Karim (Founder and Executive Director of Charmaghz) on April 27, 2023 by Melissa McNeilly of *New Tactics in Human Rights*.

Afghanistan's Mobile Libraries: A Conversation with Freshta Karim

Interviewer: Please introduce yourself.

> **FK:** So my name is Freshta Karim, and the project I'm leading in Afghanistan is called Charmaghz, which means "Walnut." It's a Persian name, and we named it "Walnut," because our main area of focus is critical thinking, so we thought we should name it something relevant and something exciting for children. And we have 16 mobile libraries working in Afghanistan, hosting 2,000 children per day. We are the largest chain of libraries in the country for children.

Interviewer: That's incredible. I didn't realize that you had so many. You've had a lot of growth in the last few years. That's amazing! So I kind of wanted to take a step back and hear a little bit about your personal story. I think we all have a unique story about what brought us into humanitarian or human rights work, and so I'd love to hear a little bit just about your background and what led you to becoming a children's rights advocate.

> **FK:** I think it's a collective of things. It's really hard to find what exactly brought this, but I think it's it's so many things coming together to make us do what we are doing right now. For me, it has been my journey of working with children and for children from a very young age. When I was 12 years old, I started working in a TV channel. I was hosting children's TV shows, and I worked there all the way until I was 17, so I grew up in a TV channel. In the couple of years that I worked in a TV channel, I was part of different programs, but one of the programs that majorly impacted my awareness, and probably my political education, was a program where I was interviewing

411

children about their challenges. And then I was going and interviewing the government officials, trying to be a bridge between children and government officials, building awareness around their situation and advocating for that situation to change. So I think that's where I built a huge consciousness and awareness of what children are going through and why it is important work and why children themselves have a voice, and why that voice needs to find a place. And since then I've been working for children in different platforms, but the major investment in children, particularly in working in the education sector, has been in the last five years where we are working through this NGO.

Interviewer: So you've been in existence for five years. Can you tell me how the Charmaghz mobile library started? Obviously it has grown a lot. What have been some of the challenges along the way?

FK: In 2018, on the 14th of February, Valentine's Day, on a lovely snowy day in Kabul, we launched our first mobile library with the vision that we need to take responsibility for ourselves and try to design a future or try to make a story together with children: a different story for our country. That was the bigger vision for it. Since then, we have been working starting from one mobile library where we collected books from our friends to turn an old public bus into a mobile library, and since then it has grown. Right now we have five bus libraries, one van library, and ten library boxes that go inside the schools and work with children there. In terms of challenges, I think working in a conflict zone, it has been absolutely challenging. We are not able to expand as much as we want. But yeah, I have been realizing that working in a conflict zone is absolutely very difficult work to do.

Interviewer: I can imagine. How many staff do you have?

> FK: We are a team of 56 people. Three of us are out of the country, and the rest are inside Afghanistan. 80% of our colleagues are women, and I am very proud to say that it is a women majority organization.

Interviewer: I'd love to hear from the perspective of a child that comes to visit the mobile library bus – What do they see? What do they do? What have been some of your favorite things to witness or experience?

> FK: So the way we have designed the libraries, they're really really bright colors. The children love it. And the buses are so huge, so when it comes to streets and communities, it immediately grabs childrens' attention. At the beginning, they were very surprised at what it is, and they had all these questions. But now they're so used to it. It's so much part of their lives that they keep waiting for when the bus is visiting them. If we come late, they make complaints of "why are we late," "you should be on time," "we want to spend more time." All the way until we leave the area and they wave their hands. They keep track of what we do and what we don't do. They give us a lot of consultation on how they want the bus to be designed. For example, one of the major things we have been hearing from children is, "We are ready to learn Mathematics, literacy or whatever you say, but it has to be through play. We want to play. Otherwise, it's boring." And we have considered that so much as part of our work, that anything we do has to have play as a big part of it.
>
> The parents are also a big part of it. Whenever we go to communities, parents make sure to bring us tea and

dried fruits and just make sure we are well-fed so we can work well with children. It's quite a community oriented program, with children and parents feeling that it's their program. And that's the part I love the most about it.

Interviewer: That warms my heart to hear and imagine – that it's their space. That as kids who are living in a conflict-affected area and may not feel like they have much of a voice, they get to have some control over making a space that feels comfortable and safe and fun for them to learn.

FK: That's how we have designed it, because we do understand the issue of agency – that children often in societies that are conflict-oriented and in many ways conservative, children are not seen as equal partners. Rather, they are seen as an "empty cup," and we are filling them. That's generally the approach towards children, and that's what we are trying to change in our work. They're our equal partners and we respect them. They are part of the decision-making process. They are part of the design process. Their voice matters. And we have taken this into really small details. For example, a child who comes into the library, he writes his name; he writes his surname; he writes his signature. And this is to tell him that "You are an individual. You're not a number for us." Most of our colleagues know the names of the 2,000 children who visit the library every day, as well as what they like and what they don't like. So, it's a lot of working around the fact that children feel respected and a sense of dignity, a sense of agency.

Interviewer: That's a beautiful perspective. They're never too young to participate and make a change. It's very inspiring. For me, the experience of having access

to books and safe space seems very powerful. Can you speak to the power of that experience and the kinds of exchange that happen within the space?

> **FK:** I think having a safe space to come and to have access to books beyond your school textbooks – many children in Afghanistan only have access to their school textbooks, not to storybooks, not to magazines. So they come here, where they have liberty to choose what they want to read, what stories they want to read, how they want to read, if they want to read in groups, with their friends, if they want to play first, for example, play chess or some of the mental health games that we have, or do they want to have painting… So there are a lot of choices. And children learn to make these choices. And based on their choice decide what they want to do. Which shows that a child starts learning how to make these decisions and imagining when they start reading these storybooks, they are able to start imagining and broaden their worldview, to see what is beyond. For example, if they're reading a storybook, to put themselves in the state of those characters, to try to understand all of these complex emotions. Which we think helps them a lot in their creativity, understanding, empathy, compassion – all those really important things. And probably at times, I also think there is escape. Personally for me, libraries have always been an escape from the world around us, and the truth of a world in conflict is that it's a very stressful world. And even if conflict is not right near your door, the fact that there is conflict in other parts, that there is political tension – this creates a huge stress. You need a place to go where you feel safe, where you think "the books are my friend. I can read, and I'm not going to be judged" – a place where you can concentrate on one thing.

Interviewer: I can tell you're exuding passion about this.
So, you do have permission to operate as a primary
education initiative. You have support from local
authorities. I think I read somewhere that there was
collaboration with the Ministry of Education to expand
services in schools. Are those plans still underway? Are
there additional plans for expansion and collaboration
with schools in Kabul?

> Yes. So since we launched, we have been working
> with schools, and we're trying to expand to as many
> schools as we can. We understand that as the political
> crisis is deepening, we realize a sense of responsibility
> as the demand is increasing. The opportunities for
> children to feel safe, to experience learning
> opportunities beyond their school have deteriorated
> so much. That's why our work is becoming even
> more important, and we are committed to continue
> for as long as we can.

Interviewer: From the perspective of an outsider, I just
have a desire of *"What can I do?"* Do you have any
suggestions for what your average globally and civically
minded citizen can do to support women and girls who
are living in crisis in Afghanistan, and if you want to be
more specific, what can people do to support the
Charmaghz mobile library?

> **FK:** So I think on the bigger issue of what people can
> do – I feel as citizens of this world, we all are
> responsible to ensure that the foreign policy of each
> country is just. I think we are in the 21st century, and
> we all know that we all are human. I could have been
> born in the UK or America, and you could have been
> born in Afghanistan. By chance, we are where we are.
> And I feel we are responsible to make sure that our
> governments and their foreign policies are not unjust

toward other people. And I think that's what I expect from people – to be part of politics in their countries, to be active participants in it. Let's connect "national interests" to "human interests" – human interests of everyone , not just people who are within the geography of my country, but people everywhere. That's what I feel – that there needs to be a revolution in the international politics and foreign policy of countries. That is for world citizens I think.

And with regards to what they can do for Charmaghz, I think we need huge financial support to continue our work. We are open to receive donations from people to expand and ensure that we are able to hire more staff and reach more children. And together with children – create a new story. I believe the situation is so dark, but I am still hopeful, because I feel there is no other alternative. We need to be hopeful that we have certain agency, even if it is really small, that we can bring those changes. And if each one of us have a small sense of agency, then we can bring it together, we can mobilize each other and try to change.

Interviewer: You always have to maintain hope. The beautiful thing is you have a lot of support globally. Hopefully the international community takes action so the situation can improve.

FK: I think one of the problems with living under conditions of political uncertainty is that over time you start doing self-censorship, and then you stop dreaming. And I think that is the worst part. Because if you don't have dreams – how are you going to change the situation? And I hope we all could continue dreaming. Because at the end of the day, I also realize that as much as we have all these problems, we also have each other. Just looking around ourselves, there is so much good in humanity, and there has been this good in humanity for a long time. The world has seen World War I, World War II – so many wars. But in all these wars, we have been able to come out of it better because we have had each other, people who could even see humanity in their oppressor. And I think that constantly inspires me, that there is still hope.

Interviewer: There is a conversation we have a lot with activists at New Tactics, and you mentioned taking care of your staff. How do you protect your own mental health – your own wellness and resilience? Do you have any specific advice that you give your staff or things that are your go-to coping strategies?

FK: Yes, I think we have been becoming more conscious of the fact that if we want to work sustainably, we have a long struggle ahead of us. To be able to sustain in that, we need a lot of self care, and that should be at the core of our work – each of us individually and then taking care of each other as a team. For us, it has been showing a huge solidarity to each other, listening to each other. Just talking. Just knowing that we are here to listen to each other.

And knowing that we can be extremely sad, but we can still allow ourselves to have moments of joy. To joke, to find a little humor in life. I think that combination of celebrating little things in our lives – those little things have been really hopeful for us: to be able to laugh, to be able to cry together and allow that space to cry. That has been very helpful for us. But I think we are still learning what self-care means for people working in human rights. There is still so much for us to learn – that it's not always about

giving – it's also about receiving. It's also about
creating our boundaries. It's also about adding joy in
our struggle. It's about play, adding play into it. These
are all important bits and pieces from our side.

**Interviewer: I love that you model that mindset for the
children as well. I think a common struggle across the
human rights and humanitarian field is how to not burn
out when you're dealing with such heavy issues all the
time. And I think the answer for a lot of people is just
there's no other choice. You have to keep up the good
fight for the long haul, and in order to do that, we have
to prioritize our own wellness. The only other option is
not continuing forward and not reenvisioning that new
world forward.**

FK: Exactly. I do give credit to people working in
human rights. It's absolutely so difficult. I sometimes
feel like my entire heart – I feel this huge pain in my
heart looking at human misery. It sometimes looks so
impossible to witness. To witness human misery to
this level and still remain alive. We are strange
creatures. We have a huge capacity to still remain alive
after experiencing so much pain in our lives – some
of it beyond our imagination, something one had
never imagined a human is capable, a system, a
government or authorities would be capable of doing
something like this to humanity. And you live with it
– day one, day two, day three, and this pain becomes
part of you. And you carry your pain within you. And
I think that's the most difficult part of working in this
area because you don't just carry the pain, but you
also have to work. So how do you carry the pain and
work in a way where your pain doesn't turn into
hatred, but you continue working out of love for
humanity? I find it a big challenge.

Interviewer: That was beautifully stated – you're very poetic with your words. It's amazing how resilient we are as human beings. And that's the work that we do at CVT – helping survivors of horrible atrocities, survivors of torture, survivors of human rights violation – helping those communities heal. And there's always joy and hope in our collective community and the way that we're able to care for one another. Is there anything else you would like to share that we didn't cover in the conversation today?

FK: It looks like what we're doing and the conditions we're working in, sometimes it looks like it's a story I'm reading, a novel I'm reading – with the challenges that are coming, with the resilience my colleagues are showing, with the passion they're working with, with the reaction of people, with the support of parents. I look at it, and I feel a lot of hope. I feel like if we have a group of people in the middle of a situation where it's hard to keep hope, but people wake up with energy and think "Today, what can I do for children?" And probably that's what a lot of people working under very difficult circumstances do – you wake up and you think "What can I do for humanity today?" And I think as long as we have that question – "What can I do today? How can I fight injustice today?" – I remain hopeful. And I think that, to me, is really important.

And another strength that our colleagues have shown is that we are providing services to children – to children of everyone. And you're still trying to understand and find humanity in all sides of the conflict and hope for a future where all people could sit together for justice to take place. This shows a lot of resilience to me, and I'm very grateful to have had the opportunity to work with people in this situation and in this time. It feels to me that it has made me a better person. I can feel my heart, and I am not numb. And I'm so grateful that I'm not numb.

Interviewer: Congratulations on everything you've accomplished. It's truly incredibly impressive. When I saw the story, I was like "How? How are they able to operate and so successfully?" It's such a beautiful, joyful story to see from a place where a lot of the stories are not that. I really appreciate you being so open in telling us about your work. Do you want to tell us your website and where people can find you online?

FK: Yes, our website is www.Charmaghz.org, and we are having an online fundraising campaign and global campaign right now. We are very active on Instagram – that's our main place.

*****

Samir Noor serves as a high school assistant principal in Northern California, bringing over a decade of valuable experience in education. His journey includes roles as an elementary school teacher, Pearson edTPA scorer, middle school vice principal, and now, a dedicated high school assistant principal. Samir holds a Bachelors of Arts in Psychology from the University of California, Davis. His educational journey continued with a Multiple-Subject Credential from Sacramento State University and a Masters of Arts in Teaching and Administrative Credential Services from San Diego State University. Currently, Samir is pursuing his Doctor of Education at University of California, Davis. With an interest in artificial intelligence in education, Advanced Placement programs, and school attendance, Samir Noor remains deeply engaged in exploring and contributing to key aspects of the educational landscape.

Authors: Since you have both teaching experience and administrative experience, how do you motivate students to do better and learn? More specifically, how do you help students who like to procrastinate?

SN: If students don't understand why they are doing something, it is unlikely they will be motivated to complete the task and learn from it. Stating the objectives of the lesson at the beginning of the lesson is essential to achieve student learning. More specifically, I would start with a 'hook'. A hook should capture the attention of the students by embedding realia at the beginning of the lesson. After the hook, I would introduce the objective that clearly states what they will be learning, how, and why. Outside of creating an engaging lesson, it is key to provide specific and timely feedback for students. General feedback: "Good job on your essay". Specific feedback: "Your introduction paragraph captured my attention by including a thought-provoking question".

Parkinson's Law states that a task will typically take as long as the time allotted for it. Personally, I have been able to complete bigger tasks in a shorter amount of time when I have an approaching deadline. As a teacher, I've noticed this pattern with most students. In an effort to decrease the chance of procrastination among students, I create multiple deadlines for a project/assignment over a span of time. In doing so, it allows students to reach different sections of a unit project/assignment while reaching the objective at the end of the unit. I've noticed that when students are able to complete smaller tasks, they are more likely to continue on to the next one. When I am creating a plan for project, I break it down into smaller sections with multiple deadlines. Ultimately, they will complete all the parts of the projects covering the different standards, but it will happen over multiple deadlines. This is an effective way to provide ample feedback and avoid procrastination on a project.

Authors: In your opinion, what are the qualities of a good elementary school principal and high school principal?

SN: I believe having effective communication skills and compassion make a good principal or leader at any level. Communication from the principal is key in building the school culture. The principal is responsible for communicating the vision and mission of the school to all stakeholders. Being a compassionate leader who effectively communicates to students, staff, and families.

Authors: Why is it important for a school to have an improvement plan?

SN: As an educator that practices a growth mindset, having an improvement plan is an essential part of increasing student achievement. In order to continue to grow, we need to implement strategies and make data-driven decisions, review the results and reconvene with a professional learning community to reflect and repeat the process. It's important to repeat the process with the professional learning community.

Authors: What methods do you implement to help teachers improve their instructional methods, and what types of professional development would you seek out for faculty?

SN: Teachers are routinely evaluated by an administrator. The administrator will complete two informal evaluations and one formal evaluation. An informal is a thirty minute walkthrough where the administrator attends unannounced and a formal is scheduled prior to the visit and for fifty minutes. Prior to completing any classroom evaluation visit, the teacher and administrator schedule an initial conference to discuss their standards and goals during the evaluation cycle for the teacher. It is an essential part of the coaching process to allow the teacher to self-assess their teaching practice using the standards used in the evaluation cycle. Outside of the evaluation, I complete instructional walkthroughs that focus on effective teaching practices. I typically implement a 'glow and grow' method during my walkthroughs. I understand that I only see a snapshot of the teaching when I am there for ten to fifteen minutes sometimes. Timely feedback is key and my goal is to leave a non-evaluative note for every teacher's classroom that I visit that includes something I noticed that went well and something I am wondering about or an area of growth.

Every school year, administrators and instructional coaches who are experts in their subject area complete walkthroughs together to calibrate the walkthrough process. After completing the walkthroughs with the instructional coaches, we debrief altogether to discuss what we observed in each visit. While we debrief, we tie the observations to the California Standards for the Teaching Profession (CSTP). This allows us to calibrate and learn from one another. It's a very powerful way to become a more effective instructional leader as I always learn from other people's perspectives just by debriefing after observing the same lesson. I am a big proponent of having teachers visit other schools and classrooms as professional development. I believe we can learn a lot from stepping into another classroom to observe different teaching strategies, styles, etc.

Authors: Based upon your experiences of teaching and also observing many teachers in the classroom, what are some examples of how teachers use "*creativity*" in the classroom?

> **SN:** Student-centered learning presents more creative opportunities for students. One way to create a student-centered learning environment is to give students choice. In the book *Learning to Choose, Choosing to Learn: The Key to Student Motivation and Achievement* (Anderson, 2016), it states when students are given more autonomy in their learning they are more likely to develop skills that include critical thinking and creativity. I've noticed that students are far more creative when they have the ability to take ownership of their learning by having a choice. Another effective strategy is to use real-world problems tied into the learning targets.

Authors: When dealing with students and discipline, at what point is it appropriate to involve parents, and how do you support them in helping students succeed in school and at home?

> **SN:** I personally like to involve parents more often than not. Ideally, the first form of communication to parents should be a positive one. Any discipline that takes the student out of instructional time (on campus suspension, detention, suspension, etc.) will require a phone call to parents to notify them of the incident. Prior to contacting parents administrators will complete the investigation to have as much information as possible to share with parents.

Authors: How do you build a positive school culture or climate?

SN: Building a positive school culture takes a team effort and takes time. It starts with laying down a foundation like a school vision and mission that everyone is constantly working towards. The vision and mission should be visible and constantly referred to by all stakeholders. Ensuring that every student, family, and staff member feels welcome and heard is another key factor into building a positive school culture.

Authors: How do you make sure that each staff and faculty member understands their role in student and campus success?

SN: Reiterating and emphasizing our school mission and vision regularly in staff meetings is one way to reinforce our role as educators. The more we can refer back to the mission, the more likely we are to increase student and campus success. We also continue to offer professional developments in multiple focus areas to enhance learning opportunities for all of our staff.

Authors: What role does the internet/technology play at your high school for teachers and students?

SN: The internet and technology play a vital role in our high school as all students have a Canvas account where they access learning materials for all of their classes. Every teacher uses Canvas for grades, assignments, and sometimes assessments. Parents can also access Canvas to stay updated with their child's grades and assignments.

Authors: Do you agree with the flipped classroom model?

SN: The flipped classroom model can be an effective model to increase student achievement. The model is designed to give students the opportunity to gain lower levels of comprehension outside of the classroom. In the classroom, the goal is to apply and analyze what students learned outside of the classroom with their peers and support from the teacher. Utilizing the flipped model creates a learning environment that is student centered because they are coming with background knowledge on the content prior to engaging in discussions in class.

Authors: What are your thoughts on online education? Is it an effective medium for teaching/learning assuming that electricity and internet is not an issue?

SN: I believe online education can be effective depending on the learning preferences and needs of students. Online learning can be an effective tool to supplement in-person learning at the high school level. I am a big proponent of utilizing strategies in moderation and having a variety of tools to do so. There are many ways that online learning can effectively enhance learning, but kinesthetic learning opportunities will be difficult to create using an online learning platform. I emphasize the importance of balancing auditory, visual, and kinesthetic learning for all students.

Authors: What are your personal thoughts on standardized tests (e.g. SATs)? Do you find them to be fair and/or equitable?

SN: I think standardized tests can be a way to determine a students' academic ability on a specific topic. On the contrary, standardized tests can be inequitable. One inequity can be socioeconomic status that may result in someone not having test resources to prepare for the exam. Another inequity can be cultural biases in test questions. A standardized test that considers the inequities and minimizes them can be an effective measuring tool. I still wouldn't advise to utilize the scores as the sole determining factor for a job or college admission.

Authors: How important is class rank for a high school student when applying to a college in the US?

SN: Class rank plays an important role in the college acceptance process. Class rank can be an indicator of determining what colleges they may have a chance to get into. For example, some University of California colleges guarantee admission to students that are in the top 9% of their class. Also, achieving the top rank in the graduating class will give a student the valedictorian title that will be factored into their college admission choice.

Authors: What are your thoughts on CTE programs? What CTE programs are offered at your high school? Are CTE programs beneficial to students and future employers?

SN: Our Career Technical Education (CTE) programs are a great way for students to explore and learn practical skills that they will use in the workforce. The real-world application is another benefit that students will experience if enrolled in the CTE classes. The courses below are offered in our CTE program:

- Academy Internship with Industry Partners
- AP Computer Science A

- Business Communication
- Business and Personal Finance
- Child Development
- Computer Keyboarding
- Computer Programming
- Fire 101: Intro to Fire Fighting
- Fire 102: Fire Behavior and Combustion
- Intro to Mass Media
- Intro to Broadcasting
- Sports Broadcasting
- Microsoft Office Basics
- Computer Service and Repair 1
- Computer Service and Repair 2
- Exploring Computer Science
- Health Career Core
- Virtual Enterprise
- Mock Trials, Moot Courts and Trial Advocacy
- Teaching and Learning Careers
- Culinary Arts 1
- Culinary Arts 2
- Percussion Ensemble Studies
- Advanced Percussion Ensemble Studies
- Jazz Band 2
- Music Theory and Technology

Authors: What are your thoughts on magnet schools?

SN: I am not too familiar with magnet schools. I think magnet schools can be beneficial for some students and families depending on what they are looking for.

Authors: Do you agree with requiring teachers to have a specific teaching credential in the subject that they will be teaching? If so, explain why.

SN: I believe that a teacher should have their credential or be enrolled in a program that is related to the subject they will teach. Acquiring a teaching credential in California for a public school requires the teacher candidate to complete courses related to their subject as well as methods classes that specifically teach teaching strategies. In addition to completing a full-time year program, the teacher candidate will also be required to complete a field placement. The field placement requires the candidate to work with a supervisor teacher that guides them as they observe and begin to teach their own lessons. Learning how to create a structured lesson plan is essential to effective teaching. At the end of the program and field placement, teacher candidates submit their portfolio that includes a lesson plan, video clip teaching a lesson, and other materials that may include student samples. As a former Pearson edTPA scorer, I would review and score the teacher candidate portfolios.

Authors: Describe the administrative credentialing program and exam(s) that you were required to complete to become a vice principal.

SN: I completed my administrative credential at San Diego State University. It was a full time year long program. My principal at the elementary school I was working with at the time was my administrator mentor throughout the program. I created a professional learning community with three other teachers and focused on implementing learning strategies for English learners in 4th and 5th grade. I had to record portions of the meeting I facilitated with our professional learning community as we reviewed data, implemented strategies, and discussed findings. As I was working on this, I completed a three cycle project called Cal APA (cycle 1, 2, and 3). Cal APA stands for California Administrator Performance Assessment. The Cal APA is a fairly new requirement for those that are in administrative credentialing programs in California.

Authors: As an Afghan American with significant experience in education, what are your thoughts, suggestions, or recommendations when you see the following stats regarding Afghanistan:

- **An estimated 3.7 million children are out-of-school in Afghanistan – 60% of them are girls (UNICEF, 2023).**

SN: In short, it is heartbreaking that 3.7 million children are not in school. As a first generation Afghan-American, education has been a big part of my life. Receiving an education has opened so many doors of opportunity for me and my family. My simple suggestion would be to open schools for all children. Boys and girls should have access to an appropriate education. Basic needs like shelter, food, and water should be a top priority and education should follow that. The government should ensure that all children receive their foundational education. Ideally, education should empower students to be able to critically think and communicate effectively. It begins with acknowledging that there is an issue. From there, creating a team to specifically address these issues is key to making a change.

- **In Afghanistan, the gap in adult literacy between men (52.1%) and women (22.6%), is larger (29.5) than the gap of the South Asia aggregate, 15.7. Adult literacy rate is the percentage of people ages 15 and above who can both read and write with understanding a short simple statement about their everyday life.**

SN: I would recommend gathering disaggregated data to identify specific regions that have higher literacy rates among adults. Reviewing programs and the education structure in those areas can assist with how to address the alarming low adult literacy rates in other areas. I strongly recommend a team of individuals that solely focuses on the low literacy rates should create a plan to address this as it will take a lot of time and resources to tackle this problem. Collaboration with neighboring countries that have literacy rates of 70% or higher is another way to address this. The literacy rate for women is substantially lower than men; the access and use of the internet to provide instruction (self-paced or live instruction virtually) can be another way to address this. I would also recommend building and/or expanding an adult school program in different regions in Afghanistan to help increase the literacy rate. Some jobs in specific areas in Afghanistan may not require being literate, but being able to read and write will empower those that cannot.

- **After spending 4 years in primary school (elementary school), around 65% of Afghan students have only fully mastered Grade 1 Language curriculum and less**

than half of them mastered Grade 1 Mathematics curriculum.

SN: When I see this statistic, I think of the grade level teaching standards and strategies that can help guide quality and effectiveness of instruction. I am curious as to who is reviewing this data and what standards are being followed, if any. It is a good practice for teachers to continue reflecting on their teaching strategies. Effective teachers do this regularly. My suggestion here would be to assign a team of instructional leaders (coaches) to work with grade levels that focus on data collection and assessing what the areas of strength and weakness are in each department. After gathering data and reviewing it as a collaborative team, I would recommend creating an action plan that focuses on key language and mathematical skills for each grade level. Formative assessments should be designed to regularly check for student understanding and adjusting instruction as needed. As mentioned above, the assessments should tie to a set of standards that are grade level specific.

- **Most Afghan principals (97%) were not knowledgeable of their schools' performance, in terms of teacher absence, teacher content knowledge, and learning outcomes.**

SN: It is imperative that principals are informed of their schools' performance, especially information that directly affects student achievement. Teacher content knowledge and learning outcomes can be observed by the principal as they are the instructional leaders on campus. I would recommend the principal makes weekly visits to classrooms to observe lessons.

In addition to the regular classroom visits, I also recommend collecting data to track progress and address areas of need with the teachers.

- **In the US, a student's high school GPA is very important when applying to college. However, in Afghanistan, high school GPA is irrelevant when applying to a public college. It all comes down to one exam (Kankor). What are your thoughts on this? Do you agree with this?**

SN: I personally believe in considering multiple factors when reviewing a student's college application to get a more comprehensive assessment of a student's abilities. I think having an exam as one of the measuring tools can be beneficial in the application process, but I wouldn't recommend it being the only factor considered. A student's ability to be creative, think critically, and lead is difficult to measure using an exam. A student's grade point average (GPA) gives an indication of how the student performed in the different courses throughout their high school years. Extracurricular activities like sports, clubs, and other programs can provide more insight into what a student is capable of.

Authors: Discuss a typical day at work for you....

SN: For context, I am an assistant principal at a high school with about 2,700 students in the East Bay Area, California. Our administration team includes the principal and five assistant principals who lead different programs and projects. We have four offices that students are assigned to (SLC A, B, C, and D). I oversee about 800 students, about 5 clerical staff, two counselors, and 30 teachers. Advanced Placement (AP), Attendance office, Homework HELP tutoring, Science department, World Languages department, and Back to School Night are some of the programs and teams that I lead. We meet with our administration team at least two times a week, I meet with my secretary once a week, and meet with both of our counselors biweekly.

A typical day for me at work includes following up on anything that I've been working on the previous day that is time sensitive. For example, it can be a follow up with a student regarding their attendance trends or a teacher question about resources for their project in an upcoming lesson. Before getting intothe follow up, I briefly check in with my secretary about what the day will look like (meetings, phone calls, messages). After following up, I plan to walk into a couple of classrooms to observe and give some feedback on lessons. These are about 15-20 minute non-evaluative walk-ins in classrooms. Depending on the day, I can be in an Individualized Education Plan (IEP) meeting, 504 Plan meeting, or other meetings that come up between parents and students, or with staff. During non-instructional time (passing period, before or after school), I will step out of the office to be present around campus as students are walking to class, eating lunch, or going home. I enjoy being out and interacting with the students during this time. It is difficult to explain a typical day as they are all so different. As a high school assistant principal, there are days where we have sporting events, board meetings, and other activities that will extend our days sometimes until 10:30PM. Attending these events are great opportunities for us as educational leaders to interact and get to know our students and community at a more personal level which in turn creates a more welcoming environment for all on our campus.

*****

Code to Inspire (CTI) is the brainchild of Fereshteh Forough (Founder and Executive Director), an extraordinary individual who, born as an Afghan refugee in Iran, overcame countless barriers, including the denial of educational opportunities. In 2015, driven by an unyielding sense of purpose, Fereshteh felt compelled to establish Code to Inspire, the first-ever advanced computer coding school in Afghanistan. The organization aims to educate young women and girls, empowering them to pursue a seemingly distant dream: the opportunity to study and evolve into the fullest versions of themselves.

Authors: As the visionary behind Code to Inspire, what unique blend of leadership and technical skills do you believe are essential for your role? Could you share the pivotal experiences or learning moments that shaped your skill set?

> **FF:** As the founder and executive director of Code to Inspire (CTI), I emphasize a unique blend of leadership and technical skills. On the leadership side, inspiring and motivating teams, communicating a compelling mission, fostering collaboration, and empowering individuals are essential. Effective communication and strategic thinking are key components of my leadership approach.
>
> Technically, a strong understanding of coding is crucial for guiding the organization successfully. My technical background enables me to comprehend project nuances, address student challenges, and make informed decisions aligned with our mission. It

436

facilitates effective communication between leadership and our talented educators and students. Having worked in the tech industry and as a professor in Computer Science at Herat University, I witnessed technology's transformative power, inspiring the establishment of Code to Inspire.

Navigating organizational challenges has been a significant learning experience, honing my leadership skills. Continuous learning through conferences and collaborations keeps me updated on technological advancements, contributing to Code to Inspire's success and positive impact.

Authors: Navigating the dynamic landscape of education and technology can be intricate. Could you delve into specific instances where Code to Inspire encountered challenges and elaborate on the innovative solutions or strategies you implemented to overcome them?

FF: CTI has shown exceptional adaptability in the face of challenging circumstances. The Taliban's ban on education for girls above the 6th grade presented a significant obstacle to CTI's mission. Nonetheless, our immediate decision to shift from a physical location to an online platform reflects our commitment to providing education, irrespective of external challenges. This experience showcases CTI's ability to overcome adversity no matter the difficulty.

For our online education, we are using Google Classroom to demonstrate CTI's capacity to leverage digital tools for teaching and learning. This includes further curriculum development, video content creation, and interactive exercises tailored to the needs of our students. The students' limited access to laptops and the internet necessitated innovative solutions, such as conducting surveys and distributing essential hardware and connectivity packages.

Authors: Reflecting on the organization's journey, how has the operational landscape of Code to Inspire evolved amidst external factors, such as changes in the political climate pre and post Taliban? Can you shed light on any notable adjustments or adaptations made during these transitions?

FF: In the wake of the Taliban's takeover of Afghanistan in August 2021, which included the prohibition of education of women and girls beyond the 6th grade up to university level, Code to Inspire was compelled to modify its facilities. This decision was made to ensure the safety of our staff and students, given the circumstances surrounding the ban on the education of women and girls. However, our commitment to our mission remained unwavering, and we swiftly adapted by transitioning our operations to an online platform while awaiting the opportunity to reopen our physical school.

To facilitate this transition, we opted for Google Classroom as the medium through which we could provide educational content to our students, encompassing a wide array of resources such as videos, presentations, and interactive exercises. However, this digital shift was not without its challenges. The limited availability of laptops and reliable internet connectivity among many of our students' households caused significant problems in our ability to educate.

Recognizing the pressing issue, we conducted a comprehensive survey to help meet the needs of our students. Subsequently, we embarked on a distribution initiative that provided laptops and monthly internet packages to each student's home, thus mitigating the digital divide.

Thanks to this concerted effort, we successfully managed to reintegrate approximately 80 percent of our students into our online learning environment, thereby ensuring their continued access to education.

Authors: Your commitment to education is commendable. Could you elaborate on the societal impact you believe Code to Inspire has had, and how does this align with your personal philosophy? Do you identify as a social entrepreneur, and if so, how does this perspective influence your approach?

FF: CTI is dedicated to transforming Afghan women's lives through technology education, fostering inclusivity and breaking down barriers. Our primary goal is to bridge the education gap for women in Afghanistan, offering free, high-quality coding and graphic design education. By empowering women with these skills, we enable their participation in the digital economy, addressing educational disparities and promoting social empowerment.

Driven by a commitment to narrowing the gender gap in education, CTI creates a supportive environment for female students to thrive economically. Our free programs provide unique opportunities for Afghan women to excel in the technology sector, fostering confidence and independence. Beyond individual empowerment, CTI's impact extends to the overall economic growth of Afghanistan, aiming for a multiplier effect where our students' success

contributes to broader economic advancement and
sustainability in local communities.

**Authors: Expanding access to quality education is a
pressing concern. Have you explored integrating online
education platforms to extend the reach of Code to
Inspire? How do you envision leveraging technology to
bridge gaps and provide coding skills to a broader
audience?**

> **FF:** Code to Inspire is integrating online education
> platforms like Google Classroom to overcome
> geographical constraints and provide quality coding
> education to students from diverse regions. In
> addition, the organization is developing its own online
> learning platform, offering a variety of tech skills in
> Farsi and Pashto. This initiative promotes self-paced
> learning, aligns with industry standards, and fosters a
> sense of community through virtual forums and
> collaborative elements.

**Authors: Recognizing global shifts in education, do you
envision a parallel benefit for Afghan students if coding
were integrated into primary school curricula? How
might this influence both individual skill development
and contribute to the broader economic landscape?**

> **FF:** Introducing coding at the primary level fosters
> computational thinking, problem-solving, and critical
> creativity, providing foundational tech literacy
> applicable in various aspects of life. This early
> exposure enhances problem-solving skills,
> contributing to a versatile skill set applicable across
> disciplines. Moreover, it breaks gender stereotypes by
> promoting inclusivity, ensuring that all students,
> including girls, are prepared for the evolving tech
> landscape and fostering a diverse workforce.

Authors: Celebrating the success of your graduates is crucial. Could you share specific success stories and highlight industries or sectors where your alumni have found meaningful employment after completing the program? How does this align with Code to Inspire's mission?

FF: We have provided education to over 550 girls in our coding and graphic design classes. Over the past years, our alumni and students have successfully completed 50 remote projects in coding, graphic design, and animation, totaling $60,000 in value. These projects were delivered to clients located in the United States, Europe, and Afghanistan.

Based on the data gathered from the alumni survey conducted in July last year, 80% of our alumni work in Afghanistan helping to improve the overall economy of the region. 88.5% of students/alumni believe that CTI has had an impact on their personal well-being. 94.4% of students/alumni believe that the skills and knowledge they received from CTI's program contribute to their personal growth and development. 86.6% of students/alumni believe that CTI helped improve their employment opportunities. Students and alumni of CTI report that they spend a large amount of their income on their healthcare, savings, education, personal/professional development, and the reinvestment of themselves.

Momtaz, one of our graphic design graduates says: "CTI has completely transformed my life. Through their comprehensive program, I not only became a skilled graphic designer but also had the opportunity to work on several paid graphic design projects, earning income for the first time. These experiences not only improved my skills but also instilled a sense of financial independence. With an enhanced portfolio and gained experience, CTI opened doors for me that I never imagined possible. Through CTI, I secured an internship at Binance, one of the largest cryptocurrency exchanges in the world, where I worked on their social media promotional materials. This opportunity has been truly life-changing, providing me with invaluable experiences and opening new horizons for my career.

I am immensely grateful to Code to Inspire for paving the way to financial independence and empowering me to pursue my passion. CTI has not only equipped me with the necessary skills but has also provided a supportive community that believes in the potential of Afghan women. I cannot thank CTI enough for the life-changing opportunities and the platform they have provided me to thrive as a graphic designer."

Wajiha, one of our Front-end coding graduates says: "Code to Inspire (CTI) has been the pivotal point in my life, where curiosity met opportunity. This transformative coding school for Afghan girls provided me with a nurturing environment that encouraged me to explore the vast world of technology.

CTI became my guiding light, equipping me with the knowledge, skills, and unwavering support to pursue my dreams and thrive as a full-stack developer. The comprehensive curriculum and dedicated mentors at CTI struck the perfect balance between theoretical knowledge and practical experience, enabling me to sharpen my coding skills and embark on a rewarding career path.

Armed with the invaluable education and experience gained at CTI, I confidently embraced the role of a full-stack developer. This career not only fulfilled my professional aspirations but also became a means of supporting my extended family. Each milestone I reached allowed me to contribute to their financial stability and well-being, uplifting them towards a brighter future.

I am grateful to Code to Inspire for unlocking my potential, shaping my career, and providing opportunities that transcend geographical boundaries. With their support, I am embracing a future filled with possibilities, making a positive impact on the tech industry and creating a better life for my loved ones."

Authors: Diving into the heart of education, could you provide insights into the creation of Code to Inspire's curriculum? Were there specific philosophies or industry needs that guided its creation? Additionally, how does the curriculum ensure graduates are well-equipped for entry-level coding roles?

FF: Code to Inspire's curriculum, rooted in student-centered and project-based learning, emphasizes hands-on experience and practical coding application. It's designed to be engaging, interactive, and tailored to diverse student needs. Updated regularly to align with industry trends, the curriculum collaborates with experts to enhance graduates' employability. Recognizing diversity, it's inclusive, accommodating varied learning styles and backgrounds. The iterative curriculum development process, fueled by feedback from students and industry partners, ensures constant improvement and relevance to evolving industry needs.

Authors: Bridging the gap between traditional education and the demands of the tech industry is a unique challenge. How does Code to Inspire tackle the shift from memorization-focused education to fostering critical and logical thinking? Have there been notable challenges or successes in this regard?

> **FF:** Code to Inspire places a strong emphasis on project-based learning. Instead of memorization, our educational model revolves around hands-on projects that require students to apply coding concepts in real-world scenarios. This approach not only enhances their technical skills but also fosters critical thinking as they problem-solve and create tangible outcomes. We believe in the power of collaboration. Our learning environment encourages students to work together on projects, share ideas, and learn from each other. This collaborative approach helps develop not only technical skills but also interpersonal and communication skills, crucial for success in the tech industry.

Authors: Looking ahead, what strategic visions or expansions do you envision for Code to Inspire in the next decade? Could you elaborate on any plans to empower graduates to contribute to the establishment of vocational schools across different provinces, creating a ripple effect of positive social and economical impact?

> **FF:** In the next decade, Code to Inspire envisions an expansive approach to empower women economically. This includes the extension of educational and job placement programs throughout Afghanistan, ensuring that women in various provinces have access to coding and tech education. The organization also plans to launch a comprehensive online educational platform,

providing a flexible learning environment for women who may face geographical or logistical challenges.

Additionally, recognizing the displacement of Afghan refugees, particularly women, Code to Inspire aims to expand its operations into neighboring countries with significant Afghan refugee populations. By reaching out to these communities, the organization seeks to provide educational opportunities and support the economic empowerment of Afghan women who may be rebuilding their lives in new environments.

Furthermore, the establishment of a mentorship hub is integral to this vision. The mentorship program will connect experienced professionals with aspiring women in the tech industry, fostering a supportive network that goes beyond formal education. This mentorship initiative aims to guide women in making informed career choices, navigating challenges, and building successful pathways in the tech sector.

Authors: Do you believe engaging the diaspora (Afghans living in the west) for support is pivotal? What specific roles or contributions do you believe Afghans in the West can play in supporting Code to Inspire? Are there collaborative initiatives or partnerships you envision that could amplify the impact of your cause?

FF: The Afghan diaspora can financially support Code to Inspire, funding infrastructure, technology, and scholarships for students. With diverse skills, they make valuable mentors, guiding students in tech education and career development. They can also facilitate job placements by connecting with tech companies, enhancing employment prospects. Partnerships with diaspora organizations, community groups, and businesses can amplify impact through joint projects and awareness campaigns. Engaging the diaspora in advocacy efforts enhances visibility and support, raising awareness about empowering Afghan women through technology education.

Authors: Many educational initiatives face resource challenges. How has Code to Inspire overcome resource constraints and ensured sustainability, especially in the context of financial or infrastructural limitations as Afghanistan continues to face political challenges and crises?

FF: Code to Inspire actively fundraises, reaching out to donors and partnering with organizations committed to empowering women through tech education. Recognizing the importance of tech access, the organization distributes laptops and provides internet support for students facing financial constraints. Collaborations with tech companies secure additional resources, including in-kind donations and financial support. Building community engagement is crucial for sustainability, fostering collective responsibility and grassroots support for educational programs.

Authors: Technology is always changing - considering the growing influence of artificial intelligence in various industries, how does Code to Inspire incorporate AI and other emerging technologies into its curriculum? Are there specific initiatives or strategies to prepare students for the evolving landscape of technology?

FF: Code to Inspire's curriculum integrates the latest technology advancements, focusing on AI, machine learning, and emerging technologies. Students gain a foundational understanding and practical skills through hands-on projects, implementing AI algorithms and analyzing data. This approach enhances problem-solving skills and prepares them for AI applications in various industries. The curriculum also emphasizes ethical considerations, educating students on responsible AI practices, promoting fairness, transparency, and accountability for well-rounded and responsible technologists.

Authors: I really appreciate you being so open in telling us about your work. Do you want to tell us about your website and where people can find you online?

FF: You can learn more about our work by visiting our website: https://www.codetoinspire.org/

*****

Dr. Bahaudin G. Mujtaba is a Professor of International Management and Human Resources and has 25 years of higher education experience locally in Florida, nationally in the United States, and globally in over ten different countries such as Afghanistan, Pakistan, China, Vietnam, Thailand, Morocco, and several others. He also has 16 years of corporate and management experience.

Authors: What are the implications of girls not being allowed to go to school?

BM: It is devastating for the people of Afghanistan, the country's national productivity, and overall talent pool in the country.

Authors: From your perspective, why is it important for a country such as Afghanistan to offer PhD programs?

BM: Having a rigorous and quality doctorate program in Afghanistan will enable research possibilities based on science and facts, and it will empower talented Afghans to become regionally and globally competitive with any workforce in developed economies.

Authors: In Afghanistan, which 3 departments should start with offering PhD programs and why?

BM: Afghanistan needs Ph.D. scholars in all subject matters. I would recommend starting with faculty areas such as education, information technology, and business administration as these departments can be initiated with the least resources. And, the best option might be to partner with accredited foreign universities so Afghan students can have access to the latest available research.

Authors: Why is it important to have faculty members with PhDs or doctoral degrees?

BM: Doctorally-qualified professors will provide students the guidance and rigor needed for research so Afghan leaders can become the drivers of major decisions through science and evidence.

Authors: Where would you like to see Afghanistan in 10 years in regards to education?

BM: Through a focus on quality and equitable education of young men and women in Afghanistan, the country can become not just a competitive regional economy in South Asia, but it can also compete with other nations around the globe. I would like to see Afghanistan as a thriving economy, following the example of Singapore, South Korea, and other such successful nations.

Authors: Why is international accreditation so important for different programs being offered at Afghan universities?

> **BM:** International accreditation in Afghanistan is a necessary starting point so Afghan graduates can research with and find jobs in any university across the globe. However, after accreditation, universities must find their narrow niche and differentiate themselves from others in Asia, Europe, and North American through excellence.

Authors: With English being the business language of the world, would you agree that it's important for Afghan students to also learn the basics of English?

> **BM:** If Afghanistan is to become competitive with the regional workforce in South Asia, Afghan high school students and college graduates must become proficient in English by going beyond the basics. Speaking English is a necessity for the national economy to grow and thrive quickly.

*****

Abdul Waqar Danishyar is a management expert with over a decade of experience in the education sector in Afghanistan. He is currently working on his Ph.D. degree and possesses a context-oriented and deep understanding of the education sector. He is currently managing around 30,000 students in Community Based Education (CBE), Accelerated Learning Program (ALP), Temporary Learning Classes (TLC) and Child Friendly Spaces (CFS) classes in western Afghanistan. He has developed many proposals and concept notes for improving the educational landscape of the country, including a NGO-based CBE implementation policy.

Authors: Who is to blame for the education status in Afghanistan?

AWD: The challenges in Afghan education are the result of historical conflicts (e.g., Soviet invasion, civil wars, Taliban regime), which disrupted social and educational structures. Political instability and changes in governance have led to inconsistent education policies. Economic hardships have limited government spending on education. Cultural norms in some areas restrict access to education, especially for women and girls. The lack of educational infrastructure and trained teachers is a significant barrier. Foreign influences have sometimes prioritized strategic interests over educational development. Assigning blame is not straightforward as these factors are interlinked and compounded over time.

Authors: What are the requirements for high school teachers in Afghanistan?

AWD: Historically, a Bachelor's degree in a relevant field or in education was the basic requirement. Over the years, with international support, there has been an effort to standardize and improve teacher qualifications. Rigorous requirements are important for quality education but must consider the current educational levels and teacher shortages. Balancing higher qualification demands with practical training and ongoing professional development could be more effective.

Authors: Please discuss teacher training programs in Afghanistan.

AWD: Teacher training programs usually combine theoretical education with practical training, but their quality and duration vary. The preparation of teachers to handle actual classroom situations may be inconsistent due to varying standards of training programs. The curriculum of these programs typically includes pedagogy, subject-specific knowledge, and classroom management skills. Post-employment evaluations of teachers can be irregular and lack standardization, depending on the region and resources.

Authors: Please discuss the correlation between high school grades and university admissions.

> **AWD**: The reliance on entrance exams over high school grades is possibly due to the lack of a standardized grading system across schools. This approach aims to provide a level playing field for students from diverse educational backgrounds. The disconnect between high school performance and university admissions can impact student motivation. Reforms that integrate high school performance into university admissions criteria could incentivize students to consistently perform well.

Authors: What is the purpose of the class ranking system?

> **AWD:** The class ranking system in high schools is primarily for internal assessment, motivation, and recognition of academic achievement. It encourages a competitive academic environment and helps in identifying and supporting students who may need additional help. While not directly linked to university admissions, it can be influential for scholarships, internships, or other educational opportunities.

Authors: What are the inter-provincial teacher qualifications?

> **AWD:** A teacher from a different province, assuming linguistic proficiency, should be qualified to teach in

Kabul. However, challenges may include differences in regional curricula, teaching methods, and cultural contexts. Adaptability and understanding of the local educational and cultural environment are crucial for effective teaching. There may also be administrative or regulatory hurdles in transferring qualifications between provinces.

Authors: Please discuss the Kankor Exam and Teacher Qualifications.

AWD: Selecting teachers based on Kankor exam scores alone may not always yield the best candidates, as teaching requires skills beyond academic knowledge, such as pedagogical techniques, communication, and empathy. Relying heavily on Kankor scores can overlook these essential teaching qualities. Developing a more holistic teacher selection process that includes teaching aptitudes and skills would be beneficial.

Authors: Please discuss how teachers prepare students for the Kankor Exam.

AWD: Teachers might focus on Kankor exam content, leading to a teaching approach that emphasizes test preparation over comprehensive education. This can limit students' broader learning and critical thinking development. While this approach helps with Kankor exam performance, it might not fully prepare students for university-level studies or practical life skills.

Authors: What are your thoughts on a National Uniform Curriculum in Afghanistan?

AWD: Afghanistan has attempted to implement a national uniform curriculum, but its effectiveness varies greatly due to regional differences, conflict, and resource limitations. The curriculum aims to standardize education but faces challenges in consistent implementation.

Authors: How do teachers teach in Afghanistan?

AWD: Traditionally, there has been a greater focus on rote memorization and understanding basic concepts. Less emphasis is placed on developing higher-order thinking skills like analysis and evaluation, which are crucial for comprehensive learning and real-world application.

Authors: Discuss the grading system in Afghan high schools.

AWD: Grading typically includes exams, homework, and sometimes class participation or attendance. The balance among these components can vary, with a strong emphasis often placed on exam performance.

Authors: Discuss the fairness of the Kankor Exam.

AWD: The Kankor exam's fairness is questionable due to disparities in educational quality across regions. It tends to favor students from better-equipped schools or those who can afford private tutoring. Students who don't perform well have limited alternatives, such as private institutions or vocational training, which may not be accessible to all.

Authors: Discuss the school hours and days in Afghanistan.

AWD: The number of hours and days students spend in school can vary. Primary school typically has shorter days than secondary school. The academic year usually spans around 200 days but can be affected by regional stability and cultural practices.

Authors: How does one become a school principal in Afghanistan?

AWD: Requirements for becoming a school principal often include having a certain level of education (such as a Bachelor's or Master's degree) and teaching experience. However, these requirements can vary and may sometimes be influenced by local dynamics or connections.

Authors: Discuss the knowledge, skills, and abilities of Afghan School Principals.

AWD: The lack of awareness among principals about their schools' performance is concerning as it impacts the ability to make informed decisions and improvements. This issue points to a need for better training and resources for school leadership.

Authors: Discuss the effectiveness of vocational programs.

AWD: Vocational programs vary in effectiveness, often limited by resources and regional disparities. Current programs include trades like carpentry, mechanics, and tailoring. Expanding and improving vocational training, aligned with market needs, is crucial for future employment opportunities.

Authors: What are your thoughts on online education in Afghanistan?

AWD: Online education has potential in Afghanistan, especially in bridging educational gaps in remote or conflict-affected areas. However, challenges include internet access, technological infrastructure, and digital literacy.

Authors: What are your thoughts on out-of-school children, particularly girls?

> **AWD:** The high number of out-of-school children, especially girls, is alarming and reflects deep-seated issues like conflict, poverty, cultural norms, and security concerns. Addressing these requires multifaceted strategies including community engagement, security improvements, and policy reforms.

Authors: Why does Afghanistan have such a high literacy rate?

> **AWD:** The high illiteracy rate is attributed to prolonged conflicts, lack of access to education, especially for girls, and economic hardships. Solutions include government commitment to education, international support, community-based education programs, and special focus on girls' education.

Authors: Why is primary education in Afghanistan suffering?

> **AWD:** The low mastery level in primary education highlights issues in educational quality and resources. This requires curriculum reform, teacher training, and improved educational infrastructure.

Authors: What are your thoughts on the Taliban's performance in education?

> **AWD:** The Taliban's approach to education has been restrictive, especially regarding girls' education. Their policies have often been criticized for undermining educational progress and human rights. Balancing traditional values with modern educational needs is a significant challenge under their regime.

*****

455

Born in Logar, Afghanistan, Mr. M. Homayoon Stanakzai is an accomplished engineer and aviation safety professional with extensive experience in the mechanical and aviation sectors. He graduated from Kabul University's Faculty of Engineering, specializing in Mechanics, after completing his education at Nadria High School. Mr. Stanikzai is the proud father of three Afghan born daughters who have all completed their Masters degrees in the USA.

Authors: Throughout Afghanistan's history, education has never been a major priority. Who is to blame for this?

> **MHS:** Afghanistan was once at the heart of the Silk Road and ancient civilization. Some of the major poets such as Mawlana Jalaludin Balkhi (Rumi) were born in Afghanistan. Education is very important for Afghanistan. However, given that the country has been suffering from four decades of continuous war, it has impacted all sectors of the country, including education. War and poverty are the main reasons why the Afghan educational sector remains underdeveloped. Even after the foreign intervention, much of the international assistance was focused on war and not education. The previous governments are to be blamed for this.

Authors: What are the requirements to become a high school teacher in Afghanistan? Have the requirements to become a high school teacher changed over the years? Do you think the requirements need to be more rigorous? Please explain.

> **MHS:** In order to become a teacher in Afghanistan, it is sufficient to have a high school graduate diploma. Unfortunately, due to corruption and, of course, lack of proper governance, there are no other

requirements, and teachers are not even evaluated properly before being hired, which has also impacted the quality of education.

Authors: Please describe the teacher training program to become a high school teacher in Afghanistan. How long is the program and how prepared is a person to teach in their area after completing the teacher training program? What do aspiring teachers learn in the teacher training programs? Once hired as a teacher, how are high school teachers evaluated?

> **MHS:** There are educational institutes that offer two years of education for teachers. Some students go to those institutes after they have graduated from high school and after 14 years of education, they become teachers. However, there are no programs to train teachers after being hired. Previously, some NGOs provided training for teachers, but it was not nationwide, and it was very selective. Currently, there are no other programs to train teachers or evaluate them.

Authors: Why are high school grades not considered for admissions at public universities in Afghanistan? Why would a student work hard in high school if their grades are insignificant? What are your thoughts on this?

> **MHS:** It's not fair that school grades are not taken into consideration when admitting students to universities. However, since there are no national standards for all the schools and some schools have more talented teachers and advanced teaching methods than others, it also makes sense to have the Kankor exam.

Authors: What is the purpose of the class ranking system if it is not used for admissions at a public university?

> **MHS:** The purpose of the class ranking system is to motivate students to compete with each other and reward the students who are paying more attention to their students, and also inspires other students to work harder.

Authors: Would a teacher from a different province be qualified (assuming no language barriers) to teach in Kabul? Do you see a problem with this?

> **MHS:** Yes, of course a teacher from a different province would also be qualified to teach in Kabul. In fact, some provinces, for example Herat and Mazar, have better education systems than many districts of Kabul.

Authors: Since Afghan high school teachers entered the teaching profession because of their Kankor exam scores (most likely average scores), are they the best candidates to eventually teach high school students? Do you see a problem with this?

> **MHS:** In Afghanistan, the Kankor ranking system is unfair. The smartest students are sent to medical school while teaching is a very important profession. I think early education is very important and unfortunately, teachers are underpaid so many students after graduating school don't aspire to become teachers. Only when someone doesn't find a job, do they then choose to become a teacher.

Authors: Do high school teachers throughout Afghanistan know in advance what will be on the Kankor exam and as a result, teach their students the

information that will be on the exam so the students will be able to pass the Kankor exam? Please explain.

> **MHS:** Everything in the Kankor exam is in Afghanistan's educational curriculum, but it's not always taught very well, and teachers don't do a good job of covering everything.

Authors: Does Afghanistan have a national uniform curriculum? Please explain.

> **MHS:** In theory, Afghanistan has a national uniform curriculum, but all the books are not distributed equally or taught in all the schools. Additionally, with every new regime, the school curriculum changes and it's not consistent.

Authors: In Afghanistan, do teachers focus more on teaching students how to remember and understand concepts or analyze and evaluate information? Please explain.

> **MHS:** In Afghanistan, teachers focus more on information and less on concepts. The country also doesn't have laboratories in the schools, and teachers don't have in-depth knowledge of many concepts, so the education system is very behind.

Authors: How are students graded in high school? For example, only exams, or exams and homework, or exams, homework, and attendance? What criteria is used?

> **MHS:** Currently, in Afghanistan, the students are graded based on their exams. Homework and attendance are not taken into consideration.

Authors: Do you think the Kankor exam is a fair assessment for all students throughout Afghanistan? What are your thoughts on this? If a student does not perform well on the Kankor exam, what other options do they have?

> **MHS:** Kankor is not a fair assessment for all students throughout Afghanistan. One exam shouldn't determine someone's career. Additionally, Afghanistan is diverse, and people in remote areas don't have access to the same quality of education as people in Kabul so it's not a fair system and doesn't serve everyone.

Authors: How many hours per day are the students in class in primary school and secondary school? Also, how many days per year are the students expected to go to school?

> **MHS:** In primary schools, children go to school for three hours. From fourth to sixth grade, they go to school for three hours and 45 minutes, and in middle school and high school, they go to school for four hours and thirty minutes a day.

Authors: How does someone become a school principal in Afghanistan? What are the requirements?

> **MHS:** The minimum requirements for becoming a principal are a bachelor's degree and two years of teaching experience. Many who work as teachers later get promoted to principal in the same school. However, in recent years, mostly due to corruption many unqualified people have been hired as principals.

Authors: According to one study, most Afghan principals (97%) were not knowledgeable of their

schools' performance, in terms of teacher absence, teacher content knowledge, and learning outcomes. What are your thoughts on this?

MHS: This shows that many principals are not qualified for their jobs and don't know how to conduct them. It's necessary that a principal must have working experience of more than 5 years as a teacher and fully understand her/his duties before being assigned as a principal.

Authors: How effective are vocational programs in Afghanistan? What vocational programs do we currently have in Afghanistan? What suggestions do you have for implementing more vocational programs in the future?

MHS: Vocational programs can be very effective in educating people and providing them with more employment opportunities. Given that not all students can get into University, some vocational programs have enabled students to have hope for the future. There are very few vocational programs, and they certainly should be expanded to other provinces. Currently, only Kabul, Herat, and Balkh have vocational training centers.

Authors: What role will online education play in the future of Afghanistan?

MHS: The world is fast developing, and everything around the world is now internet-based so we certainly can't deny the important role online education can play in Afghanistan. Especially, for girls who are not allowed to leave their homes in many remote areas of Afghanistan. However, with a lack of electricity and access to the internet all over Afghanistan, it's not going to be achievable.

Additionally, people are poor and won't be able to afford the equipment. But we must start from somewhere so where it's possible, I think online education should become more accessible.

Authors: According to a report by UNICEF, an estimated 3.7 million children are out-of-school in Afghanistan – 60% of them are girls (UNICEF, 2023). What are your thoughts on this?

MHS: That's a very sad phenomenon. Unfortunately, due to poverty and lack of an effective educational system, many children, especially girls are being deprived of education. I think more education-friendly policies must be implemented and education must be prioritized by any government in Afghanistan.

Authors: Why do you think the literacy rate in Afghanistan is so high (about 50%)? What are some solutions to this important problem?

MHS: War, poverty, and lack of a uniform national educational plan have led to many Afghans being deprived of education. I think, instead of investing in war or other sectors, the donors and international community focus more on education in Afghanistan. More schools must be built, and the government should be persuaded to promote education as well. Additionally, Afghanistan is a traditional society so people go to mosques. In my view, all the mosques in Afghanistan should lead dialogues to encourage more people to pursue education.

Authors: According to one study, after spending 4 years in primary school (elementary school), around 65% of Afghan students have only fully mastered Grade 1

Language curriculum and less than half of them
mastered Grade 1 Mathematics curriculum. What are
your thoughts on this?

> **MHS:** The lack of a uniform educational curriculum
> educated teachers, and an effective educational system
> has led to such results. In my view, the teachers
> should be paid well so more educated people are
> encouraged to join the Afghan educational system,
> and that will improve the overall quality of education.

**Authors: From your perspective, please critique (good
and/or bad) the Taliban's performance in the area of
Education in Afghanistan.**

> **MHS:** Unfortunately, not allowing girls and women
> beyond grade six to go to school is a very sad issue.
> Not much has changed since the Taliban takeover so
> can't say there has been any good changes. So far, it's
> been only bad.

******

Education Reform in Afghanistan

Ending the Cycle of Poverty, Instability, Inequity, and Dependency

ISBN: 979-8-218-42972-0

Printed in the United States of America.

Institute of Management, Education, and Arts Development
Mountain House, California

9 798218 429720